The Arnold and Caroline Rose Monograph Series
of the American Sociological Association

Class, Race, and Worker Insurgency

The League of Revolutionary Black Workers

Other books in the series

J. Milton Yinger, Kiyoski Ikeda, Frank Laycock, and Stephen J. Cutler: *Middle Start: An Experiment in the Educational Enrichment of Young Adolescents*

Paul Ritterband: *Education, Employment, and Migration: Israel in Comparative Perspective*

John Low-Beer: *Protest and Participation: The New Working Class in Italy*

Volumes previously published by the American Sociological Association

Michael Schwartz and Sheldon Stryker: *Deviance, Selves and Others*

Robert M. Hauser: *Socioeconomic Background and Educational Performance*

Morris Rosenberg and Roberta G. Simmons: *Black and White Self-Esteem: The Urban School Child*

Chad Gordon: *Looking Ahead: Self-Conceptions, Race and Family as Determinants of Adolescent Orientation to Achievement*

Anthony M. Orum: *Black Students in Protest: A Study of the Origins of the Black Student Movement*

Ruth M. Gasson, Archibald O. Haller, and William H. Sewell: *Attitudes and Facilitation in the Attainment of Status*

Sheila R. Klatzky: *Patterns of Contact with Relatives*

Herman Turk: *Interorganizational Activation in Urban Communities: Deductions from the Concept of System*

John DeLamater: *The Study of Political Commitment*

Alan C. Kerckhoff: *Ambition and Attainment: A Study of Four Samples of American Boys*

Scott McNall: *The Greek Peasant*

Lowell L. Hargens: *Patterns of Scientific Research: A Comparative Analysis of Research in Three Scientific Fields*

Charles Hirschman: *Ethnic Stratification in Peninsular Malaysia*

Class, Race, and Worker Insurgency

The League of Revolutionary Black Workers

James A. Geschwender
Professor of Sociology
State University of New York at Binghamton

Cambridge University Press

Cambridge
London   New York   Melbourne

Published by the Syndics of the Cambridge University Press
The Pitt Building, Trumpington Street, Cambridge CB2 1RP
Bentley House, 200 Euston Road, London NW1 2DB
32 East 57th Street, New York, NY 10022, USA
296 Beaconsfield Parade, Middle Park, Melbourne 3206, Australia

First published 1977

Printed in the United States of America
Typeset by Telecki Publishing Services, Yonkers, New York
Printed and bound by the Murray Printing Company, Westford, Massachusetts

Library of Congress Cataloging in Publication Data
Geschwender, James A 1933−
Class, race, and worker insurgency.
(The Arnold and Caroline Rose monograph series
of the American Sociological Association)
Includes bibliographical references and index.
1. League of Revolutionary Black Workers − History.
2. Detroit − Race relations.
3. Detroit − Riot, 1967.
4. Trade-unions − Afro-American membership.
I. Title. II. Series: The Arnold and Caroline Rose monograph series in sociology
F574.D49N44   329'.07'0977434   76-62581
ISBN 0 521 21584 6 hard covers
ISBN 0 521 29191 7 paperback

For Laura Ellen
May she come to understand the nature of the struggle
May she choose to participate in her own time and her own way

Contents

Tables

Preface

Several research techniques were utilized during the course of this project although not all lend themselves to ready classification in terms of standard textbook methods. I was a member of the sociology faculty at Wayne State University in Detroit from 1964 to 1968. During this period I came to know several of the principals involved in the League of Revolutionary Black Workers as either they or their wives were students in my classes. As a result I was able to observe at close hand the activities of Uhuru and its evolution into subsequent forms up to the time that DRUM was born. I spent the period from 1968 to 1970 at the University of Western Ontario in London (120 miles from Detroit) before moving to the State University of New York at Binghamton. I watched Detroit television stations and read Detroit newspapers in London, Ontario, and thus kept up with media coverage of League developments. I received a more intimate picture of developments through personal communications, visits to Detroit, informal discussions and formal interviews with participants.

It is not proper to classify me either as a participant observer or an objectively neutral observer. The League of Revolutionary Black Workers was a black Marxist—Leninist organization. I would have been excluded from membership or active participation on the grounds of race even if I had met all other requirements. I was able to gain access to conduct the research eventuating in this monograph because several members of the executive committee knew me and my orientations. They recognized me as a Marxist and were somewhat familiar with my orientations as a result of classroom lectures and out-of-class discussions. We were able to relate to one another as Marxists and engaged in discussions as to the proper tactics and strategy for a Marxist—Leninist organization. I never interacted with members of the League as a white giving advice to a black organization as to the correct line of struggle for black liberation. However, I did interact with them as a Marxist discussing the correct line of struggle for a Marxist—Leninist organization to follow as part of the larger proletarian struggle. It was not until the fall of 1970 that I finally decided to write a historical analysis of the League. This decision was communicated to all concerned as soon as it was made.

I developed an understanding of the historical evolution of the League of Revolutionary Black Workers through observation and discussion. This was supplemented by some formal interviews, by reading all items written about the League by either movement people or journalists, and by reading as much of the League's own writings as was available. I managed to collect a virtually complete set of the DRUM newsletters, a slightly less complete set of ELRUM newsletters, some newsletters from FRUM and other revolutionary union movements, most copies of the *Inner City Voice*, as well as a set of League pamphlets.

I have adopted a somewhat unusual strategy of citations for material incorporated as part of the following presentation. In many cases I will cite an article or interview written by someone else as the source for information of which I have independent knowledge. I do this so that the interested reader may more readily check a source and see the context in which a particular statement was made. This technique enables me to have confidence in the veracity of the quote because I have independently ascertained the same information. The alternative strategy of citing myself as source for this information would make it more difficult for the interested reader to determine whether a particular statement was correctly interpreted or cited out of context.

I have utilized two additional checks on the accuracy of my accounts and interpretations. A first draft of this material was prepared in 1973 and sent to several key members of the League and to a representative of the UAW International leadership. I then interviewed these persons regarding their perception of the accuracy of the manuscript. A second draft was completed in 1974 and subjected to the same treatment. I carefully considered and responded to all suggestions of factual error. I also carefully considered, but was less responsive to, suggestions of errors in my interpretations. I believe that it is my responsibility as a scholar to get the historical record straight and to make my own interpretations in light of that record and in relation to a theoretical focus. I have sometimes departed from strict literal accuracy in reproducing quotes from revolutionary union movement literature. I retained their own expressions but sometimes corrected misspellings. I believe that there is nothing to gain by using the traditional "sic" indication next to spelling errors. That procedure subjects persons to needless embarrassment without corresponding profit.

I should also state that this monograph does not represent the account of a disinterested or dispassionate observer. I have retained some of my contacts with League members to the present. I had, and have, a positive emotional tie to the League and its members. I am firmly convinced that the United States is in dire need of a basic transformation of the type that can only be brought about by an organized body of workers consciously struggling in their own collective interests. I believe that black workers occupy a position in the American system of production that makes it inevitable that they will play a prominent role in any such change-oriented movement. Thus I have conducted the following analysis of the career of the League of Revolutionary Black Workers development, partially because of the importance of the League as a social and historical development, partially because of what it reveals about the nature of racial stratification in America, and also partially because of what may be learned for future use. If we can determine the set of factors that contributed to the growth of the League, and the set that contributed to its demise, then it may be possible to build a stronger and more successful worker's movement in the future.

I would like to state at this point that *Class, Race, and Worker Insurgency* was not my original choice for a title. I had wished to use as a title, *But the Beat Goes On: An Analytic History of DRUM and the League of Revolutionary Black Workers.* I chose that title because of the various connotations and symbolisms associated with it. The phrase "but the beat goes on" is often used in Detroit to refer to the almost ceaseless pounding of the assembly lines that produce so many of the nation's cars. This has an obvious tie-in to the content of this monograph. Beat also bears an obvious relation to DRUM as an organizational name and the use of drums to decorate the DRUM newsletters. But I really wished to convey far more than this. I wanted to convey the notion that DRUM and the League of Revolutionary Black Workers may have been the organizational forms that embodied the beat of black worker militance during the time of their existence but that they were neither its cause nor the only possible vehicle for this expression. Chapter 11 of this work demonstrates that the "beat" of black worker militance continued to find expression in rebellion even after DRUM and the League disappeared from the scene. At the publisher's request, I selected the present title so that the content of the book might be clarified for an international audience. Although it is an adequate title, it does not convey the meaning or have the impact of my original choice, "But The Beat Goes On."

It is impossible ever to acknowledge all the debts one incurs in conducting research of this nature. I owe a great debt to all members of the League of Revolutionary Black Workers, who proved to be so cooperative and helpful. To single out any individuals for special citation is to run the risk of omitting others who should also be mentioned. Nevertheless, I would be derelict if I failed to thank Ken Cockrel, Luke Tripp, John Watson, and John Williams for having been especially helpful. I am also grateful for the cooperation of Jordan Sims of the United National Caucus, and Homer Jolly and Douglas Fraser of the United Automobile Workers. The staff of the Detroit public library was extremely helpful as was the staff of the Archives of Labor History and Urban Affairs at Wayne State University.

Portions of the material included within this monograph were previously published in *The Journal of Ethnic Studies* 2:2 (Fall 1974) and in Raymond L. Hall (ed.), *Black Separatism and Social Reality: Rhetoric and Reason* (New York: Pergamon Press, 1977). These materials are included herein with the permission of the original publishers.

Many persons have been kind enough to read various drafts of this monograph and to make suggestions that substantially improved its quality. These include, in alphabetical order: William H. Form, Barbara N. Geschwender, Martin Glaberman, Lewis M. Killian, Arthur Liebman, James Petras, James Rinehart, Elliott Rudwick, Theda Skocpol, and Immanuel Wallerstein. Patricia Dolaway made an invaluable contribution in typing and editing various drafts. I am also indebted to the Research Foundation of The State University of New York for funding a portion of the research involved in preparing this monograph.

James A. Geschwender

June, 1977

Abbreviations

AFL	American Federation of Labor
BSUF	Black Student United Front
BEDC	See NBEDC
CORE	Congress of Racial Equality
CRU	The Committee for Real Unionism
DRUM	Dodge Revolutionary Union Movement
ELRUM	Eldon Avenue Revolutionary Union Movement
FRUM	Ford Revolutionary Union Movement
GOAL	Group on Advanced Leadership
HUAC	House Un-American Activities Committee
IBA	International Black Appeal
IFCO	Inter-Religious Foundation for Community Organization
KKK	Ku Klux Klan
LSDF	National Black Labor Strike and Defense Fund
NAACP	National Association for the Advancement of Colored Peoples
NAC	Negro Action Committee
NBEDC	National Black Economic Development Conference, later simply called Black Economic Development Conference (BEDC)
NIRA	National Industrial Recovery Act of 1933
NLRB	National Labor Relations Board
NRA	National Rifle Association
PASCC	Parents and Students for Community Control
RAM	Revolutionary Action Movement
SDS	Students for a Democratic Society
SMSA	Standard Metropolitan Statistical Area
SNCC	Student Non-Violent Coordinating Committee
TUEL	Trade Union Educational League
TULC	Trade Union Leadership Conference
TUUL	Trade Union Unity League
UNC	United National Caucus
WCO	West Central Organization
YSA	Young Socialist Alliance

1. Sociology and the dialectics of class and race

The League of Revolutionary Black Workers had a relatively brief history. It first appeared on the Detroit scene in 1968 when the Dodge Revolutionary Union Movement (DRUM) was formed. All visible signs of League activity were gone by the spring of 1973. The League during its brief existence organized black workers, conducted demonstrations, held wildcat strikes, participated in union electoral politics, and generally fought to improve the lot of the black worker as part of the process of transforming American society. The struggle led by the League resulted in objective improvements in the areas of safety, working conditions, elevation of blacks into positions of authority in local unions, increases in numbers of black foremen, and in the elevation of level of consciousness on the part of the black worker. This alone would justify a close examination of League history. However, the League experience has a significance that is much greater than simply a half-decade of struggle in Detroit. An examination of the experience of the League may tell us much about the larger dialectic of race in America.

The study of race in America

Much of the study of race in America has suffered from two major defects. It has failed to locate its subject matter in the larger context of the evolving world capitalist system and it has tended to treat blacks as victims without comprehending the dialectical nature of racial exploitation. It is not possible to understand the basis for racial exploitation without an analysis of the world capitalist system. It is only by examining conditions in the world economy that we can understand the necessity for racial exploitation as one element in the social organization of production. However, more is needed than the recognition of the relation between the world political economy and racial exploitation. It is possible to understand the economic basis of racial exploitation without recognizing that it is a fundamental error to see blacks only as vic-

1

tims and ignore their active contribution to the shaping of their own destiny. It is this active contribution that is described herein as the "dialectic of race."

The dialectic could be described roughly as follows. The state of the world capitalist system at any given time sets the parameters for racial exploitation. It determines the nature of the need for labor by amount, type, and probable source. A more or less *organized system of racial exploitation* frequently emerges to fill the need. The exploited group presents a *challenge* to the system through its resistance by any means possible. The exploiting group generally does not wish to give up its advantage so its *response* usually takes the form of an attempt to crush resistance. If the resistance is too strong to be crushed, then the exploiting group may be forced to *retreat* through a partial abandonment of the system of racial exploitation. Retreat does not mean total defeat. The exploiting group retreats because the resistance of the exploited has made maintenance of the existing system too expensive. Retreat usually takes the form of *retrenchment* in a new system of racial exploitation which provides many of the advantages of the old system at lesser cost. This new structure, in turn, stimulates a new collective challenge on the part of the subordinate group against those benefiting from the new systematic exploitation of a racial minority.

The actual operation of the dialectic of race is more complex because it interacts with the dialectic of class. It is not possible to subsume either dialectic within the other. The dialectic of race is neither a subprocess within the dialectic of class nor the larger process subsuming the dialectic of class. Both exist simultaneously and confound the simpleminded analysis of either. A complete analysis of the dialectic of race will not be attempted here but a brief sketch of its broad outlines will be provided to aid the reader in interpreting the meaning and significance of the League of Revolutionary Black Workers.

The analysis must begin with the rape of Africa and the proletarianization of the African people which, in turn, has to be understood in relation to broader processes. Wallerstein notes that:

If it seems that we deal with the larger system as an expression of capitalism and the smaller systems as expressions of statetism . . . we never deny the unity of the concrete historical development. The states do not develop and cannot be understood except within the context of the development of the world-system. The same is true of both social classes and ethnic (national, religious) groupings. They too came into existence within the framework of states and of the world-system, simultaneously and sometimes in contradictory fashions. They are a function of the social organization of the time.[1]

Slavery existed as a mode of organization of production and Africa functioned as a supplier of slaves prior to the introduction of Africans into the American colonies.[2] Slavery resulted from the need for large amounts of unskilled labor for labor-intensive industries. Africa was selected as a supplier of slaves because Europe needed a large population pool that was readily accessible but outside its economic system, so that the negative economic consequences of the removal of manpower would not harm the European economy. Thus the precedent was set, and when American agriculture changed to a mode of agriculture compatible with a labor-intensive system of production it was natural to turn to Africa as a supplier of labor.[3]

Blacks did not respond to slavery with complete docility.[4] Slaves resisted their masters through noncooperation, sabotage, maiming and killing animals, running away, conducting strikes, conducting organized rebellions, and engaging in guerrilla activities. White slaveowners attempted without success to crush all resistance. Ultimately the combination of the activities of slaves and of the Union army (which included many former slaves) combined to destroy the Confederacy and to put an end to slavery.[5]

The end of slavery did not mean an end to the need for cheap unskilled agricultural labor in the South. It was necessary for the dominant classes to come up with a different system of racial exploitation. A system of peonage was developed.[6] It took the form of sharecropping, tenant farming, and debt peonage. This too was resisted. Blacks joined the Sharecroppers Union and the Tenant Farmers Association as well as migrating to cities when jobs became available.[7] Black resistance combined with mechanization of agriculture to bring an end to the system of agricultural peonage.

This occurred at about the same time as expansion of American industry and a consequent growth in need for industrial workers in the United States. Immigrant white labor had satisfied most labor needs during the early period of industrial expansion.[8] However, the immigrant flow ended around the time of World War I while industry was still expanding. A new source of labor was needed and black workers filled the void.[9] Their earliest introduction to industry often had been as strikebreakers but they were now needed as more permanent workers.

The newly emerging system of racial exploitation was one that operated on a basis of racial discrimination. Blacks were systematically shunted into the harder, least desirable, more dangerous and more poorly paid jobs. The black struggle against this form of exploitation is still continuing. It produces changes and accommodations but it never results in complete victory — that is, in the complete abolition of racial exploitation.

A class dialectic operated simultaneously with the above described racial dialectic, in which racial divisions were exploited to the detriment of white as well as black workers.[10] Slave labor was used in competition with free labor to lower the costs of the latter. After slavery was abolished the presence of large numbers of easily exploited blacks made it possible to keep white tenants and sharecroppers in circumstances little better than those of their black counterparts. Early attempts at industrial organization among white workers were undermined by the use of blacks as strikebreakers. The presence of blacks in lower-status, less desirable jobs inhibited white militancy. Employers could always use the threat of replacing white strikers with black workers. The post—World War II period saw a greater integration of blacks into industry but not on the basis of equality with white workers. The black workers found no greater degree of equality in the unions than in the factories. The civil rights movement brought advances on social issues but no basic change in the economic position of black Americans.

These are the broad developments that set the stage for an examination of the history of The League of Revolutionary Black Workers. As a result of the continued evolution of the American system of production, whites have largely moved out of production jobs in heavy industry to be replaced with black workers. The whites who remain in heavy industry hold down the best jobs and dominate the union structure, while blacks are largely excluded from union decision-making posts as well as being concentrated in the least desirable jobs, departments, and shifts. The activities of the League were simply a manifestation of the continuing black struggle as part of both the racial and class dialectics as they are manifested in heavy industry in northern industrial cities.

Racial stratification theory

Contemporary American sociology does not have the theoretical or conceptual tools that would enable us adequately to analyze the interplay between racial and class dialectics. Perhaps this inadequacy results from a refusal to recognize that racial stratification is only a special case of social stratification. Stated in overly simplistic terms, social stratification is the unequal distribution of scarce resources associated with the unequal distribution of power. Those classes of persons who influence the distribution of scarce resources utilize their advantage to insure that they and others like themselves receive more than their proportionate share.[11] Members of the ruling class attempt to maintain their power advantage in order to maintain their material advantage. They often manipulate the distribution of scarce resources so as to maximize the number of persons receiving more than their share and thus feeling that they also have a stake in perpetuating the status quo. The unequal distribution of scarce resources may accord with a "divide and conquer" policy in which certain groups receive more than others and consequently develop loyalty to the ruling class despite the fact that it maintains the lion's share of resources for its own use. The ruling class seizes upon any possible ideological rationalization that may divide the exploited into mutually distrustful groups. The most frequently manipulated lines of cleavage are those between men and women, skilled craftsmen and unskilled laborers, and those who "work with their heads" as opposed to those who "work with their hands."[12] Perhaps historically the most important of such lines of cleavage has been the division of society into racial and ethnic groups, whose hostility has frequently been manipulated to facilitate the perpetuation of existing systems of privilege.[13]

Existing theories of racial stratification are not adequate to the task. In fact there is very little in the way of theoretical work on racial stratification in American sociology. The bulk of all scholarly work that relates in any way to race in America is concerned with the topic of race relations rather than stratification, *per se.* Most of it purports to have relevance for the analysis of racial stratification and, in fact, some does. There are four major models currently used by American sociologists in the analysis of racial stratification. These are the assimilationist model, the white racism or prejudice model, the class model, and the internal colonial or submerged nation model. Each of these will be discussed separately and contrasted to the theoretical approach that dominated the field when first created.

Robert Ezra Park

Serious scholarly work dealing with race was initiated by Robert Ezra Park. Park rooted his theory of race relations in an analysis of developments in the world political economy.[14] Situations of race contact, which Park called racial frontiers, were created by European expansionism and exploration in search of markets and raw materials. The earliest frontiers were created by the desire for trade and resulted in competition between groups differing in custom and behavior.[15] Ethnocentrism helps competition to become racially defined.[16] Races are socially defined units. They come into existence when differences are recognized and are interpreted as being biological in origin.[17]

Competition between racially conscious groups may lead to prejudice and the transformation of competition into conflict. Conflict might prove disruptive of commerce; therefore, it tends to be replaced by systems of accommodation.[18] Accommodation is nothing more than institutionalized systems of dominance—subordination (e.g., slavery or caste) that facilitate exploitation by eliminating conflict. Struggle does not return until the system of accommodation begins to break down. Prejudice results from the attempt by members of the subordinate group to rise up out of their assigned station.[19] The system of accommodation may also break down because the oppressed people develop a sense of nationhood, which may lead to the struggle for self-determination and possibly national independence.[20]

Park recognized that racial frontiers may be created by immigration into a host society of large numbers of persons differing from the host population in terms of either race or culture.[21] Park saw no basic difference between frontiers involving racial differences and those involving cultural differences except that race facilitates the identification of individuals in terms of group membership.[22] However, national movements arising in immigrant situations were less likely to seek national independence and more likely to seek room to operate in the larger society free from discrimination.[23]

Park believed that there was a long-term trend toward assimilation and the elimination of racial minorities as such. The development of modern states was such that it appeared probable that minorities would increasingly be absorbed into, and take on the characteristics of, the dominant group.[24] The modern world was perceived to be developing in such a way that more and more nations would be incorporated into a common world political economy in which race, *per se,* would become decreasingly important. The emerging world system would not end conflict and exploitation but it would ultimately transform its nature from race to class.[25]

This approach provides an adequate framework for the analysis of racial stratification in America. It provides the basic concepts and perspectives that facilitate examining race as a socially derived concept, emerging out of a world political economy in which one people finds it desirable to exploit others either for reasons of trade, land, or labor needs, and in which racism and prejudice emerge as rationalizations for such exploitation. Prejudice is explained as the result of competition over status as accommodation systems break down. Many of Park's students continued this initial approach but, over time, the field of American sociology drifted to less meaningful perspectives on race. The most popular of these is embodied in the assimilationist school.

The assimilationist school

The assimilationist perspective dominates contemporary American sociology. There are several varieties but they share certain central propositions. All versions perceive race as relatively unimportant. Blacks are seen as being in essentially the same position as all other minorities. Each entered American society in a disadvantaged position. Each lacked the knowledge of American culture, the skills and the competencies that would enable them to compete. It is assumed that a certain amount of assimilation took place during slavery but that the process had not progressed sufficiently by abolition to enable blacks to move into American society on a basis of equality.

The traditional assimilationist perspective assumes that all minorities, over time, learn the dominant cultural perspectives and become integrated into American society. It was not assumed that minorities would become identical to the dominant group but that they would become a fully accepted part of a smoothly functioning social system. Most social scientists expected minorities to vary in their rate of assimilation as a consequence of variations in the extent of majority group resistance. Members of the majority group were expected to develop prejudice in response to various features of the minority group. Higher levels of hostility would be generated against groups that were racially or culturally different from the majority. Racial differences were thought to produce the more intense response. Majority group members were also expected to perceive large concentrations of minority group members as a threat. Each of these factors was expected to stimulate majority group prejudice leading to majority group resistance, retarding, but not entirely halting, the rate of minority group assimilation. All minorities were expected to become acculturated eventually and to develop the skills and competencies necessary for effective competition in American society. This would lead to a reduction in majority group prejudice and eventual assimilation of the minority into American society on a basis of total equality.

Oscar Handlin accepted most elements of this model but he deviated in one respect.[26] He argued that blacks came to New York City and faced a situation similar to that faced by all earlier immigrant groups but differing in two important respects. The amount of prejudice directed against blacks was greater than that directed against other groups and the internal communal strengths of blacks were less. Handlin felt that blacks were weaker in communal voluntary organizations, in community business, and that they were less aware of the importance of political participation.

Glazer and Moynihan further modified the basic assumptions of the assimilation model.[27] They no longer assumed that the tendency was for minorities to become completely assimilated into the dominant society. The first edition of *Beyond the Melting Pot* argued that minorities would become integrated within racial and religious groupings but that race and religion would continue to provide the basis for distinct social groupings. The second edition suggested that ethnicity was reemerging in importance while race and religion were receiving decreasing emphasis in modern American society. Glazer and Moynihan continued the trend begun by Handlin of shifting the locus of responsibility for lack of black assimilation from majority group prejudice to minority group deficiencies.

It had been assumed initially by Glazer and Moynihan that blacks would achieve full legal and civil equality. It was argued that all previous minorities had started at the bottom, had moved up without massive governmental help, and that no institutional racism existed to prevent blacks from doing likewise. Glazer and Moynihan acknowledge the existence of prejudice but argue that all previous groups also faced prejudice and managed to overcome it. They suggested that any failure of blacks to make significant progress was largely the consequence of their own deficiencies. Blacks tended to perceive actual gains as psychological losses and consequently to develop a sense of deprivation and impending doom. They failed to take advantage of political opportunities by refusing to register and vote in sufficient numbers. They did not develop the economic or leadership strength that results from a strong minority involvement in business. They failed to develop the strong self-help community organizations that were essential if defects in black family structure and black education were to be overcome. The opportunities existed but blacks failed to take advantage of them. True discrimination remained but other minorities had continued to prepare themselves and were ready to seize opportunities when barriers were lowered. Blacks are not doing this. What is worse, blacks have turned to a separatist rhetoric that alienates their white friends and tends to close doors that would be open to an assimilationist-oriented black population. More would have been gained if they had chosen to identify themselves as an ethnic group rather than a racial minority.

It is difficult to find in the writings of the assimilationist school any indication that European immigrants were brought to the United States because the dominant economic class could profit by their importation in the same manner that this class profited by the importation of Africans. There are important differences between the importation of Europeans and Africans but there are also significant similarities. Africans were imported to fill the need for cheap controllable labor generated by the developing plantation system just as European immigrants were imported to fill the need for cheap controllable labor generated by developing industries. Each was brought to America because members of a particular class, differing racially or culturally from the immigrants, found it profitable. This is not basically different from the colonial situation created by European incursions around the world in search of markets, labor, and raw materials. In each case institutionalized systems of superordination—subordination emerge to facilitate exploitation and receive their ideological justification through the development of a system of racist beliefs.

All of this escaped the attention of the assimilationist school, as does the role of prejudice in dividing exploited groups into mutually hostile racial and ethnic camps. This succeeds in weakening the exploited and facilitating the perpetuation of a small class in a position of power and privilege. The concept "exploitation" is almost totally absent from the writings of the assimilationists. They ignore the fact that exploitation is the driving force behind race and ethnic relations. Their refusal to confront the central issues leads to a concern with the process of cultural assimilation. The assimilationists cannot ignore the fact that racial groups tend to remain somewhat separate from, and in an inferior position to, the dominant society, even after cultural differences are removed. The attempt to explain this has led to a concern with similarities and differences between blacks and European ethnic groups.

Irving Kristol agrees with Moynihan and Glazer that blacks today are essentially the same as ethnic immigrants of earlier periods.[28] While blacks are old Americans, they have only recently migrated to cities and face the same problems confronting earlier immigrants. They start at the bottom with the least desirable jobs and residential areas but may be expected to repeat the cycle of skill acquisition, movement up the occupational ladder, improved incomes and migration away from the ghettos. Any failure to do so is not the result of majority group prejudice because this attitude confronted all immigrant groups. Glazer charges that blacks and poor whites today are simply not willing to do the kind of hard and/or demeaning work that immigrants gladly did a generation ago in order to get the first leg up the ladder.[29] Nor are blacks willing to work to prepare themselves for opportunities that may not be readily apparent but are nevertheless real.

The Kerner Commission shared the basic premise that blacks are recent immigrants to the cities but argued that the situation has changed. [30] European immigrants arrived in the United States at the time of an expanding economy and much of their collective progress resulted from changes in the occupational structure. Blacks are moving into the cities at a time when the economy is mature and the opportunities earlier available to white immigrants have disappeared. Greatly increased levels of education are required for even the least desirable jobs. The cities themselves have changed. They are no longer growing and expanding. Immigrants gained control over cities with budgets that could be used for group progress. Blacks are gaining control over cities that are bankrupt. The Kerner Commission concluded that blacks are recent immigrants to the cities but they are faced with greater prejudice and fewer opportunities than any previous immigrant group.

This debate is misleading because it concerns itself with the wrong questions. Attention is directed away from the central fact that blacks and European immigrants were both brought to the United States to fill a need for cheap exploitable labor and each has been exploited ever since. Any approach that fails to begin with an analysis of exploitation and the role of racism as an ideological rationalization simply cannot provide an adequate basis for the analysis of racial stratification or the evolution of the black revolt in America.

White racism or prejudice school

None of these problems is resolved by the second most popular perspective among American students of race, the racism or prejudice school. The racism perspective is best associated with the work of Winthrop Jordan.[31] Jordan argues that Europeans were struck by the blackness of Africans from earliest contact. Preexisting cultural elements gave blackness a negative connotation. This combined with savagery and heathenism to stimulate a total rejection of Africans by Europeans. Europeans thus developed a need to debase blacks. Jordan recognizes the fact that Africans were exploited but he believes that exploitation is simply one variant of the need to debase. Racism is seen as a prime cause rather than as a rationalization for exploitation.

This approach is appealing because of its basic optimism. It suggests that all that is necessary is to educate racism out of existence and all race relations problems will disappear. One need not examine the possibility that basic economic transformations may be required in America prior to the elimination of racism. Despite its appeal, the approach is inadequate. There is ample evidence that slavery was not established because of European racism.[32] A number of factors converged to produce slavery in the American colonies but the prime determinants were political and economic. The agricultural economy evolved in such a manner as to create a need for a large controllable labor supply at the same time that the supply of European indentured servants was drying up. Political and power considerations precluded the enslavement of Indians or whites. There was ready access to a supply of Africans and both West Indian and European precedents for using them in a system of coerced labor. There is no need to resort to racism in the explanation for the origin of slavery but there is need to use it in explaining the ideological justification for it.

The variation within the overall attitudinal approach that focusses on prejudice rather than racism does not provide an analysis that is any more adequate than that provided by Jordan.[33] Prejudice is an individual attribute tending to be associated with certain personality characteristics. Variations in child-rearing tactics produce individuals who vary in level of security. Insecure individuals tend toward prejudice and authoritarianism. This is reinforced by threatening situations that stimulate the frustration-aggression-displacement cycle. Much research on prejudice has been focussed on societal conditions or social situations stimulating the expression of prejudice but, even then, resultant antipathies are usually explained in individual terms.

The prejudice school recognizes the existence of exploitation but tends to give it a minor role. It recognizes that high levels of prejudice develop in situations in which members of minority and majority groups are perceived to be competing for the same scarce resources (e.g., jobs and homes) but does not seem to consider the possibility that this perception of competition may be artificially induced in order to stimulate hostility and conflict and to prevent all exploited groups from joining together to end their mutual exploitation. This deficiency results from the failure to examine race relations from a historical and world systems perspective. The broader perspective inevitably forces the recognition of the primary role of exploitation and the secondary nature of prejudice as a set of attitudes created in a complex, hierarchically and racially stratified society.

The capitalist exploitation or class model

The capitalist exploitation or class model appears to have more potential utility than either the assimilation or white racism perspectives.[34] There is general agreement among scholars sharing this perspective that capitalism is the basic source of the oppression of black Americans. Capitalism is a system of production for profit that requires people to be proletarianized — that is, they must be divested of all resources except their labor power, which must be transformed into a marketable commodity. All workers are exploited under capitalism and potentially could join together to overthrow the capitalist order. The capitalist class does all in its power to prevent this from happening.

European expansion produced exploitative colonial relations between white and nonwhite peoples. Accommodative systems of superordination—subordination developed as a means of facilitating exploitation with a minimal expenditure of time and money upon direct coercion. These systems took many different forms but they included slavery at one extreme and wage labor at the other. The nature of exploitation of colonial peoples differed from that of internal labor sources in that it involved the proletarianization of an entire people instead of a single class. Because colonial powers shared the human desire to view themselves as moral peoples, they developed an ideology of racism and/or race prejudice to rationalize their behavior.

The American colonies imported African slaves to fill a particular labor need and simultaneously imported the ideology of racism as its justification. The conflict between two white capitalist classes resulted in the abolition of slavery in the United States. The exploitation of black labor continued beyond the death of slavery, as manifested in debt peonage, tenant farming, sharecropping, and eventually wage labor. The latter became increasingly important as blacks moved north to become part of the industrial labor pool. These changes were accompanied by a change in the function of race prejudice. It now served to divide the working class racially, keeping it weak and exploitable. A system of white skin privilege evolved, through which white workers were led to believe that they had a vested interest in the status quo and black workers were led to believe that white workers were their enemies. Thus black workers could be used as a reserve army of the unemployed and as strikebreakers.

There is little question that this model does reflect a great deal of reality. Capitalism is a system that exploits all workers and most blacks are workers. The capitalist exploitation or class model does an adequate job of describing the location of blacks in the American racial stratification order and thus may serve as a useful starting point for the analysis of the class dialectic. However, a note of caution must be introduced. Not all blacks are members of the proletariat. There are a few minor black capitalists. None is engaged in primary production to a significant extent. There are no black-owned General Motors or General Electrics. However, there are black-owned capitalist enterprises that do have a significant dollar-value business. These firms are linked into the free enterprise system and the blacks who own and operate them do have a vested interest in maintaining the existing capitalist system. There are also a few — a very few — blacks who are employed in the corporate hierarchy of the American business structure. They also have a stake in the existing order. Thus while the majority of blacks are proletarians some are clearly integrated into the capitalist system.

The internal colonial or submerged nation model

The colonial model also appears to have much to offer. It has two basic historical phases. The first was from about 1928 to 1957 and had its roots in the Communist Party advocacy of the submerged nation thesis.[35] It suggested that black Americans in at least one section of the country comprised a submerged or oppressed nation. They were perceived to meet all the criteria of a nation as specified by Stalin's classic definition that "a nation is a historically evolved stable community of language, territory, economic life and psychological makeup manifested in a community of culture."[36] They met the requirement for a common language with English. The fact that they shared the same language with their oppressor was not considered to cause any special problem. This had also been true for the peoples of Scotland, Ireland, and Wales. Blacks also qualified as having a common culture shaped by their common experience of oppression in America. Blacks developed an intelligentsia contributing to art, music, and literature. The requirement for a common territory meant far more than simple residence in a common area. It also meant the existence of an integrated economic system with a certain amount of internal differentiation. The Black Belt met these requirements.

The Black Belt is that area of the South that was named for its particularly rich soil. The rich soil lent itself to plantation production of cotton and consequently became an area of high black population concentration. As of 1948 there were some 180 Black Belt counties with a black majority. They were immediately contiguous to another 290 counties ranging from 30 to 50 percent black. This produced a combined area that was over 50 percent black and included a majority of all American blacks. The plantation system of the Black Belt, both during and after slavery, produced an agricultural economy shared by all of its black residents. The black population was dependent upon the plantation system which was, in turn, dependent upon external northern capital. Thus the entire area comprised an internal dependency. The black relationship to the plantation system produced the historically evolved stable community essential to nationhood.

The Communist Party abandoned its belief that blacks comprised an oppressed or submerged nation as a result of changes in American society. They suggested that industrialization stimulated migration of blacks out of the Black Belt and into the cities along with occupational differentiation as more blacks left agriculture for industrial jobs. The concentration of blacks in the Black Belt further diminished as whites moved into the area replacing some of the blacks who left. Eventually whites comprised the majority of all residents. The Communist Party concluded that the conditions for black nationhood ceased to exist and they changed their official position to conform to the class model. This was not the death of the concept. Numerous scholars eventually adopted the thesis in one of several related forms and referred to blacks as an internal colony. All current versions share certain key elements.[37] All proponents agree that blacks were brought to the United States because it was profitable for whites, that black culture was undermined, that blacks have always lived under a system of white domination profitable to whites, that black liberation requires independence, and that whites will resist black independence. They all agree that blacks are not simply another immigrant group, that there is no hope for black equality within the system, that independence does not insure equality, and that some spokesmen for black independence may not serve black interests because they may unwittingly (or even wittingly) serve as agents of indirect rule.

Perhaps one of the most important features of this model is its recognition of the importance of indirect rule. Proponents argue that blacks do not have to be concentrated in the Black Belt to comprise an internal colony. Blacks are concentrated in urban ghettos despite dispersion around the nation. Colonialism traditionally develops some form of indirect rule as a means of accommodation — that is maintaining a system of superordination—subordination at minimal cost to the ruling power. This indirect rule may be manifested in internal class differentiation among black Americans. Middle-class blacks may be recruited, educated, socialized, and financed in order to induce loyalty to the system and to the exploiters. A class develops within the subject peoples with a vested interest in perpetuating the system of exploitation even though it does not itself interpret the situation in this manner. The existence of such a class minimizes the probability for the development of a successful change-oriented movement among the oppressed.

Conclusions regarding the four models

It is important that we recognize that none of the dominant theoretical positions used for the study of race in American sociology is totally adequate for the study of this problem. Most American sociologists who are at all concerned with race study race relations and not racial stratification. The overwhelming majority accepts some combination of perspectives derived from the assimilationist or white racism and prejudice approaches. In other words, the majority accepts theoretical perspectives that have little potential utility. A small, but significant, number of American sociologists accept some variety of the colonial model. This has some utility but is less than completely adequate for the task. This model helps us to understand many aspects of the racial dialectic but entirely ignores the class dialectic. A small number of American sociologists accept the capitalist exploitation model. This also has some utility without being completely adequate. It helps us to understand aspects of the class dialectic but ignores the racial dialectic. A new model is needed which can explain the simultaneous impact of, and interplay between, the dialectics of race and class. One object of the present monograph is to attempt the first steps toward the construction of such a model. This question will be returned to in Chapter 12 after a consideration of the historical development of the League of Revolutionary Black Workers. However, a brief overview of the layout of this monograph is appropriate before examining that history.

The structure of the monograph

The dialectics of class and race provide the general context for analyzing long-term struggles but all concrete struggle occurs within a particular social context that influences its mode of expression and sets parameters for its range of possible outcomes. Therefore Part I of this monograph examines the social context out of which the League emerged in two chapters describing the history of blacks in the auto industry and in Detroit. Part II includes seven chapters that analyze the growth and development of the League of Revolutionary Black Workers from its inception as DRUM to its split and demise. Part III consists of two chapters. One explores the post-League scene in an attempt to predict the future course of the racial dialectic. The second includes an analysis of the theoretical contribution of this study as well as the significance of current societal developments. The introductions to each Part provide a more complete presentation of their contents and an explanation of how each chapter relates to the overall development of the monograph.

PART I

Historical context

This Part is designed to present the historical context within which the League emerged. The broad general schema of the racial dialectic within a world capitalist system was presented in Chapter 1, as a basis for the understanding of concrete developments. However, the picture is not complete without adding details of a more local nature. It is true that all American industry has certain features in common in its historical relations with black workers but there are also features unique to each industry. In Chapter 2 the history of blacks in the auto industry and in the United Automobile Workers (UAW) is presented. The peculiar combination of a radical leadership in the UAW and Ford's use of black workers in an attempt to create a docile labor force stand out as features setting auto apart from other industries. Nevertheless the broad pattern of racial exclusiveness, racial divisiveness, and racial exploitation is similar to that of all American industry.

Similarly Detroit has certain features that set it apart from other American cities. It is an industrial city more heavily dependent upon a single industry than any other comparably sized American city. It is also somewhat unique in the level of radical political activities concentrated within its borders. Only New York rivals it in this regard and even New York probably does not compare with Detroit if radical political activity is measured on a per capita basis. It is probable that there is a mutually reinforcing linkage between Detroit's dependence upon the auto industry and its high level of radical activity. Detroit also shares many characteristics of other northern industrial cities. In Chapter 3 the history of blacks in Detroit is examined.

It is undoubtedly the case that the League of Revolutionary Black Workers developed as it did as a result of broad societal and world system trends. However, its development was probably influenced also by factors unique to Detroit and the auto industry. Hopefully the material in Part II will aid in sorting out the effects of each.

2. Black workers, the auto industry, and the UAW

The UAW has the reputation of being one of the most progressive labor unions in America. It feels that it has a right to be proud of its record of concern over societal issues and particularly of its record in the area of race relations. It is probably true that, relative to other unions, it has an admirable record of support for the black drive for equal rights and equal job opportunities in all their manifestations. Nevertheless the UAW has come under severe criticism from many blacks and has been called a "racist organization." This apparent contradiction can best be understood through a close examination of the role that black workers currently play, and have historically played, within the automobile industry and within the UAW. As is often the case, an understanding of the present can be best arrived at through an examination of the past.

The beginning

Northrup concluded that "Perhaps if there had not been a shortage of labor during World War I, Negroes would never have found employment in the automobile industry."[1] The validity of that statement is attested to by the fact that there were only 569 blacks among the 105,758 gainful workers in the automobile industry in 1910.[2] This is slightly over one-half of 1 percent. The migration of southern blacks and southern whites to Detroit was initially spurred by Henry Ford's announcement of January 5, 1914, that he would pay all workers a wage of five dollars a day.[3] A survey in 1917 of the twenty largest urban Detroit employers (not limited to the automobile industry) found a total of 2,874 black workers.[4]

The northern migration of both southern whites and southern blacks was intensified by labor demands resulting from war production. A repeat survey of the same twenty firms in 1919 found about 11,000

18

black workers — approximately 6,000 of whom worked at the Ford River Rouge plant.[5] An additional 4,000 blacks were estimated to be employed at the Ford Highland Park plant. No accurate employment figures are available for the auto industry as a whole until 1930, when blacks comprised about 4 percent of the gainful workers (25,895 out of 640,474).[6] This would suggest that blacks had slightly better opportunities in the auto industry than elsewhere in Detroit. Van Deusen notes that blacks constituted about 3 percent of Detroit's labor force in 1929.[7] However, this should not be interpreted as indicating that the industry practiced fair employment practices. Blacks represented about 8 percent (120,000 out of 1,500,000) of Detroit's population.[8] Blacks were underemployed in Detroit industry, but to a lesser extent by automobile manufacturers. The proportion of blacks in the automobile industry remained relatively constant throughout the decade of the thirties. Blacks still accounted for about 4 percent of employed persons in 1940 (23,015 out of 617,132).[9]

Blacks were not randomly distributed within the auto industry. They tended to be highly concentrated regionally, by employer and by job level. Bailer notes that:

With respect to geographic distribution, Negro workers have been unduly concentrated in Michigan, and more particularly in the Detroit area. In 1940 Michigan accounted for 60 percent of the white workers as compared with 83 percent of the Negro labor force. Probably 70 percent of all Negroes in the industry were employed in the Detroit metropolitan area alone.[10]

Bailer suggests three reasons to account for the concentration of black workers in Michigan: (1) Michigan had a greater labor shortage than elsewhere as a result of a more rapid rate of industrial expansion; (2) the occupations in which blacks were concentrated were largely confined to Michigan; and (3) antiblack attitudes were more prevalent in the other parts of the country where auto plants were located. Two of the three reasons are structural and, in large part, beyond the employers' control. If there are insufficient white workers to fill available jobs, blacks must be hired. If, in a time of labor shortage, whites refuse to work at certain tasks, blacks must be so employed. Black job opportunity in the auto industry came about, for the most part, because jobs remained after all available white workers were employed. Bailer states that attitudes and receptivity make up the third factor leading to a concentration of black workers in Michigan. The material presented in this chapter lends support to Bailer's conclusion that attitudinal receptivity was the least significant of the three factors. In fact it raises questions as to whether it should be included on the list.

Black workers in the auto industry were also concentrated by employer and plant. Bailer furnishes data on the distribution of black auto workers among the ten largest employers of blacks during the period 1937–1941.[11] Almost half of all blacks employed in the auto industry worked for Ford where they constituted 11,000 out of 90,000 employees. Ford employed more than four times the number of blacks employed by any other concern despite ranking third in the production of finished vehicles. The degree of concentration is revealed as even more pronounced. Of black workers employed by Ford in 1937, 99 percent worked at the River Rouge plant in Dearborn. Similarly Chrysler employed 2,000 blacks among their 50,000 employees, but the majority worked at Dodge Main in Hamtramck. General Motors had 2,500 blacks out of 100,000 employees, the majority of whom were employed at Buick plant 70 in Flint; the Pontiac foundry in Pontiac; Chevrolet Forge, Spring and Bumper in Detroit; or Chevrolet Grey-Iron Foundry in Saginaw. This should be interpreted in the context of the knowledge that there were several Buick plants in Flint, five major Pontiac plants in Pontiac, and several Chevrolet plants in the Detroit area.

The two auto plants having the highest proportion of black employees, Midland Steel Products (1,250 out of 4,100 employees) and Bohn Aluminum and Brass (688 out of 2,798), are both primarily engaged in foundry operations. Dodge Main included the largest Chrysler foundry operation. We may note from their names the prominence of foundries among the plants listed above as employing the most black workers. This is consistent with the general distribution of black workers by type of occupation.

Robert Dunn found that black auto workers in the late twenties were primarily concentrated in the less desirable and most-unskilled manual occupations.[12] Bailer analyzed the 1930 census and found that about three-fourths of the black and one-fourth of the white auto workers were in unskilled positions.[13] Approximately half of the white, and one-eighth of the black, auto workers were in skilled or white-collar occupations. Bailer feels that these statistics tend to underestimate the degree of skin color advantage given to white workers:

for jobs within the same classification as to skill vary greatly in their desirability. Outside of the core room nearly all foundry jobs are unpleasant, yet a substantial portion of them are semi-skilled and skilled. The same holds true for the heat-treat and sanding and paint operations. Yet most of the semi-skilled and skilled Negroes were found in such departments, where they were confined to the most hazardous or otherwise undesirable occupations. . . . Likewise, Negro unskilled workers filled the more undesirable jobs in that broad occupational category. In brief, Negroes were not only concentrated in occupations requiring less skill but were also attached to the worst jobs within each occupational classification. The sole exception to this general characterization was the Ford Rouge plant — though here . . . the difference was largely one of degree.[14]

There was a negligible number of black foremen outside of Ford. There was a slightly larger number of black strawbosses but they were always in charge of all-black work crews. Almost all blacks in assembly plants outside Michigan were either janitors or in similar occupations. It has been stated above that the Ford Rouge plant was different. Bailer notes that:

Negroes were used in every major department in the plant. Moreover . . . they performed practically every operation relating to automobile manufacturing. . . . Negroes were engaged in every occupation in the plant. It was nevertheless true that Negro wage-earners were disproportionately concentrated in the less desirable occupations and divisions. Thus they constituted nearly half of the production workers and over one-third of all workers in the foundry, but less than 1 percent of the tool and die makers. In the most disagreeable jobs the proportion of Negro workers was over 50 percent. . . . Thus, at Ford's, as in the rest of the industry, Negroes were employed in the greatest numbers in those sections where the general nature of the work was least desirable. Yet the Rouge plant was the only instance in the industry in which Negro workers were used in every occupation. In addition, the number of Negro foremen in the plant, though small in relation to the volume of Negro employment, exceeded the total for the rest of the industry.[15]

It appears that, with the exception of the Ford Rouge plant, black auto workers were initially hired only when there was a shortage of white workers available and were largely restricted to occupations that whites were most reluctant to accept. It is not entirely clear whether blacks were also discriminated against in terms of wages. Carlson notes that during the 1920s there were a few plants in which differential pay was given for the same work.[16] This was done by giving blacks lower payroll classifications than justified by actual work performed. Bailer found that this differential had largely disappeared by the 1940s.[17] He presents data showing that black annual income averaged $209 less than white income in 1939 ($1,092 compared with $1,291). This difference was less than in most major industries but may indicate more inequality in treatment than is readily apparent, due to the black concentration in Michigan, which paid higher wages to auto workers than did other areas of the United States. It is not possible to determine whether blacks earned less than whites because they were concentrated in lower-paying occupations or whether the occupations paid less because they were defined as black occupations. Both factors probably interacted.

Why was Ford different?

The preceding Section describes the Ford River Rouge plant as different from other auto plants. It hired more black workers, both absolutely and proportionately, than any other employer and was virtually the only plant in which blacks had an opportunity to get skilled production and supervisory jobs. It is worth examining the degree of these differences. Northrup states that:

> The story most frequently told is that at the beginning of the 1921 depression, a delegation, composed of Negroes employed at River Rouge and prominent members of the Detroit Negro community, approached Henry Ford and expressed their concern over discrimination in layoffs. Mr. Ford then adopted the policy of employing the same proportion of Negroes at River Rouge as the proportion of Negroes in the population of Greater Detroit. . . . Actually, the proportion of Negroes at River Rouge usually exceeded that.[18]

It should be emphasized that this policy included placing blacks in all occupations and departments but it did not extend to the point of full equality in employment practices. It has been noted that black workers were disproportionately concentrated in lower-status and less desirable jobs. Blacks were not proportionally distributed by department. Nor was there inclusion of blacks in all Ford plants. Ford had nineteen Michigan automobile plants but only five employed blacks (the ones in northern Michigan were most likely to be all white).[19] Virtually all black Ford workers located in Michigan in 1939 worked at River Rouge (9,825 out of 9,882). Ford employed almost no black workers in the American South except for a small number of janitors and porters. Similarly when Ford purchased the Lincoln company it did not extend to it the policy of proportionate hiring of blacks.[20] Northrup gives Henry Ford the benefit of the doubt in concluding that:

> There is no evidence that Henry Ford originally decided to employ large numbers of Negroes at River Rouge for other than altruistic reasons. His move naturally won him great respect and admiration among Negroes, especially those in Detroit. At a later date, the support of Negroes proved to be a valuable ally for the propagation of Mr. Ford's ideas on politics and unionism, as he well realized.[21]

An examination of the manner in which this policy was carried out might shed some light on the degree of altruism involved. All unpopular policies established at the top have the potential of being sabotaged by uncooperative lower-level supervisory officials. In order to avoid this Ford appointed two blacks to the Ford service department.[22] These individuals were apparently selected both for loyalty and visibility in the black community. One, Donald Marshall, had worked at Ford for an extended period of time while the other, Willis Ward, had been an All-American football player at the University of Michigan. The Ford service department combined the functions of a company police force and a personnel office. All blacks were hired through Marshall and Ward and all issues related to blacks were referred to them. Line supervisors tended to carry out company policy after Marshall and Ward demonstrated that they had sufficient authority to insure compliance.[23]

Howe and Widick describe the process through which Henry Ford gained favor in the Detroit black community.[24] He donated the parish house of St. Matthew's Episcopal Church where Donald Marshall also taught Sunday School. He gave substantial financial aid to the Second Baptist Church. Henry Ford also helped to finance the village of Inkster (then all black). He also publicly invited George Washington Carver to his home and sponsored appearances of Marian Anderson and Dorothy Maynor on the "Ford Sunday Hour."

The links forged in this manner were strengthened through Ford hiring practices. Northrup states that:

Most Negroes employed by Ford were recommended to Messrs. Marshall and Ward by particular individuals. Before 1938, certain Detroit ministers were the most important group who gave job recommendations. These preachers had demonstrated complete agreement with Henry Ford in matters of politics and industrial relations. In other words, they were pro-Republican and anti-Union. Prior to 1932, such qualifications invoked no hardships on the ministers, for the Detroit Negro community was overwhelmingly in accord with Mr. Ford's views. Since that date, however, a majority of Negroes supported the Democratic party in the national elections, and a minority became pro-union. The result was a growing opposition to Ford employment policies among Detroit Negroes.[25]

This relationship worked to the mutual advantage of both Ford Motor Company and the black ministers. Ford received a supply of labor that could be expected to be loyal, docile, and anti-union. The attractiveness of Ford as an employer of black workers was sufficiently great for there to be usually far more blacks seeking jobs than there were jobs available.

Not all ministers' recommendations carried the same weight with Ford. Therefore the congregations of the more influential ministers were increased by blacks seeking work at Ford.[26] Bailer suggests that Henry Ford was sufficiently interested in keeping the ministers in his debt that he would even fire blacks already working at Ford in order to give jobs to others who came well recommended.[27]

Howe and Widick describe some of the mechanisms used by Henry Ford in order to insure a docile work force:

> Several Negro churches and other institutions barred pro-union speakers. . . . When A. Philip Randolph . . . was invited in 1938 to speak at a church meeting, church members at Ford were threatened with layoffs. After Randolph spoke, some were dismissed and frankly told that Randolph's speech was the reason. When Mordecai Johnson, president at Howard University, made a pro-union speech at a Negro church, a second appearance was denied him three months later. For in the meantime, said the minister of the church, "Don Marshall heard about the speech and was very angry. . . . He said that he would never hire another member of the Bethel Church if the church allowed any more speakers to come here and criticize the company."[28]

There were many such incidents.[29] However, in 1938 a liberal black minister, Dr. Horace A. White, published a magazine article entitled, "Who Owns the Negro Churches," which exposed the association between Henry Ford and many black ministers.[30] This caused sufficient furor for the system of ministerial references for workers to be largely abandoned. Perhaps by coincidence a black Republican political organization was formed in Wayne County (Detroit plus outlying area) shortly thereafter. Most blacks believed the organization to be sponsored by Willis Ward and Donald Marshall. Large numbers of blacks joined and recommendations from the organization's precinct captains appeared to be as successful in getting jobs at Ford as ministers' recommendations previously had been.

Marshall and Ward continually attacked labor unions, stating that they did not have black workers' interests at heart. The implication was clear that it would not be wise for a black worker to join a union. It may not have been. Union members were fired from Ford and often physically harassed when their membership became known. Both Marshall and Ward were active in politics. They campaigned "as individuals" but took extended leaves of absence from Ford in order to do so. They were not reluctant to point out the displeasure of their employer when blacks began voting Democratic in large numbers.

Northrup states that there is no evidence that Henry Ford had "other than altruistic reasons" for hiring large numbers of black workers. This is true. However, indirect evidence exists that certain practices had the consequence of providing a pool of docile black workers who would not be anxious to join a union. White Ford workers might easily share their reluctance because of the knowledge that they could always be replaced by a black worker. This was especially credible because Ford had not been slow to fire white workers who resisted black employment.[31]

Unionization comes to the auto industry

The auto industry had little to fear from organized labor prior to the depression. The combination of the misery and fears brought by the depression and the hope and optimism stimulated by Franklin Delano Roosevelt's election created a surge in union-organizing activities throughout the nation. The National Industrial Recovery Act (NIRA) of 1933 simultaneously fed this drive and helped to harden employers' reaction against unionism.[32] Employers reacted against the pro-union attitudes of Roosevelt. They were confident in the belief that the Supreme Court would eventually throw out the NIRA. They instituted a national wave of repression of union activity. In the Detroit auto industry this was reflected by the firing of union sympathizers and the utilization of labor spies. Widick notes that General Motors paid the Pinkerton Detective Agency $419,000 and Chrysler spent $210,000 on spies and informers.[33]

This type of repression was only one barrier faced by those who wished to organize the auto industry. Perhaps their major handicap was the multiethnic character of the work force. The same migrant stream that brought large numbers of southern blacks to Detroit's automobile factories brought with it even larger numbers of southern whites. Many carried with them racial attitudes formed in their region of origin. These attitudes took some of the same organizational forms they had in the South. There was a minimum of 200,000 members of the Ku Klux Klan (KKK) in Michigan in 1936 in addition to an unknown number of members of its more dangerous offshoot, the Black Legion.[34] It is estimated that between 1933 and 1936 the Black Legion committed over 50 murders in Michigan. However, it is not at all clear that either the KKK or the Black Legion were transplanted from the South or that their membership was primarily southern white.

Both the KKK and the Black Legion were violently anti-union. Moreover their existence is indicative of the presence of a racial attitude that would make it difficult to jointly organize black and white workers. A large number of the nonsouthern auto workers were foreign born — primarily from Poland. Polish-American workers shared the antiblack prejudices of the southern white.[35] The origin of the Polish hostility toward blacks is not exactly clear. Widick suggests that, "While anti-Semitism was a heritage from the old country, the Polish had to be taught to hate the black man, and on that score the KKK *did* leave a permanent imprint on the immigrants."[36] Widick's thesis may receive some support from Bailer, who noted a higher level of hostility toward blacks among the younger generation of Poles.[37] However, there are alternative explanations. Employer policies of playing off one racial/ethnic group against the other may have been sufficient to account for the development of racist attitudes without resort to blaming educational practices of southern whites or the KKK. Regardless of the origin of the attitude it is a fact that Polish-American auto workers were no more anxious than southern whites to join together in solidarity with black workers.

The circle is completed when one considers the attitudes of black workers. Bailer notes:

Negro workers have been slow to accept unionism. The causes are not difficult to determine. Largely because of their unfortunate experiences with some unions, Negro workers generally have been traditionally skeptical of organized labor, and Negroes in the automobile industry were no exception. Moreover, the effect of this historic suspicion was reinforced by their background of experiences. Beginning with World War I, most of them had migrated from the rural south. Possessing little experience with trade unions, they were easily influenced by those who counseled abstention from unionism. In fact, the bulk of the Negro middle class in the automobile centers . . . was decidedly anti-union in sentiment. Again, an awareness of the racial attitude of many of their white fellow workers made Negroes reluctant to join in common cause with them. Finally, the general community pattern of race relations has made it difficult for the union to practice racial equality in most localities and thus has restricted correspondingly the ability of Negroes to take advantage of full participation.[38]

Black workers generally viewed labor unions as organizations of white men concerned with white men's problems. They saw little reason to expect that whites who had displayed ample evidence of their bigotry in the past would be any more egalitarian in unions than elsewhere. Employers consistently argued that the bigotry of white workers forced them to restrict the number of black workers and the range of jobs open to blacks. It was only an employer like Ford — one willing to act like a dictator — who was able to employ large numbers of blacks and to employ any outside the most undesirable jobs. Labor unions would only give more power to workers known by blacks to be racist.

This fear was reinforced by a strike at American Can in Toledo several years before the sit-down strikes began.[39] A strike broke out in a department with a large number of black workers. The strike was lost and the white workers blamed the blacks. Management promptly fired all black workers. This experience could be interpreted as a message that blacks were asking for trouble whenever they cooperated with whites. It is hardly surprising that few black workers were involved in the sit-down strikes that hit the auto industry in 1936 and 1937.[40] The most typical response of black workers was simply to go home and stay there until the conflict was resolved.

Unions were cognizant of black reluctance to support unionization drives. They also knew that employers were more than willing to use black workers as strikebreakers.[41] They concluded that the black workers had to be won over to the union cause if there were to be a realistic chance for lasting unionization. The UAW made special efforts to win over black workers.[42] The UAW consistently stressed the theme of racial equality in its publicity. Organizers exhibiting overt prejudice were dropped. Blacks with leadership potential were put into highly visible and somewhat responsible posts (e.g., Sam Fanroy, a black worker, was put on the strike committee at Chrysler during the March 1937 sit down).

This policy had variable successes. Plants in which blacks constituted a large portion of the work force exhibited good race relations and a reasonable proportion of the black workers joined the union. Those in which the proportion of black workers was small had some racial clashes. This may have been partially a function of black perception of security and collective power resulting from numbers. The extent to which white acceptance of blacks during unionization drives was motivated by self-interested recognition of need is exemplified by the experience of a small east-side Detroit plant.[43]

The plant was dominated by southern whites who rejected all appeals of the union agent to accept blacks into the union. The company refused to recognize the union. A strike was seen as unavoidable. A determination had to made as to the treatment of black workers. A committee of black workers was invited to a union meeting and asked to state the black position. The committee reiterated that blacks were willing to join the union and strike if they could be assured full and equal participation in the union after the strike. The whites recognized the inevitability of a strike and the need for blacks if the strike were to be won. They agreed to all demands. Blacks joined, a strike was fought and won, and blacks attended the victory dance without any vocal opposition. Self-interested concern was also manifested in a reputed offer by white union officials to pay black workers' dues if they would join the union during the 1936 Lansing Oldsmobile strike.[44] The offer had few takers.

Automobile manufacturers were also aware of the potential use of black workers for their own purposes. They systematically exploited racial cleavages as a means of destroying the union movement. The most flagrant example came in 1939.[45] The Dodge Main plant (Hamtramck) was closed October 6 in response to what management called a slowdown instigated by the union. A shutdown of all Detroit Chrysler plants followed. Several black foundry workers returned on November 22 to pick up their paychecks. They "somehow got the impression" that they would be put to work if they returned within ten days. On November 24 about sixty black workers returned and attempted to pass the picket line. Violence broke out, stones were thrown, two policemen and six workers were hurt. Most blacks succeeded in getting inside the plant but were sent home after a few hours' work.

The union attempted to prevent a recurrence of this incident.[46] They brought in black union members from other locals and put them on the picket line. Many black leaders in the community feared a possible race riot. The reality of this fear was attested to by the fact that Hamtramck was almost entirely a Polish-American community, the white work force at the plant was heavily Polish, and the Poles had high levels of racial hostility. A leaflet was put out over the signature of many prominent blacks including Rev. Horace White of the Plymouth Congregational Church, Rev. Charles Hill of the Hartford Avenue Baptist Church, Michigan State Senator Charles Diggs, and Louis Martin, the editor of the *Michigan Chronicle.* The leaflet warned that the back-to-work movement might cause race riots and would not be of value to black workers. It stressed the class appeal that black workers could only gain in combination with white workers.

Nevertheless 181 blacks and 6 whites attempted to return to work on

November 27 under police protection. There was a well-disciplined picket line of several thousand and no violence resulted. Several black leaders spoke urging blacks not to cross the picket line and urging the pickets to refrain from violence. Once again the strikebreakers were sent home after a few hours' work. It was almost as if Chrysler felt that nothing was to be gained if violence could not be provoked.

The dilemma faced by the black worker was clear. He could see that management was cynically using him and exploiting racial antipathy in order to destroy the union movement. He could see that white workers were antagonistic to blacks and that they had restricted black opportunities in the past. White workers appeared to be every bit as cynical as management in laying aside racial bigotry when it was in their self-interest to do so — when blacks were needed for successful union-organizing drives. Thus it was easy for black workers to say "the hell with everybody," and pursue what they perceived as being in their own self-interest. The real dilemma came in determining what constituted self-interest — when were actions productive of short-range gains also productive of greater long-range losses?

The UAW attacks Ford

One factor that could never be totally left out of the equation was the fact that Henry Ford, whatever his private motives, had always provided more black jobs than any other Detroit area employer and, in fact, at times provided more black jobs than the rest of Detroit employers combined. Ford Motor Company was also the strongest holdout against the union movement. Henry Ford had a violent hatred of unions. The possible future gains to blacks of unionization weighed little in balance against the reality of present jobs. This was especially true because the elusive gains of unionization would be dependent upon the goodwill of white auto workers — workers who were predominantly southern white or Polish-American.

This dilemma became very real when the UAW decided to move against Ford. The UAW had to face the fact that the success or failure of this movement would largely be determined by black workers. Blacks could not sit this fight out. They were forced by their very numbers to take sides. The earliest confrontation involving blacks occurred in May 1937 at the infamous "Battle Of the Overpass." Blacks were among Harry Bennett's goon squad (employees of the Ford Service Department) that attacked and severely beat Walter Reuther and other union organizers attempting to pass out leaflets at the gates of the Ford River Rouge plant.[47] Despite the fact that the sixty UAW members, the majority of whom were women, had a permit, they were severely beaten by the Ford Service people. Newspaper photographers had their cameras stolen. The *Detroit Times* published an account of the action and Ford withdrew its advertising for more than one and a half years. Three months later the UAW returned to leaflet again. This time they were not molested — perhaps because they brought along a thousand rather well-constructed union members who did not appear to be inclined toward pacifism.

The next three years were filled with violence as the UAW pushed its attempt to unionize Ford. Dearborn passed ordinances effectively barring the passing out of leaflets at Ford River Rouge. Over 1,000 UAW people were arrested. However, blacks did not play another significant role in the conflict until 1941. As 1941 approached it became increasingly evident that the union would stand or fall depending upon what happened at the River Rouge plant and that a strike could not be avoided.[48] The River Rouge management began hiring large numbers of blacks during the early months of 1941.[49] The word was spread in the Detroit ghetto that any man who wished a job could get one at Rouge.[50]

The strike at River Rouge began as a spontaneous walkout on April 1, 1941.[51] The union leadership endorsed the strike once it was in progress but they did so with great reluctance. They were unsure and concerned regarding the possible role of the 17,000 blacks employed by Ford. An estimated 2,000 persons, mostly black, remained in the plant.[52] The next morning, April 2, picket lines were formed and barricades set up by 6:00 A.M. Howe and Widick describe what happened next:

An hour later the first fighting broke out. "Iron bolts and nuts flew through the air in a wholesale barrage from the factory roof, while several hundred Negroes with steel bars and knives charged out of the main gate, No. 4, of the Rouge plant in two assaults on the UAW—CIO picket lines there." Thirty-six unionists were hurt and treated at the union's hospital. The pickets had not expected this attack and their lines were broken. Picket lines were soon reformed and at 9 A.M. another assault took place from within the factory. This time the pickets were ready and slugged it out with baseball bats, fists and sticks. The battle was brief, bloody, and decisive for the lines held, and. casualties aside, the union had shown it could close the plant.[53]

There were two developments at this point that had serious racial implications. First, the black workers remaining inside were not inclined to leave and were arming themselves.[54] It was rumored that they were being paid their normal wages of $1.00 an hour for a full 24-hour day. Second, Homer Martin appeared in the Detroit ghetto as an American Federation of Labor (AFL) organizer, addressed an assembled crowd of 3,000 blacks, and attempted to organize a "back-to-work" march.[55] Both of these developments had the potential to further inflame levels of racial tension.

The back-to-work drive was beaten by a coalition of Detroit black leaders having essentially the same composition as the one that had fought the earlier Chrysler attempt to use blacks as strikebreakers. The problem of the black workers inside Ford was harder to handle. Walter White, executive secretary of the National Association for the Advancement of Colored Peoples (NAACP) came to Detroit and met with officials of the UAW who told him that the strike might be lost because of the activities of black workers.[56] He obtained from them a promise that union seniority rules would not be used against black workers when employment declined and then set about attempting to get blacks out of the plant.

His first job, and a rather difficult one, was to convince the leadership of the Detroit NAACP that the black community and the black workers stood to gain most from a union victory achieved by black and white cooperation. The NAACP hired sound trucks, rejecting the union's offer to provide them, and circled the Ford plant urging the black workers to come out. Walter White describes both the reasons why many blacks might have wished to support Ford and why they may have been afraid to leave the plant:

I walked the picket line around the plant and attempted to talk to a Negro inside who brandished a frightening weapon several feet in length made of tool steel which he had sharpened to razor keenness. In answer to my plea that he come out of the plant he told me in exceedingly profane and biological language what he thought of unions in general and of me in particular. He said that Ford's was the only place in Detroit where he had been able to find a job to support himself and his family, and that the union had not done a blankety-blank thing to break down employment discrimination in other Detroit plants.

After a few hours, however, our loudspeaker appeals began to produce results. Across the main entrance of the River Rouge plant stood an apparently impregnable wall of human flesh made up of armed guards placed there to prevent not only entrance into the plant of unauthorized persons, but also to prevent departure of those inside from the plant. Across the road, which formed a kind of no man's land, was a solid mass of strikers. I remember one sturdy Negro from the plant standing poised on the other side of the guards like a halfback waiting for the ball to be snapped. As one of the guards momentarily turned away the Negro charged through the split-second opening and across the road. A great cheer arose and he was greeted warmly by the strikers.[57]

Not all blacks left the plant but approximately one-third of those inside did. Eventually the rest were talked out by a federal conciliator carrying a safe conduct pass from the UAW. A compromise settlement was reluctantly accepted by both Ford and the UAW. A National Labor Relations Board representational election was held in late May. The UAW won with 58,000 out of 80,000 votes cast. Only about 4 percent of the votes was cast for "no union."

This should not be taken as an indication that most blacks had deserted Ford and were won over to the UAW. Bailer concluded that the bulk of the votes cast for the AFL union (20 percent of the total cast) were cast by black workers who believed that they were doing what Henry Ford wanted them to do.[58] This interpretation is buttressed by evidence indicating that the black ministers who had previously allied themselves with Ford supported Homer Martin and the AFL union.[59] Once the issue was lost Henry Ford signed a closed shop contract despite the fact that this was not common to the industry. This greatly increased the number of blacks in the UAW because they had to join or give up their jobs at Ford. This may have been interpreted by blacks as one more case in which they were sold out by whites when they were no longer needed. In this case, however, it was white management that had previously tried to appear as a friend of blacks.

Impact of unionization

Unionization had little impact upon the lives or working conditions of black automobile workers prior to the beginnings of World War II. Northrup states that as of 1941 the union was unable to bring about any substantial alterations in the racial occupational distribution.[60] Bailer notes that union action brought insignificant amounts of upgrading in some Detroit area plants.[61] This is best understood in the context of the tensions between local and national union leadership.[62] National UAW leaders appear to have been sincerely committed to racial equality and attempted to further it. Local leadership usually reflected the attitudes of the membership because the leaders were part of the local and because they depended upon membership votes. National leaders were more committed to the development of the union than to racial equality. They did not usually carry their commitment to racial equality to the point where it might disrupt the union movement. Black men's interests were sometimes sacrificed to achieve harmony among whites.

An example is provided by an Atlanta UAW local that unionized a plant employing a few black janitors. The national UAW leadership wanted full integration. White workers in the Atlanta local wanted the blacks fired. The national leadership would not allow the firing but they did not push the issue of integration. They compromised and allowed a segregated UAW local in Atlanta.

Bailer states that some of the greatest progress achieved by the union was in the area of improved race relations.[63] It is difficult to understand this statement unless Bailer considers it improved race relations simply to get jobs for blacks without provoking violence or wildcats. Many areas of strain were clearly in evidence. Blacks were not usually welcome at union social activities. Some locals ceased to sponsor dances rather than face the tensions that would result if blacks came. In some cases black union members were not even particularly welcome at union meetings.

The seniority system proved an even greater source of tension.[64] There are a number of possible bases for a seniority system: occupation, occupational group, department, division, plant, and company. Each of these has its own set of problems and implications for black workers. It is generally the case that during periods of full employment blacks benefit most from the widest possible seniority base (plant or company). Seniority might then be used as a vehicle for upgrading and promotion. Unfortunately the operation of the system was never that simple. Promotion rules generally specified that both skill and seniority must be considered in promotions. All too often skill meant either being white or being acceptable to those workers with whom the newly promoted individual would be brought into contact (e.g., being white). No system is fair unless it is implemented in a fair and impartial manner.

It is generally the case that during bad times blacks benefit most from a narrow-based seniority system (departmental or occupational). The high concentration of blacks in certain occupations and departments provides a protection against being bumped by whites. Unfortunately opting for this type of protectionist system closes the door on upgrading and promotion opportunities. Some plants had the worst possible combination, departmental seniority for promotions and plant seniority for layoffs.[65] This undoubtedly reflected the racial distribution of power.

The impact of World War II

The industry's conversion to war production which began in the last half of 1941 threatened to worsen the Negro's already inferior position. . . . the influx of thousands of additional workers, chiefly from the South, weakened the union's grip upon its membership and strengthened opposition to fuller Negro participation in the union and the industry. Due to the initial decreased importance of the jobs in which they were most heavily represented, Negro employees found fewer openings in their traditional occupations. . . . and management made little effort to retrain and upgrade them.[66]

The first labor shortages appeared in the skilled occupations and black workers were not upgraded to meet these shortages. A major strain was felt by blacks with the opening of the Chrysler Tank Arsenal in late 1941.[67] White workers were transferred from Dodge Main to the tank arsenal while blacks with more seniority were passed over. Black protests got little results until they culminated in a series of wildcat work stoppages. The local union then established a committee to discuss the matter with management but no change in policy was effected. The federal government intervened, management admitted discrimination but blamed the local union (not totally without justification). The national leadership of the UAW also intervened and eventually some blacks were transferred. It should be noted that at the end of 1941 only 170 out of 5,000 employees at the Chrysler Tank Arsenal were black and all of them were janitors.[68]

This provides an indication of the degree of seriousness that can be attached to written agreements such as the one negotiated by the Office of Price Administration on September 17, 1941. In it automobile manufacturers and unions agreed that all transfers would be based on industry-wide seniority with workers within the industry having first priority for all war production jobs.[69] If this agreement had been lived up to, it would have forced the transfer of large numbers of blacks to new jobs and forced them to be upgraded from traditional "Negro jobs." Attempts to implement this policy, even at a token level, were greeted with less than enthusiasm by many white workers.

Two black metal polishers were transferred to war production at the Packard plant in November 1941.[70] This touched off a wildcat strike on the part of white workers that was not settled until the blacks were withdrawn. Three wildcat sit-down strikes took place at the Chrysler Highland Park plant in February of 1942 in response to the transfer of black workers to war production. These strikes ended when the UAW national leadership informed the strikers that they could either return to work or give up their jobs. The Dodge Truck plant was shut down on June 2, 1942, by another wildcat strike protesting the transfer of black workers from another Chrysler plant. Once again the UAW national leadership had to intervene in order to get the whites back to work.

The Hudson Naval Ordnance Plant illustrates the degree of difficulty involved in interpreting any events as indicating attitudes held by an entire group. The plant was owned by the government but run by Hudson. Blacks worked primarily as janitors before the war. In February 1942, two blacks were placed on the union local's executive board. The board went on record as favoring the upgrading of blacks. On June 18, 1942, eight blacks were placed on machine operations and white workers walked off the job. It was only after the Navy Department and the UAW jointly informed the strikers that they would not only be fired, but blacklisted from all war industry jobs, that they returned to work.

Management and labor did not take as firm a stand during two strikes that occurred in response to upgrading of black workers at Timken-Detroit in July 1942. Blacks were traditionally allowed to be hammerman helpers but were barred from the position of hammerman. One black worker was upgraded to hammerman, a strike followed, and he was withdrawn. The issue was discussed at a series of local meetings and it was finally decided that the black worker could keep the hammerman post. Apparently this was considered an exception to the rule because the upgrading of a second black to hammerman caused a second wildcat strike. He also eventually won the right to retain his new job.

The most serious series of racially motivated wildcats took place at the Packard Airplane Motor Plant in the spring of 1943. Three black workers were upgraded to the final motor assembly line in late May. White workers staged a wildcat and the blacks were withdrawn to allow for discussion. The withdrawal stimulated about 60 percent of the 2,500 black workers to walk out in response. The company had immediately responded to the demands of the white wildcatters but they simply talked the blacks into returning to work until discussions on the issue were completed. The three black workers were reinstated on the assembly line on May 30, and on June 3 a wildcat began which included over

90 percent of the white workers. With great bitterness the white workers returned to work on June 7 after discovering that the united front of management, the federal government, national and local union leadership could not be budged. The union was viciously attacked for being undemocratic and failing to reflect the will of its membership. To its credit it did not represent their will on this particular occasion.

This series of strikes over black upgrading highlighted a number of conditions that might have remained latent if it were not for the war. First, the degree of difference in orientations between the national leadership and the rank and file membership was brought into startling focus.[71] The union was dominated at the national level by people with an ideological commitment to the just society. This represented a range from the Communist Party, through Trotskyists, to democratic socialists and "welfare-state" liberals, but all were sincere in their desire to build a better America. Local unions were predominantly led by persons sharing the "bread-and-butter unionism" orientation of the bulk of the membership. That is, in many ways, an overly simplistic picture as many rank-and-file workers were more advanced on racial and social issues than was the national leadership. But the general tendency was the reverse.

This split fed directly into the conflict between the national leadership and mass white membership (with local leadership vacillating between) over the issue of equal rights for blacks. The national leadership believed in racial justice but most union members wanted the union to protect jobs, improve wages and working conditions, and allow retention of individual prejudices. The resolution of disputes demonstrated that the national union could achieve social objectives only if it was in a secure position of power that could not be shaken by the membership. The backing of a federal government, stung into taking action by the need for black support of the war effort, made possible the needed concentration of power in the hands of the national leadership.

The series of events also demonstrated that black workers would not any longer sit patiently by and wait for whites to give them things out of the goodness of their hearts. They were beginning to reach the stage where they would openly battle for their rights. They also were becoming increasingly suspicious of a union in which they had little direct access to power. They actively sought a more direct voice in order to bypass the channel of an often bigoted local leadership.

Northrup argues that the sensationalism of the wildcat strikes distracts us from actual progress which occurred.[72] He states that most plants were integrated without major trouble and that, in most plants, there was little overt resistance to black upgrading into new occupations. He points particularly to the Briggs Manufacturing Corporation where the proportion of black workers increased from 10 to 20 percent between 1940 and 1944. This was accompanied by occupational upgrading. Northrup acknowledges union complicity in discrimination but feels that much progress was made toward its elimination. He concludes by blaming blacks for contributing to the continuation of discrimination throughout the war years:

UAW—CIO leaders continued to be hindered in their attempts to secure equality of opportunity for Negroes by the failure of Negroes in some plants to give the union their full support. Rather typical is the case at the Buick plant in Flint, Mich., where a strong stand by the union leaders resulted in the upgrading to production jobs of more than 500 Negro foundry workers who are now well-integrated on all types of work throughout the plant. Yet in July 1942, less than 50 percent of the Negroes were union members as compared with 90 per cent of the white workers. If Negroes hope to maintain the unqualified support of union officials, they must recognize their responsibility to join and take an active part in union affairs.[73]

Ford provides an ironic footnote to the war years. During the early part of the war the Ford River Rouge plant continued its earlier pattern in upgrading black workers with little or no problem.[74] Ford also continued its earlier pattern by keeping its Willow Run plant virtually all white. Noticeable changes in policy began to appear about mid-1943.[75] Ford officials became concerned over the level of militancy exhibited by black workers in Local 600 (the River Rouge local) and by an alleged decline in quality of black job applicants. When Ford was almost alone as an employer of blacks, it could pick and choose and select the "one-in-four" black applicants that it really wanted. However, the labor shortage meant that it had to draw from the same pool of recent southern migrants as all other employers.

Donald Marshall and Willis Ward were removed from the Ford personnel office (no longer the Ford service department). They were replaced by Jesse Owens who also was transferred when the Negro division was abolished in May 1943. Local 600 charged that the hiring of black workers had come to a virtual standstill. This charge was not without substance. Ford moved full circle from the company giving the greatest opportunity to black workers at a time of widespread discrimination to a company excluding them from employment at a time of the lowest level of discrimination in industry history. Ford consistently acted in terms of perceived self-interest. The second irony arises from the fact that black workers, who had been used by Ford in order to fight unionization, were now left to rely upon that self-same union to protect their rights.

Reconversion to peacetime industry

The end of the war did not cause significant alterations in economic opportunities in the auto industry. There was a short-term loss of jobs during reconversion to civilian production but this was soon reversed. Civilian automobiles had not been manufactured since 1942 and the aging of existing vehicles produced a pent-up demand. Further stimulus was provided by the accumulation of money due to high wartime earnings and by returning GIs with their muster-out pay. There was no real alteration in demand for auto workers, nor were there immediate major alterations in industry racial practices.

There were about 75,000 black workers, including women, employed by the auto industry in 1945.[76] Women suffered the major pains of reconversion. Dodge Truck laid off thirty-one black women without taking into account their contract rights.[77] Union protests were replied to with the statement that there was a lack of available work that the women were physically capable of performing. A union grievance was eventually resolved in favor of the women and they won $55,000 in back wages.

Management was not alone in its antiblack activities. There were several wildcat strikes in the late forties against black upgrading.[78] The UAW pressured the companies into penalizing the wildcatters. One strike occurred when blacks were upgraded to metal finishers in a shop employing 2,000 workers (about half southern white and most of the rest Polish or Italian-Americans). The white workers refused to "break-in" the blacks and walked off their jobs. They eventually returned after a hostile union meeting in which it was made clear to them that they either returned to work or lost their jobs.

A similar turmoil, four months in length, resulted from the upgrading of four blacks to assembly-line work at the Chrysler Kercheval plant.[79] However, events were not entirely consistent. A black woman was disciplined at Hudson in November 1948. White and black workers walked out in a wildcat protest against her punishment, which was believed to be unfair. The penalty was removed but a rumor circulated at a nearby plant, and was believed for a day, that the strike resulted from a race riot during which a black worker stabbed a white worker to death. An ironic sidelight to the wildcat came three days earlier when a local union official had police prevent three black couples (the males were union members) from attending a union Halloween party to which they had been sold tickets.

One can see similar patterns of inconsistency in the fact that black and white workers cooperated without apparent tension during the May 1948 Chrysler strike but most white workers did not support a move to desegregate restaurants located near the plant.[80] Social activities stimulated the bulk of remaining racial tensions. Blacks and whites played baseball together but when Walter Reuther started a separate bowling league (after the American Bowling Congress refused his requests to desegregate) white workers were less than enthusiastic in their support.[81] Apparently, bowling may be considered to be a more intimate form of social activity than baseball because women are more likely to accompany men.

This should not be taken as indicating that all economic problems were resolved. Jordon Sims, president of UAW Local 961, had this to say about his job-hunting experiences in 1948 after graduation from a primarily white high school in Hamtramck with a good record:

Me and 16 other of the good white brothers that I had shared athletic endeavors with, shared text books with, went right down to the Dodge Main (also located in Hamtramck) to get a job. They hired all the white boys and told me they weren't hiring. A friend of mine told me how to get a job. So I got the word. He said you have to go out to the plant, you have to go out once and make an application and they'll send you away. You should always come back the following week, and the week after that if it's necessary, *to let the man know that you sincerely want to work.* That's how I got the job (at Eldon Avenue Assembly not at Dodge Main). I followed that recommendation.[82]

The implication is that white applicants demonstrated that they "sincerely want to work" simply by applying for a job but that more was demanded of black applicants. The racial difference did not end there, as indicated by Mr. Sims' further comments:

When I came to a place like Eldon, I was told what a big break I was getting. Because a few decades prior to that time blacks wouldn't even qualify, be considered qualified, to operate machinery in a sophisticated place like Chrysler because it was too complicated for the black mind to comprehend. . . . I guess that they make certain assessments as to who would be available in what area and why. They told me they were giving me a break. I wasn't going to go in Department 25, the janitorial department, or someplace like that. They were going to make me a machine operator because of my exceptional background and abilities. Now aint that Hell because of the God-damned factory you have to have all that just to become a machine operator — and this is the poor working class white I'm talking about who actually had these ideas. The man told me, you know, that this was almost the height of industrial work available for blacks — you see we didn't even think about skilled trades. Just getting on a machine, if you get off the singular machine where you have just one singular operation . . . you start getting to the area where you can handle the multi-operational machines — well then you're supposed to be outstanding.[83]

The postwar period affected the big three auto manufacturers in different ways. Chrysler came out of World War II with the highest proportion of black workers (17 percent of 71,000 employees were black in 1946).[84] The number and proportion of blacks working at Chrysler continued to grow in the postwar years. By 1952, 22 percent of Chrysler's 100,000 Detroit area workers were black (blacks comprised 13.5 percent of Detroit's population). The bulk of the increase was concentrated in production jobs with few blacks getting white-collar or craft jobs. Chrysler had hard times in the late 1950s with their total employment dropping from 176,356 in 1955 to 91,678 at the end of 1958. Black workers had less seniority and suffered most. In a single year black employment at four Detroit Chrysler plants fell from 20.3 percent in 1957 (9,242 out of 45,584) to 14.7 percent in 1958 (3,345 out of 22,776).

The postwar years affected blacks employed by Ford in a different manner from those employed at Chrysler.[85] The recession of 1957–8 had a similar impact on black and white workers as both lost jobs at about the same rate. This resulted from the fact that blacks had high levels of seniority due to Ford's early employment policies. It was Ford's rationalization of production shortly after the war that had the greatest impact upon black employment. When Henry Ford shifted to scientific management of company operations instead of management according to personal whim, River Rouge was decreased in size and in proportional amount of production within the Ford empire. Blacks suffered disproportionately because of their greater concentration at River Rouge and Ford slipped to second place in proportionate hiring of blacks.

General Motors never hired as high a proportion of blacks as either Ford or Chrysler but, due to its larger size, it had more black employees at the end of World War II than either of the others.[86] This poorer record in hiring blacks may be partially explained by the wider geographic dispersion of General Motors factories but it is also true that General Motors was slower to move toward fair employment practices. However, General Motors had a higher proportion of black workers in its southern plants than did Ford. Blacks lost jobs at a disproportionately high rate during the recession of the late 1950s due to their lesser amount of seniority at General Motors.

McCarthyism and anticommunism exacerbated racial tension in the auto industry in the 1950s.[87] The House Un-American Activities Committee (HUAC) began hearings on communism in the auto unions in late February 1951. The committee disproportionately concentrated its attention upon black unionists whom they perceived to be either Communists or Communist influenced. Local 600 at River Rouge came in for special attention. Peterson notes that it was in this local that Communists were especially successful in gaining a foothold in the UAW.[88] He further notes that this was the local with the highest concentration of black workers and implies that the two factors are closely linked. More will be said about this below. The significant point is that the identification was made in the eyes of the public between blacks and communism. This identification was also made in the eyes of white workers with latent, or manifest, hostile attitudes toward blacks. This carried into the workplace and union halls and became the cause of greatly increased racial tensions.

The negative impact of the recession upon black employment was intensified by the forced closings or consolidations of the smaller automobile manufacturers. The loss of Hudson, Studebaker, and Packard and the consolidation of American Motors sharply reduced the amount of jobs available in auto plants in the Detroit area. Both white and black workers lost their jobs in large numbers, but black workers had greater difficulty in finding new ones. Nevertheless the recession did not completely wipe out the gains of the decade. The proportion of blacks among workers holding jobs in the auto industry was higher in 1960 (9.1 percent) than in either 1950 (7.8 percent) or 1940 (3.7 percent).[89]

However, most black auto workers were still restricted to blue-collar occupations. At no time during the decade of the fifties did blacks exceed 1 percent of the combined category of white-collar occupations nor did they ever exceed one-half of 1 percent of craftsmen. Chrysler only had 24 blacks among 7,425 skilled workers and only 1 black apprentice out of 350.[90] General Motors had 11,125 skilled workers in the Detroit area, of whom 67 were black. Ford River Rouge once again presented the best picture with 250 blacks out of a total of 7,000 skilled workers. In other words the plant with the best record in 1968 employed only 1 black among each 28 skilled workers.

Recovery from recession – the decade of the sixties

The major employers in the auto industry made a strong comeback from the recession decline as indicated by the employment growth of the big three (General Motors, Ford, and Chrysler) from 723,556 in 1960 to 1,020,783 in 1968. Smaller manufacturers did not fare as well. Several went out of business and American Motors declined in its share of production. Black workers shared in the general industry gains. Table 2.1 presents data for 1970 on total employment and occupational distribution of workers by race and sex. Note that the proportion of blacks employed within the auto industry increased from 9.1 to 13.4 percent during the decade of the sixties. The proportion of blacks among employed males exhibited a similar increase, from 9.6 to 13.8 percent, and the proportion of blacks among female employees increased from 5.1 to 10.6 percent. The data presented in Table 2.1 reveal that blacks are still disproportionately concentrated in lower-ranking and less-desirable occupations despite improvement over earlier years. Black males are underrepresented in white-collar occupations. They make up less than 1 percent of the managers, less than 2 percent of the professional or sales personnel, and 8 percent of the clerical workers. While blacks are underrepresented among clerical workers, it is only here at the bottom of the white-collar hierarchy that we find any sizable number of blacks. Blacks are underrepresented among the craft occupations and overrepresented in all lower blue-collar occupations, with the degree of overrepresentation increasing as the status scale descends.

The situation among females is different in detail but parallel in the general tendency for blacks to be underrepresented in the higher-, and overrepresented in the lower-, status occupations. Blacks account for less than 5 percent of the professional and clerical occupations and are totally excluded from managerial posts. They constitute almost 10 percent of a very small category of female sales personnel and are overrepresented in all blue-collar occupations.

The full extent of black occupational concentration is best appreciated if the data are reorganized. The final two columns of Table 2.1

Table 2.1. *Race and sex by occupation in the motor vehicle and motor vehicle equipment industry: employed persons, 1970*

	Number			Percent		
Occupation	All employees	White	Black	Black of all emp.	Distrib. whites	Distrib. blacks
Males						
Prof.-tech	79,792	77,998	1,444	1.8	10.1	1.2
Managers	26,251	26,020	210	0.8	3.4	0.2
Sales	8,312	8,179	133	1.6	1.1	0.1
Clerical	56,118	51,422	4,488	8.0	6.6	3.6
Craftsmen	227,932	209,253	17,738	7.8	27.0	14.2
Oper. (exc. trans.)	410,160	328,789	79,725	19.4	42.4	63.9
Trans. oper.	31,814	25,673	6,014	18.9	3.3	4.8
Labor	35,899	27,600	8,078	22.5	3.6	6.5
Service	26,510	19,580	6,871	25.9	2.5	5.5
Total	902,788	775,514	124,701	13.8	100.0	100.0
Females						
Prof.-tech	4,086	3,830	197	4.8	3.3	1.4
Managers	733	733	0	0.0	0.6	0.0
Sales	164	148	16	9.8	0.1	0.1
Clerical	45,394	43,430	1,842	4.1	37.3	13.2
Craftsmen	5,035	4,305	688	13.3	3.7	4.8
Oper. (exc. trans.)	69,944	59,673	9,956	14.2	51.2	71.6
Trans. oper.	721	632	89	12.3	0.5	0.6
Labor	2,005	1,585	397	19.8	1.4	2.9
Service	2,858	2,115	743	26.0	1.8	5.3
Total	130,940	116,451	13,908	10.6	99.9	99.9
Grand total	1,033,728	891,965	138,609	13.4	—	—

Source: Constructed from United States Department of Commerce, Bureau of the Census PC(2)-7C, *Occupation by Industry*, Tables 1 and 2.

present the proportional distribution of black and white workers by occupational classification with sex controlled. Over four-fifths (80.7 percent) of all black males are concentrated in the three lowest blue-collar occupational categories (operatives, service or labor) while slightly more than half (51.8 percent) of white males are similarly employed. White males are almost twice as likely (27.0 to 14.2 percent) as black males to

be craftsmen and are more than four times (21.2 to 5.1 percent) as likely to have a white-collar occupation. Similarly about four-fifths (80.4
percent) of black females and approximately 11 out of 20 (54.9 percent) of white females are in lower-status blue-collar occupations. Black
females are slightly more likely (4.8 to 3.7 percent) than white females
to hold a job as a craftsman. White females are more than two and one-
half times (41.3 to 14.7 percent) as likely as black females to have a
white-collar occupation.

The data presented in Table 2.2 reveal a continuing high degree of
geographical concentration in the automobile industry despite some dispersion compared to earlier decades. The North Central region includes
75.6 percent of all males and 77.5 percent of all females employed in
the auto industry. Blacks are only slightly more regionally concentrated at this gross level of geographical categorization. The North Central
region includes 80.0 percent of all employed black males and 78.5 percent of all employed black females. It is at the state level that sharp differences begin to emerge. Michigan includes within its borders 42.8
percent of all males (and 44.3 percent of all females) employed in the
auto industry but it includes 56.4 percent of all black male (and 55.4
percent of all black female) auto workers. The geographical concentration is even greater in that 26.9 percent of all male (and 27.5 percent of
all female) auto workers are located within the Detroit Standard Metropolitan Statistical Area (SMSA). In the absence of precise figures, it
may be estimated that 46.0 percent of all black male (and 39.7 percent
of all black female) auto workers are located within the Detroit SMSA.[91]
Thus the Detroit SMSA contains within its boundaries about 9 out of
every 20 blacks (45.4 percent, both sexes combined) employed in the
automobile industry.

A second mode of considering the geographic concentration of black
workers is to examine the regional proportions of blacks among employed auto workers. These data are also presented in Table 2.2. Blacks
constitute 13.8 percent of the male auto workers nationwide, 14.6 percent in the North Central region, 18.2 percent in Michigan, and an estimated 23.7 percent in the Detroit SMSA.[92] Black females are concentrated to a slightly lesser extent. They constitute 11.2 percent of females
nationwide, 11.5 percent in the North Central region, 14.0 percent in
Michigan, and an estimated 16.7 percent in the Detroit SMSA. This degree of concentration tends to vary from plant to plant, department to
department, and shift to shift.[93] In 1968 Ford River Rouge was about

Table 2.2. *Employment in the motor vehicle and motor vehicle equipment industry, by race, sex, and region, 1970[a]*

Region	Male Total	Male Black	% Black of total	Female Total	Female Black	% Black of total
United	(99.9)	(99.9)		(100.1)	(100.1)	
States	884,239	122,275	13.8	128,068	14,372	11.2
	(4.7)	(3.1)		(3.6)	(1.3)	
West	41,699	3,838	9.2	4,604	183	4.0
	(9.1)	(8.6)		(7.2)	(11.5)	
South	80,561	10,510	13.0	9,213	1,651	17.9
North	(10.5)	(8.2)		(11.8)	(8.8)	
East	92,826	10,078	10.9	15,060	1,263	8.4
North	(75.6)	(80.0)		(77.5)	(78.5)	
Central	669,153	97,849	14.6	99,191	11,275	11.5
	(42.8)	(56.4)		(44.3)	(55.4)	
Michigan	378,383	68,950	18.2	56,702	7,961	14.0
Detroit	(26.9)	(46.0)		(27.5)	(39.7)	
SMSA	237,598	56,263	23.7	34,195	5,712	16.7

[a]The figure within parentheses is the proportion that the specified category of persons employed within the region is of those employed in the total United States. The figures for number of black males and black females employed in Detroit are estimates (see note 91 for computational procedure).
Source: Constructed from United States Department of Commerce, Bureau of the Census: PC(1)-D1, *Detailed Characteristics, United States Summary*, Tables 236 and 299; PC(1)-D24, *Detailed Characteristics, Michigan*, Tables 184 and 185.

42 percent black overall with much higher ratios in several production areas. The proportion of blacks among those employed in plants in the Detroit area frequently ranges between 30 and 70 percent and is sometimes higher. Second shifts are less desirable and, consequently, tend to have even higher proportions of black workers. The combination of geographic, occupational, and shift concentration tends to produce interacting work groups that are often nearly all black. The implication that this has for the development of collective action will be discussed in the concluding section of this chapter and in more detail in Chapter 9.

Table 2.3 presents regional data on the 1969 median incomes, by

Table 2.3. *Earnings of experienced males in the motor vehicle and motor vehicle equipment industry working 50 to 52 weeks in 1969, by race*

	Median income		% Black income of male income
Region	All males	Blacks	
United States	9,545	8,140	85.3
North East	9,098	7,647	84.0
North Central	9,798	8,402	85.8
South	7,789	5,946	76.3
West	9,141	7,856	85.9

Source: Constructed from United States Department of Commerce, Bureau of the Census PC(1)-D1, *Detailed Characteristics, United States Summary*, Tables 301–302.

race, of male auto workers who worked between fifty and fifty-two weeks. There is relatively little variation between regions in the relative earnings of blacks. With the singular exception of the South, the black median income tends to approximate 85 percent of the median for all workers. It may not be a simple coincidence that the South has the lowest median income for all workers, the lowest median for blacks, and the lowest ratio of black median to overall median. It is possible that worker attention may be diverted from general income level and focused on relative racial income levels. Racial discrimination may serve to lower the income of all workers.

The role of the Communist Party

It is not possible to understand developments within the UAW as they relate to black unionists without a basic sense of the historical relationship between the Communist Party, the UAW, and its black members. The Communist Party was a strong and growing force on the American left during the 1930s. Lens states that they grew from a membership of 7,500 members in 1930 to 41,000 in 1936 with an additional million unaffiliated friends and supporters.[94] They had a major spurt in growth over the next two years with their membership growing to total more than 100,000 by 1938.[95] All of this strength was put to the cause of organizing workers into a strong union movement.

William Z. Foster led a long, bitter, and unsuccessful steel strike in

1919.[96] Foster then organized the Trade Union Educational League (TUEL) in 1920. This was in conformity with the Communist Party program of "boring-from-within." They wished to help to build strong unions within the AFL and to establish themselves in influential positions relative to the unions and the AFL central leadership. The Communists became increasingly disillusioned with the AFL over the next decade. By 1929 they were convinced that nothing could be done to alter the elitist craft-oriented policies of the AFL so they decided to abandon the "boring-from-within" policy in favor of one stressing dual or parallel unions. Thus in 1929 they abolished the TUEL and replaced it with the Trade Union Unity League (TUUL), which was established outside the AFL. The TUUL grew to include 125,000 formal members at its peak.

The Communist Party was especially active in Detroit during the depression years.[97] They played a dominant role in the organization of the Ford hunger march on March 7, 1942. This was a march of the unemployed on the Dearborn headquarters of Ford Motor Company demanding jobs. Harry Bennett led the Ford security forces and the Dearborn police in violent resistance to the marchers. A clash developed outside Ford headquarters. Bennett drove into the middle of the disorder and got out of his car. He was immediately struck by a flying brick and was slightly injured. This touched off a wave of gunfire directed against the marchers killing four and wounding between twenty and forty more. No marcher was ever found to have been armed or to have fired a gun. The Communist Party organized a funeral, which drew approximately 15,000 persons, for the slain.

One interesting sidelight to this clash was the fact that Ford defended its actions by the need to resist communism wherever it reared its ugly head. There could be no compromise that might risk communism coming to America. Oddly enough, Soviet engineers were inside the Ford plant at the time of the confrontation receiving training in Ford's mass production techniques. Ford received $30 million from the Soviet Union for providing this training as part of a larger cooperative venture. Apparently Ford did not feel that there was anything wrong with being paid to help strengthen communism in the Soviet Union as long as communism at home was kept weak.

The Congress of Industrial Organizations (CIO) broke with the AFL in 1935 primarily over the issue of industrial versus craft unionism.[98] The Communist Party changed its policy the same year. They abandoned the dual union approach in favor of working within the CIO. Communists played a major role in building the CIO unions and consequently developed a great deal of strength. Edward Levinson, educational director of the UAW, estimated that the Communist Party controlled over one-fifth of the national unions within the CIO, totaling in excess of 800,000 members, in addition to controlling numerous locals in other unions.[99] This does not greatly differ from the estimate of Bernard Karsh and Phillip Garman that the Communist Party controlled unions with over one-fourth of the CIO membership and that they had extensive influence in unions with an additional one-fourth of CIO membership.[100] Communists and other left-center forces were able to work together with relatively little tension until the outbreak of World War II. The important contribution made by Communists in building the CIO is attested to by Alinsky:

the Communists worked indefatigably, with no job being too menial or unimportant. They literally poured themselves completely into their assignments. The Communist Party gave its complete support to the C.I.O. . . . The fact is that the Communist Party made a major contribution in the organization of the unorganized for the C.I.O.[101]

The Communist Party interest and activities in the auto industry began early. The TUUL had conducted several strikes in auto before the AFL formed their first auto union in 1935.[102] Communists came into auto industry organizing efforts in large numbers when the CIO broke away from the AFL toward the end of 1935. Communists made an even greater contribution in building the UAW than they did in helping to build the larger CIO structure. Lens notes that the UAW hired more than 500 radicals — most of them Communists — to act as organizers during 1936 and 1937.[103] They were especially active and influential during the 1937 wave of sit-down strikes and in the organization of Ford Motor Company in 1941. The latter is of special significance because the organization of Ford not only greatly strengthened the UAW but dramatically altered its racial composition. The victory brought more than 17,000 new black members into the UAW.

The Communist Party was very interested in the new UAW members. The party had been attempting to recruit black members since the early 1920s and had waged a strong campaign aimed particularly at black workers.[104] Ford Local 600 was both the largest local union in the world and the UAW local with the largest proportion of black members.[105] Thus the party directed a great deal of its organizational efforts toward black Ford workers and black UAW members in general. It usually supported the black position on all issues with any racial implications that were debated within the UAW. Harry Haywood was active in recruiting black support for the party in Detroit. The Communist appeal appears to have been relatively successful. Howe and Widick claim that "Stalinists" (Communists) controlled Local 600 for a number of years.[106] The appeal also seemed to strike a responsive chord in blacks nationally. Blacks comprised a larger proportion of the Communist Party membership in 1938 (14 percent) than they did of the nation's population.[107] The Communist Party recruiting campaign in 1944 brought in about 7,000 blacks, almost 30 percent of the 24,000 new recruits. Thus black unionists came to comprise a significant segment of the Communist faction within the UAW or, if not actually members, to lend their support to it.

The relationship between the Communist Party and Walter Reuther is complex and rather difficult to sort out completely. The first UAW president, Homer Martin, was relatively conservative. He was opposed within the UAW by a left-oriented "Unity Caucus" headed by Wyndham Mortimer and including a large number of Communists, a few socialists, and the Reuther brothers.[108] Walter Reuther is generally viewed as having been the leader of the socialist contingent within the Unity Caucus but several socialists active during the period have told me that he was so cooperative with the Communist Party that he "was cheating them out of their dues." Foster claims that for a while Reuther even pretended to be a Communist; the *Daily Worker* noted that Reuther always voted with the Communists in 1936–7; and Glaberman believes that he has uncovered evidence that Reuther was an actual dues-paying member of the Communist Party for a period of time.[109] Howe and Widick deny actual membership, stating that Reuther declined to join because he was unable to submit himself to party discipline. Whatever his exact relationship to the party, there is little question that Walter Reuther cooperated very closely with them at a time when they were strong and his own personal following was weak.

Martin appeared to have been uneasy regarding the Unity Caucus. In 1937 he fired a number of UAW officials, including Roy and Victor Reuther, whom he called Communists.[110] Then in 1938 Martin suspended five UAW officials including Mortimer, George Addes, and Richard Frankensteen — the latter for conferring with William Z. Foster. CIO president, John L. Lewis, put the UAW into receivership, fired a number of Martin aides, and reinstated the suspended officials. R. J. Thomas charged that he had been present when Martin conferred with Ford officials regarding the best method of getting the UAW out of the CIO and into the AFL. Martin was censured and in 1939 he left the CIO to found a rival AFL auto union.

These events touched off a battle for control over the UAW between a Communist-backed slate headed by Addes and Frankensteen and a socialist slate headed by Walter Reuther. The Communists had a preponderance of the voting strength but the CIO intervened to prevent a Communist victory. Phillip Murray and Sidney Hillman directed the Communist Party faction not to use their voting strength. There was some vacillation but R. J. Thomas was eventually agreed upon as a compromise candidate and elected to the presidency. This was the first step in the Reuther drive for personal power. He stepped up his campaign in 1941 when he began the red-baiting tactics with which he came to be identified. Reuther accused the Communist Party faction of being dominated by Stalin and the Soviet Union and introduced a resolution to ban Communists from holding office in the UAW. The Communist-led faction countered by suggesting that either both Communists and socialists be barred or both be allowed to run for office. Reuther and his followers called the latter proposal red-baiting.

The UAW leadership was in basic agreement that the union should cooperate with the government during World War II in an all-out attempt to win the war. The UAW leadership, including Addes, Thomas, Frankensteen, Reuther, and Nat Gantley, endorsed a no-strike pledge and agreed that there should be overtime work without premium overtime pay. The Communist faction wished to go further. In 1943 Frankensteen and Addes proposed that the union endorse piece-work incentive pay. Reuther opposed it although there is some question as to whether his opposition stemmed from principle or practical politics.

By raising the "incentive pay" scheme, the CP could appear as a champion of increased war production. Since the scheme would, in some instances, increase the *total* pay of workers, the CP could also appear as a champion of higher wages. But to the unionists the proposal was reprehensible both because it did not involve increases in hourly pay and would result in competitive speedups in the plants.

In leading the opposition to the Stalinist proposal, Reuther estimated the union situation accurately. He knew the proposal was certain to arouse bitter enmity in the plants and that whoever was identified with it was doomed to political defeat in the union. He probably also saw that by opposing the CP on these issues he would be able to soften some of the pressure being applied by dissatisfied members on *him*.

And while he believed that the labor movement had to make certain sacrifices during wartime, Reuther, unlike the CP, did not think that it should give up its reason for existence. [emphasis in the original] [111]

The jockeying for position within the UAW leadership continued throughout the war.[112] Reuther and Addes joined forces to oppose a movement in 1943 by rank-and-file workers to end the no-strike pledge. Consequently a formally organized "Rank-and-File Caucus" formed in opposition to the UAW leadership. After VE Day the Rank-and-File Caucus renewed its drive to eliminate the no-strike pledge at the 1944 convention. Three positions emerged during the debate. Gantley, the Communist whip, favored retention of the pledge. Reuther wanted to retain the pledge for all plants engaged in war production and drop it for the remainder. The Rank-and-File Caucus wanted to drop it entirely. No position could get a majority, so the issue was sent to the membership as a referendum. The no-strike pledge was retained.

Reuther continued his campaign of red-baiting after the war ended. He accused the Communist Party of selling out the workers' interests in support of the war effort. He accused them of putting the survival of the Soviet Union above all other concerns. This charge was not entirely without merit but he failed to admit that he supported virtually every policy proposed by the Communist faction. If Reuther was any less willing than the Communists to sell out worker interests, it was hardly noticeable in his behavior. Nevertheless the sell-out charge played a prominent role in Reuther's attempt to win the union presidency in 1946. He backed up this propaganda campaign with a program of practical politics including the promise of jobs in the union hierarchy in exchange for support. R. J. Thomas had never previously been part of the Communist faction but he was fearful that a Reuther victory would bring an end to democracy in the UAW. Therefore he agreed to be the candidate representing the Addes—Leonard—Frankensteen (Communist) faction. Ford Local 600 and the majority of militant and/or independent black unionists supported the Thomas-led coalition.

However, the anti-Communist hysteria of this period proved too strong for Thomas to overcome. Reuther was elected president of the union by a narrow margin of 104 votes. The Communist—Thomas coalition retained control of the UAW executive board. Reuther completed his victory in 1947 when he successfully maneuvered his supporters into the majority of the executive board positions. He then spent the next year purging his opposition from all appointed positions and throwing his full influence into local union elections in order to complete the job. By 1948 Reuther was firmly established at the top of the UAW hierarchy. There were no longer any competing factions in the union and democracy virtually disappeared from the UAW.

A black voice in the UAW

The early resistance of blacks to unionization, use of black workers as strikebreakers, recruitment of blacks into local unions only when needed to win strikes, wildcat strikes by blacks to force upgrading, wildcats by whites against black upgrading, differences in racial policy between national and local unions, and problems of black social acceptance by white workers have all been discussed above. With this history it is not surprising that black workers have generally doubted the good intentions of whites. They felt more comfortable in situations in which they had some direct control. This perceived need for participation in decision-making representation at the policy-making level of the UAW surfaced as early as 1940.[113] In 1942 the Communist Party and its followers in the UAW strongly supported the demand for a black executive board post. Black unionists may or may not have had doubts regarding the motivation of the Communists but they certainly welcomed their support.

Howe and Widick accuse the Communists of demagoguery in making this demand. They charge that the Communists revealed their cynicism by being willing to lay aside this demand, along with all other civil rights demands, in order to achieve greater unity in the effort of winning World War II. However, it should be noted that the Communists set aside the demands of all workers, white or black, for the war effort and that this policy was, for the most part, supported by the Reuther faction. If they were cynical in their support for black rights they were also cynical in their concern for workers' rights. This is not entirely inconceivable but the cynical manipulation of blacks for their own ends was not a trait unique to the Communists. Subsequent events demonstrated that the Reuther faction was even more willing than the Communists to sacrifice the black man for its own advancement.

The Reuther faction always countered the demand for black representation with arguments against Jim Crow segregation. They asserted that to place a black man in a post because of his race would be just as wrong as excluding him for that reason. Reuther and his followers consistently argued that they would be happy to back a "qualified black" for such a policy-making position. Their failure to nominate a black seems to indicate that they did not believe any qualified black existed. The issue kept reemerging at convention after convention — always pushed by the Communists and opposed by the Reuther faction. A normal pattern of opposition to black representation soon developed. The union would debate and pass another antidiscrimination resolution at each of its conventions.[114] The UAW established a Fair Practices and Anti-Discrimination Department in 1946 and funded it through constitutional provision at a rate of 1 percent of each worker's monthly dues. This represented a formalization of the Fair Practices Committee first established in 1944. Despite their apparent commitment to equality, the national leadership of the UAW allowed the Atlanta local to remain segregated until 1962 — a date of which the significance will be explained below. For the most part the resolution and committees remained as relatively ineffective window dressing despite a few concrete accomplishments.

The black demand for representation at the policy-making level was intensified by the wildcat strikes against upgrading blacks during and after World War II but it gained its greatest impetus with the complete victory of the Reuther forces over the Communist opposition. As long as the Communists were strong, blacks had a champion in the UAW. If Peterson (cited above) is correct in seeing a causal link between the proportion of blacks and the degree of Communist influence in Local 600, it is precisely the result of the Communists' fight to strengthen the black voice and to achieve racial equality. The Reuther forces could not completely ignore black demands as long as the Communists were strong. Blacks gained from each faction as long as two factions existed. There was a great fear among blacks that once Reuther achieved complete and unchallenged dominance over the UAW he would no longer feel a need for their support and that he might forget their needs.

This fear was apparently well founded.[115] Walter Reuther defeated R. J. Thomas for the presidency of the UAW in 1946, achieved control over the executive board in 1947, and purged alleged Communists and Communist supporters from appointed offices and maneuvered elections so as to drive them out of elected offices in 1948. Most independent black activists had supported either the Addes—Frankensteen faction or the coalition headed by R. J. Thomas. They may have done this for ideological reasons but there is good reason to believe that they traded their political support for backing on issues important to blacks. Reuther either did not know or did not care what reasons justified the alliance. He purged independent blacks from positions of power just as swiftly and completely as he purged those persons labeled as Communists or Communist supporters. Reuther eventually placed some blacks in influential positions but only after he determined that their prime loyalty was to him and to his faction.

This left blacks with virtually no independent voice in the UAW. The Trade Union Leadership Conference (TULC) was formed in an attempt to fill this void.[116] The TULC was comprised primarily of black unionists from the UAW but it included other black unionists in the Detroit area. TULC also admitted some white unionists in order to combat some of the charges that it would be a separatist organization dividing the union movement. TULC saw its major tasks as fighting to eliminate discrimination within the union movement, strengthening the black voice in union policy making, strengthening black support for unions, and generally acting as a liaison between the black community and the union movement.

TULC did succeed in maintaining a relatively independent stance. They were a factor in the 1958 election at Ford's River Rouge Local 600, which a black candidate lost as a result of race baiting. After the election TULC launched a strong attack against blacks who did not have the courage or sense to take an independent position, a position of black solidarity. They freely used the term "Uncle Tom" in referring to such blacks. In 1959 their independence brought them into a series of conflict situations. They endorsed an NAACP memorandum attacking discrimination within AFL–CIO affiliates, they attacked Charles Zimmerman for his castigation of the NAACP, and they criticized George Meany for his attacks against A. Phillip Randolph. The action that brought them into greatest disfavor within the UAW was the step taken by Horace Sheffield, TULC founder, in nominating a black, Willoughby Abner, for a post on the International executive board of the UAW. Emil Mazy was enraged at Sheffield for reopening the question of black representation. He demanded that Reuther fire Sheffield. Sheffield was not fired but he did not win any popularity contests with the UAW leadership.

Detroit had a mayoralty election in 1961. The incumbent, Louis C. Miriani, was endorsed by the AFL–CIO and by the UAW. He had lost favor with Detroit's black population because he instituted some very harsh antiblack police procedures through which he was making blacks the scapegoat in an anticrime drive. TULC endorsed the challenger, Jerome P. Cavanaugh, and worked to rally black votes behind him. Cavanaugh, a political unknown, defeated Miriani by 200,413 to 158,778, largely because of the votes of the black community.

This demonstrated to the UAW leadership that Detroit's black community had unified into a powerful political force that could not be ignored and that TULC was a force within the union with an ability to influence a segment of that black community. Perhaps it is only a coincidence that the next UAW convention (1962) saw a black member of TULC, Nelson "Jack" Edwards, and a Canadian elected to two at-large posts on the UAW executive board. Perhaps it is a further coincidence that in 1962 steps were finally taken to force the Atlanta UAW local to desegregate after many years of stubborn refusal. However, it is difficult to believe in such coincidences. It is much easier to believe that these events were UAW responses to a growing black strength inside and outside the UAW.

Four later developments diminished the influence of TULC. First, there were internal dissensions over the choice between two black candidates for endorsement in a congressional primary. TULC eventually followed the lead of the UAW and endorsed Richard Austin. He was defeated in the primary election by John Conyers, Jr. The TULC failure to endorse Conyers, despite a long family tie with the UAW and particularly with black activists within the union, caused a degree of bitterness that was only increased when Austin lost the subsequent election. Second, Mayor Cavanaugh had previously appointed a TULC member, George Edwards, as police commissioner. Edwards resigned and was replaced by Ray Girarden who did not, and could not, relate as well to the black community. Third, a new force composed of black ministers who had sponsored a black freedom march during the summer of 1963 emerged as a rival center of influence. Fourth, Rev. Albert Cleage developed still another center of influence around a black nationalist program. TULC continued to exist but it could no longer be viewed as either the voice of black UAW members or of the black community.

Summary and conclusions

It is not difficult to understand why many black automobile workers believe that they cannot trust anyone other than themselves to look out for their interests. There has been a history of exploitation of blacks in

the auto industry. Their earliest opportunities to gain jobs were provided by Henry Ford who apparently recruited them in order to insure a
docile, anti-union work force. They were first welcomed into the unions when it was believed that victorious strikes and successful unionization could not be achieved without them. Henry Ford seemed to lose
all concern for black workers once he was forced to unionize and they
no longer were of any particular value to him. The unions did not seem
to push black rights once they achieved power.

World War II brought upgrading and transfers to new war production
jobs only after blacks fought and struck for their rights. This upgrading
and transfer program was met with white resistance through wildcat
strikes. The national union leadership seemed to be sincerely interested
in racial equality but only if it did not interfere with their larger program of building a union. The Reuther faction was willing to see a black
voice within the UAW for "qualified blacks" but did not believe any
were to be found. No such blacks were found until TULC proved to the
national leadership of the UAW that they could not be ignored as a political force. The Communists in the UAW fought for black rights before and after World War II but during the war they put the safety and
survival of the Soviet Union first.

There were few, if any, whites who by the late 1960s had proven to
blacks that they could be counted on. Despite occupational progress
blacks remained concentrated in the dirtiest, least desirable, and least
rewarding occupations in the industry. All efforts at upgrading or promotion were hindered by the operation of seniority rules or by outright
discrimination. Job opportunities in other regions improved but black
auto workers remained concentrated in a small geographic area: Michigan and primarily Detroit. This combination of circumstances is ideal
for the development of the type of class consciousness needed to produce a movement such as that embodied in the League of Revolutionary Black Workers:[117] A group of persons who (1) share common grievances both as workers occupying similar positions in relation to the
means of production, engaging in unsatisfying and alienated labor, and
as blacks having poorer jobs and earning less money than whites in the
same industry and experiencing other forms of racial discrimination; (2)
have the opportunity to communicate their common grievances to one
another as a result of the combination of residential segregation, industrial segregation, occupational segregation, and shift segregation; (3) develop a sense of racial and class solidarity; (4) develop an awareness of a

common enemy; and (5) develop a sense of efficacy or a belief that they possess sufficient collective power to organize and achieve common goals. This sense of collective efficacy was partially produced by the activities of TULC and partially by events in the larger community. Events in the automobile industry may be separated from those of the larger social world analytically but not in the minds and experiences of black workers. For this reason racial developments in Detroit that interacted with developments in the auto industry will be explored before The League of Revolutionary Black Workers is discussed.

3. Detroit: evolution of a black industrial city

Detroit is the epitome of an American industrial city. In 1968 it ranked first among the fifteen major standard metropolitan areas in the proportion of all employed persons who were employed in manufacturing activities (39.9 percent).[1] Detroit was second only to Pittsburgh in the proportion of all persons employed in manufacturing who were employed in that city's leading branch of manufacturing (39.8 percent of 42.8 percent).[2] However, Pittsburgh has a smaller proportion of all employed persons working in manufacturing (34.0 percent) and as a consequence has less of its total number of employed persons concentrated in a single industry (14.5 percent to 15.9 percent). The degree to which employment in Detroit is concentrated in a single branch of industry is even more striking when analyzed on a sex-specific basis. In 1970, 23.7 percent of all employed males in the Detroit SMSA were employed in the manufacture of transportation equipment.[3]

Detroit is also rapidly becoming a black city. Table 3.1 presents the numbers of blacks in Detroit by decades from 1820 to 1970, the percentage that blacks constituted of the total Detroit population (beginning in 1850), and the relative rank of the Detroit black population compared to the size of other black urban concentrations in the United States (since 1910). The data reveal that the Detroit black population grew slowly and remained proportionately small between 1820 and 1910. The decade of World War I stimulated a major increase in the rate of black migration to Detroit. This rate of growth continues and barring unforeseen circumstances there will be a black majority in Detroit before 1980 if it has not already been achieved. Detroit ranks only third in terms of the size of its black population but it is the nation's leading black industrial city and the only one whose fate is so intricately bound to a single industry — automobile manufacturing. In Chapter 2 the history of blacks in the auto industry was reviewed. The present chapter will turn to a consideration of the history of blacks in Detroit.

Table 3.1. *Detroit's black population, 1820–1970*

Year	No. black population	Percent black of Detroit's population	Rank among black urban concentrations
1820	67	n.a.	n.a.
1830	73–126	n.a.	n.a.
1840	121–193	n.a.	n.a.
1850	587	2.8	n.a.
1860	1,402–1,403	3.1	n.a.
1870	2,231–2,235	2.8	n.a.
1880	2,821	2.4	n.a.
1890	3,431	1.7	n.a.
1900	4,111	1.4	n.a.
1910	5,741	1.2	68
1920	40,838	4.1	15
1930	120,066	7.6	7
1940	149,119	9.1	5
1950	300,506	16.1	4
1960	482,229	28.4	4
1970	660,428	43.7	3

Source: Donald R. Deskins, Jr., *Residential Mobility of Negroes in Detroit, 1837–1965, Before the Ghetto: Black Detroit in the Nineteenth Century* (Urbana: University of Illinois Press, 1973), pp. 7, 13, 27, 28, 59, 60, 62 (for years 1820 to 1910); United States Department of Commerce, Bureau of the Census, PC(1)-B1 *General Population Characteristics, United States Summary*, Table 67 (for 1970). Where sources disagree on exact numbers, ranges are stated. There are no disagreements from 1880 on.

The early years

It is not possible to determine exactly when the first free blacks came to Detroit but it probably was during the first quarter of the nineteenth century. Blacks were owned as slaves well into the 1830s but it appears that their owners had lived in Detroit under British rule and that no slaves were brought into the area after it passed to American control.[4] Attitudes toward slavery and toward blacks appear to have been ambivalent. Michigan enacted a series of Black Codes in 1827 that were purported to be designed to protect blacks but had the net impact of barring free black immigration into Michigan.[5] This ambivalence contributed to and was fed by the first Detroit race riot of 1833.

The 1833 riot

Thornton and Ruth Blackburn (two fugitives from Kentucky) had lived in Detroit for several years when "slave catchers" came to Detroit and accused them of being runaway slaves.[6] The Blackburns were arrested on June 15, 1833, and were unable to *prove that they were legally free.* Sheriff John M. Wilson had to choose between turning the Blackburns over to the slave hunters despite the anger of the Detroit black community or freeing them despite their inability to prove that they were legally entitled to freedom. The sheriff returned the Blackburns to jail while he pondered the situation. Armed blacks were outside the jail on June 16 and Mrs. Blackburn escaped by switching clothes with a visitor who remained in her place while she fled to Canada.

A confrontation took place on June 17 between the sheriff and armed blacks, during which the sheriff was seriously injured and Mr. Blackburn was broken out of jail. Thornton Blackburn joined his wife in Canada where they were arrested by Canadian authorities. They were later freed and remained in Canada permanently. The incident increased racial antagonism in Detroit. More attempts were made to prevent black immigration. Blacks responded by threatening to burn down the city. The jail was set on fire on July 11 and tensions remained high.

Voting rights

Slavery was abolished by the Michigan constitution of 1837 but blacks remained disenfranchised.[7] Blacks only achieved the right to vote after a long hard fight.[8] A referendum was held in 1855 on the issue of enfranchising Detroit blacks and it was defeated by a 7 to 1 margin in Detroit and by 32,026 to 12,840 in the state. Blacks received the right to vote in school board elections in 1855 but its value was limited by the fact that the Detroit school board was appointed rather than elected. A constitutional convention was held in 1867 and a constitution was drafted that granted blacks the franchise but the constitution was rejected in a statewide referendum by a margin of 110,582 to 71,733. Wayne County votes went 63.6 percent against the constitution, with the major issue being black enfranchisement. Michigan finally passed an amendment to the state constitution in November 1870, giving blacks the right to vote but the action was mute inasmuch as the Fifteenth Amendment to the federal constitution granting blacks the franchise had been ratified in April 1870.

Education

Blacks also had to fight for the right for a decent education for their children.[9] The first community effort to educate black children came in 1836 when a church affiliated school was established. This meant that blacks had to pay taxes to support public schools and also pay to support a special school for black children. The first black public school was established in 1842 but this did not provide equality of educational opportunity. Black children were not only segregated into inconveniently located schools as late as 1867 but they were restricted to six years of schooling while whites had the opportunity for twelve years.

The Michigan legislature removed the legal basis for school segregation in a bill passed on February 28, 1867, but this had little effect upon the Detroit school system. Michigan passed a school integration statute in 1869 which was also ignored by the Detroit board of education. The Michigan Supreme Court ruled in response to a court suit that both the acts of 1867 and 1869 applied to the Detroit schools but the school system continued to turn black children away from white schools. By 1871 the Detroit school board was forced to pledge full compliance with desegregation statutes and they began a slow grudging retreat. Schools came to be integrated after a fashion.

The 1863 riot

The Civil War brought a heightening of racial tensions.[10] Detroit had a sizable concentration of recent Irish immigrants who were made uneasy by the war. They did not wish to be conscripted to fight in a war in which they felt that they had no stake. They were also afraid that the war would bring a major influx of blacks who would compete for labor and service jobs. In this context of unrest a black man, William Faulkner, was accused of molesting two nine-year-old girls (Mary Brown, white and Ellen Hoover, black). He was convicted on the girls' testimony and a primarily Irish and German mob tried to lynch him. Soldiers killed one member of the mob in an attempt to prevent the lynching. The mob vented its rage on black Detroit. Two blacks were killed, many seriously injured, thirty to thirty-five homes were burned, and 200 blacks were left homeless. Faulkner was later found to be innocent when the girls admitted that they committed perjury. No one in the mob was ever punished for his actions.

Detroit blacks responded to a call to organize the First Michigan Colored Regiment to fight in the Civil War.[11] By the time the war ended over 1,500 blacks had served. All officers were white despite all troops being black. The regiment was involved in sufficient combat that 140 persons died including 3 of its white officers.

Between the wars

The period between the Civil War and World War I was a period of industrial expansion but waves of European immigrants prevented Detroit blacks from receiving any of the benefits.[12] Much of Detroit's industry was organized on the principle that work force homogeneity was associated with maximal worker satisfaction and maximum productivity. This left little place for the black worker except in service jobs, which were increasingly vacated by whites. Between 1870 and 1910 the percentage of male servants who were black rose from 9 to 20 percent. In 1910, 9 percent of all employed black males were servants as opposed to one-half of 1 percent of white male workers.

Not all service occupations exhibited a similar pattern. Barbering provided the opportunity to earn a comfortable living with a certain amount of prestige in the community. Blacks comprised 55 percent of all the barbers in 1870 but only 7.3 percent in 1910. The absolute number of black male barbers hardly changed during the forty-year period (78 in 1910 and 76 in 1870) despite an increase in the absolute number of blacks living in Detroit. Foreign-born barbers occupied the positions formerly held by blacks. This is illustrated by the figures for 1890, which found 24 percent of the male barbers to be black while 30 percent were foreign born and an additional 24 percent had at least one foreign-born parent.

Foreign-born competition also moved blacks out of dock work, which had been a traditional means of earning a living for a large portion of the black community. It would appear that persons involved in making hiring decisions preferred to give foreign-born whites occupational advantages over blacks. Table 3.2 presents the occupational distributions of blacks, native-born and foreign-born whites at several points in time. In 1870, 25.4 percent of white males and 71.4 percent of black males held unskilled or service occupations. By 1910 the percentage of blacks in these occupations had risen to 77.4 percent while the percentage for native-born whites was only 10.2 percent. Foreign-born whites occupied an intermediate position with 35.9 percent of all

Table 3.2. *Occupational distribution of Detroit males, by race and nativity, 1870–1910*

Year	Race and nativity	Occupational classification		Percent distribution		
		Profes-sional	Skilled	Semi-skilled	Unskilled	Service
1870						
	Black	2.9	10.2	15.5	28.0	43.4
	White	23.9	43.0	7.7	22.3	3.1
1890						
	Black	5.1	9.9	14.6	23.0	47.4
	For.-born wh.	19.0	38.5	11.5	27.1	3.9
	Nat.-born wh.	39.0	33.5	14.8	8.4	4.3
1900						
	Black	8.3	9.4	10.2	22.7	49.4
	For.-born wh.	20.2	44.4	10.8	20.9	3.7
	Nat.-born wh.	37.9	37.4	13.2	7.4	4.1
1910						
	Black	9.9	11.1	11.6	17.8	49.6
	For.-born wh.	18.2	34.0	11.9	31.6	4.3
	Nat.-born wh.	33.9	36.9	19.0	6.5	3.7

Source: Adapted from David M. Katzman, *Before the Ghetto: Black Detroit in the Nineteenth Century* (Urbana: University of Illinois Press, 1973), Tables 10–14, pp. 217–220.

males in unskilled or service occupations. While no direct evidence is readily available, it seems likely that foreign-born workers acted as a buffer deflecting black hostility away from native-born whites at the top toward the incumbents of the intermediate strata.[13]

Impact of World War I

The outbreak of World War I had a major impact upon race relations in Detroit. It removed some white workers from the area at the very time that it stimulated rapidly increased industrial expansion. There was a shortage of workers and several Detroit industrial firms recruited black workers from the South.[14] This produced the sevenfold increase in the size of the Detroit black population between 1910 and 1920 revealed in

Table 3.1. However, blacks were not the only group to respond to the lure of jobs. The foreign-born white population increased from 156,000 to 289,200 and the native-born white population increased from 304,025 to 636,640 during the same decade.[15] Much of the increase in native-born white population resulted from the migration of southern whites whose racial attitudes had been formed in the old South.

The extent to which the war opened up job opportunities for blacks in Detroit industry — especially in auto — was described in Chapter 2. However, its impact in terms of increased racial tension was not fully realized until sometime after the war. The KKK became a major force in Detroit during the decade of the twenties.[16] It had a membership numbering in the thousands and on June 14, 1923, it held a mass initiation ceremony in which over 1,000 people joined. Crosses were burned later the same year in front of City Hall and Wayne County courthouse. The KKK entered politics directly when it ran a write-in candidate for mayor in September 1924. The candidate, Charles Bowles, received 106,679 votes that were counted and another 17,000 that were invalidated due to misspellings and other technical errors. Those 17,000 votes tipped the election to the victor, John W. Smith, who received only 116,807 votes.

The KKK continued to be an important force in Detroit even though its more violent wing, the Black Legion, got more publicity during the thirties. It is estimated that the Black Legion executed over fifty persons in Detroit alone between 1931 and 1936 when it was finally destroyed through a successful murder prosecution. The KKK held its biggest day in the Detroit limelight through its role in the Ossian Sweet case.

Ossian Sweet buys a house

Over 10,000 people attended a KKK rally on July 11, 1925, and cheered the suggestion that they should form neighborhood improvement associations to protect neighborhoods from blacks who wished to move in.[17] This rally took place shortly after Dr. Ossian Sweet, a black gynecologist, had purchased a home in a white neighborhood and announced that he would move in on September 8. The KKK rally resulted in the formation of the Waterworks Park Improvement Association in the neighborhood surrounding Dr. Sweet's new home. The association met a few days before the scheduled move-in to map a line of activities designed to keep Sweet out of the neighborhood. Ossian Sweet notified the police that he intended to move into the home on September 8. He arrived with a supply of food, ten guns, almost 400 rounds of ammunition, and several relatives and friends. This was felt to be necessary because of recent violence directed against other blacks attempting to move into white neighborhoods.

That night a crowd assembled in front of the Sweet home. Estimates of its size ranged from 30 to over 500 and its mood was variously described as curious to hostile. Whatever the facts as to size and mood, at least one rock was thrown through a window. About the same time a car pulled up carrying Mr. Sweet's brother and another friend. The crowd surged around the two blacks and appeared to threaten them. Shots rang out from the Sweet house and a white man was killed on the porch of a house across the street. All eleven persons in the house, Mr. and Mrs. Sweet and nine black men, were arrested and charged with murder.

The NAACP was fortunate in getting Clarence Darrow to act for the defense. The trial was long and bitter. It appeared to turn on the question of whether a group of panicky blacks had shot without cause at a small group of curious neighbors or whether a black man had been forced, with some help from his friends, to defend his home from a hostile mob. Darrow introduced testimony regarding the speakers at the Waterworks Parks Improvement Association who just a few days before the shooting had urged the use of violence to keep the neighborhood white. Much to the surprise of many, Darrow won an acquittal from the all-white jury. The right of a black man to defend himself and his property from a white mob was established. However, it was established in a context that could not be said to have reduced racial tension in Detroit.

World War II

Race relations continued without much change until the outbreak of World War II. As in the case of World War I, the war produced a reduction in the number of ablebodied white workers at the same time that it stimulated industrial expansion. Once again job opportunities were opened up for blacks, and migrants flocked to Detroit producing the increased size of the black community during the decade shown in Table 3.1. The exploitation of race by Ford, which exacerbated racial tensions during the UAW Ford organizing drive in 1941, was described in Chapter 2; also the series of wildcat strikes and work stoppages held by white workers in late 1941 and early 1942 to protest against the employment or upgrading of black workers. World War II stimulated additional racial strains in the area of housing, which surfaced most visibly in the controversy surrounding the Sojourner Truth housing project.[18]

Sojourner Truth comes to Detroit

The Detroit population had long been growing at a more rapid rate than housing could be supplied. A number of public housing projects had been built during the thirties but none were in black neighborhoods or were designed for black occupancy. In September 1941 a project designed for blacks was planned for a white neighborhood. Both black and white groups objected to its location because they felt that it would cause trouble. The buildings were completed in December but remained unoccupied while political implications were hashed out. Federal officials notified the Detroit Housing Authority on January 20, 1942, that Sojourner Truth was designated for white workers. Protest led to the reversal of this decision and the project was scheduled to be opened to black occupancy on February 28.

The KKK burned a cross near Sojourner Truth on the night of February 27. When blacks arrived to move in the next day they were confronted by a white mob. Fighting broke out and continued on an episodic basis throughout the day. The white mob dispersed after it was promised that no blacks would ever be allowed to occupy the project. Police arrested 104 persons (2 were white and 102 were black) for events surrounding the riot. Many protests were launched against the refusal to allow blacks to occupy Sojourner Truth but it was not until the incident began to appear in Nazi propaganda that the decision was finally made and enforced that blacks would occupy the project. They eventually moved in two months after the riot.

The 1943 race riot

A major outbreak of racial violence came to Detroit on June 20, 1943, in the form of a four-day race riot that resulted in thirty-four dead (nine white, twenty-five black).[19] The tensions had been building toward this type of clash over a number of years. Father Coughlin based his operations in Detroit where both the racist line that he espoused and that of Rev. Gerald L. K. Smith seemed to get warm reception in at least some segments of the community. The influx of black workers into Detroit industries had caused white resentment and stimulated the job actions described above. The most serious strike took place at Packard in the spring of 1943. Both black and white workers were frustrated by wartime shortages that prevented them from fully enjoying their war-inflated incomes. Blacks felt the impact of shortages more severely than whites. It was also the black community that bore the brunt of overcrowded housing and deteriorated housing conditions. Black attempts to break out of the ghetto met with hostile rebuffs from whites.

The early war years saw a series of clashes between blacks and sailors stationed on Belle Isle in Detroit as well as between blacks and police. Tensions ran high in both areas. They were undoubtedly exacerbated by the riot of May 1943 in Mobile, Alabama, between white and black workers, the June Los Angeles riot between white sailors and black and Chicano Zoot-suiters, and the Beaumont, Texas, riot during which 10,000 whites attacked the black community. Detroit also experienced a series of small clashes, including a battle at Inkster on June 13 during which 200 sailors joined an ongoing fight involving over 300 black and white civilians. On June 15 police from three communities had to lend aid to East Detroit to quell an amusement park disturbance resulting from an attempt by 200 white servicemen and high school students to throw 100 blacks out of the park.

Sunday, June 20, was a hot and humid day. An estimated 100,000 people, mostly black, gathered on Belle Isle. It is unclear to this day exactly what happened on the island. It is known that a series of small racial incidents broke out periodically throughout the day. The island has only one bridge connecting it with Detroit and it cannot handle a heavy traffic flow. Huge traffic jams invariably are caused by the homeward rush on days of heavy island usage. On this particular Sunday the combination of pent-up tensions and the day's activities sparked a brawl that escalated into a major riot when 200 sailors stationed on the island joined the fight. Soon a mob of 5,000 whites was gathered at the bridge attempting to catch isolated blacks headed for home. The violence continued to center around the bridge until about 2:00 A.M. when the police began to make some arrests.

Rumors helped to spread the violence to other areas of the city. An announcement was made in a black nightclub that sailors had killed a black woman and her baby while similar, but reversed, rumors circulated in white areas. Black mobs looted and burned in the black section of the city and attacked some whites who wandered through. White mobs attacked blacks who were on streetcars or driving through white neighborhoods. Police played a role that could not be described as neutral. They frequently watched white mobs beat blacks without interfering. They were frequently observed turning blacks over to white mobs or participating in the beatings themselves. It is noteworthy that police shot and killed seventeen persons during the riot and that all were black. A governor's fact-finding commission investigated and found the Detroit black community largely responsible for causing the riot. The black newspaper was attacked for having incited blacks by pointing out that the war for democracy ought to include democracy at home for blacks as well as democracy abroad. Little attempt was made to prosecute those responsible for the riot beatings and killings.

Tensions remained high between police and the black community. About 1:00 A.M. on Saturday, September 11, police responded to a purse-snatching complaint in a black district in Detroit. They observed a fight between a man and his estranged wife. The police intervened, the man resisted, and he was arrested. A crowd of 500 blacks tried to take the prisoner away from the police. The police radioed for help and were reinforced by twelve squad cars and a riot wagon. The crowd was broken up by forty-two police officers using nightsticks and tear gas. No one was seriously injured and only four blacks were arrested, but the confrontation revealed a high level of tension and animosity between blacks and the police.

The period between major riots

Housing continued to be a problem in Detroit. One aspect of the wider problem may be seen in the fact that housing became more segregated in the three decades between 1930 and 1960.[20] Nevertheless there was some progress in this area — even if it had more impact on the law than it did on actual living conditions.[21] Early in 1945 Mr. and Mrs. Orsel McGhee, both black, purchased a house in a white neighborhood. A neighbor attempted to invalidate the sale on the grounds that the house was covered by a racially restrictive covenant. Both Wayne County Circuit Court and the Michigan Supreme Court upheld the validity of the covenant. Finally on May 3, 1948, the United States Supreme Court ruled that restrictive covenants could not constitutionally be enforced by the power of the state.

A continuing series of housing incidents demonstrated that a legal ruling did not change the attitudes of all Detroiters overnight — or even over a decade. A mob numbering in the hundreds committed extensive property damage on September 13, 1948, when it milled around two homes recently purchased by blacks in a white neighborhood. Only three arrests were made and the charges were reduced from "incitement to riot" to "disturbing the peace."[22] A mob of over fifty whites attempted in 1967 to violently expel Mrs. Ethel Watkins from her newly purchased home. Police protected her but arrested no one.[23] The local newspapers ignored the incident despite white hostile demonstrations, which lasted over a period of weeks. This conflict took place in the Bagley district of Detroit. Bagley was one of a series (e.g., Russell Woods and Fitzgerald) of neighborhoods that were touted as *the* neighborhoods that would become models of stable integration. However, each of the neighborhoods rapidly changed from all white to mixed to predominantly black. Each successive neighborhood took less time to move through the cycle.

There is an apparent contradiction between the fact that there was a continuing series of incidents involving blacks moving into white neighborhoods in a period in which housing was becoming more segregated. But this contradiction is resolved by an examination of population figures. Table 3.1 demonstrated that the black population in Detroit continued to grow between 1950 and 1970. However, the white population went in the opposite direction.[24] There were 1,545,847 white Detroiters in 1950 but only 1,182,970 in 1960 and 838,877 in 1970. The black population was expanding and moving into previously all-white neighborhoods while whites were leaving the city for the suburbs. It is not unlikely that the violent resistance to black moves came from those whites who were unable or unwilling to move to the suburbs.

Economic changes

The postwar problems of the auto industry and their impact upon race relations among workers were discussed in Chapter 2. Fear of job shrinkage motivated another series of white worker wildcats against black upgrading. Black Detroiters also experienced increased economic strain between 1940–60.[25] Blacks increased their completed median years of schooling more rapidly than whites (blacks improved from 8.6 years to 9.3 years while whites improved from 10.2 years to 10.3 years) while increasing their representation in white-collar occupations less rapidly than whites (gain of 11.1 percent for blacks and 17.3 percent for whites) and falling further behind in terms of income. Black median income rose from $3,130 to $4,370 while whites raised theirs from $4,120 to $7,050. This was both a greater absolute and relative gain for whites despite a flight of higher-income whites to the suburbs.

It should also be noted that in 1963 white male income averaged $1,365 more than that of similarly educated black males. Equally significant is the fact that the size of the discrepancy increased as level of education increased. White males also outearned black males at every occupational level, with the size of the discrepancy being greatest for the higher-status occupations. Black males had higher unemployment rates than white males, were more likely to be unemployed at every occupational level, and the discrepancy between white and black unemployment rates increased as level of occupational status increased. It is not likely that black Detroiters could believe that their lower economic status was the simple result of their having less education than whites.

The 1963 Walk to Freedom

The major role that TULC and the black community had in helping to elect Jerome Cavanaugh mayor of the city of Detroit in 1961 was described in Chapter 2. Cavanaugh attempted to deal with Detroit's racial problems but could not achieve any noticeable improvement.[26] By May 1963 a group of Detroit blacks were impatient both with the administration and with the older black organizations and scheduled a Walk To Freedom to be held on June 23, the twentieth anniversary of the 1943 riot. Although the older black organizations were receptive to marches in the summer of the March on Washington, they were unwilling to participate in a march led by persons they perceived to be upstarts who would not recognize them as the legitimate spokesmen for the black community. The alleged "upstarts" were a group of black ministers, led by Rev. Franklin, head of Detroit's largest black church, who had grown impatient with the inaction of Detroit's black labor-type leaders.

It appeared possible that a march would be held consisting only of Detroit's most militant blacks. Mayor Cavanaugh was afraid that this would lead to violence. He wanted to be certain that "responsible elements" would be part of any demonstration that was held. He let the "established" black leadership know that community interests would be best served if they participated in the parade and that he, Jerome Cavanaugh, would be part of it. The NAACP, Urban League and the UAW cooperated. Martin Luther King accepted an invitation to march. The march included King, Cavanaugh, Michigan Governor George Romney, and Walter Reuther as part of the group of between 150,000 and 200,000 persons who peacefully paraded down Woodward Avenue.

It appeared that Detroit was finally entering into an era of good feelings as far as race relations were concerned. People (white Detroiters) constantly bragged that Detroit had the finest race relations in the nation. There was a general aura of optimism and hope. Shogan and Craig described it this way: "There is more hope for the solution of Detroit's racial problems in 1964 than at any time in the past. Much of the hope stems from the fact that the city government at last is openly trying to come to grips with the problem."[27] This was the mood of Detroit — black discontent and white optimism — when urban insurrections began sweeping America between 1964 and 1967.

The 1967 insurrection

It may be valuable to review a few political developments that helped to set the scene for 1967.[28] William T. Patrick was elected in 1959 as Detroit's first black member of Detroit's nine-person Common Council. Patrick resigned in 1965, and a special election was held in which Thomas Poindexter, white, was elected in a campaign centering around his petition-referendum drive to give homeowners a right to racial discrimination in the sale and rental of housing. During the regular election of 1966 Poindexter was defeated and Rev. Nicholas Hood, a black minister, was elected to the council. However, his election was only achieved after considerable pressure was exerted. The analysis of votes in the primary election showed that blacks voted an interracial slate but whites only voted for whites. Black ministers then announced that they would urge their congregations to vote only for blacks. Liberal whites became concerned over their chances for election and a coalition was formed that resulted in Hood's election.

A minor racial incident occurred on August 9, 1966, when a police cruiser was involved in an altercation with a group of young blacks on Kercheval Street.[29] Later several cars driven by whites were stoned and riot police moved in to break up gangs beginning to form. A black community group went door-to-door to try to keep the neighborhood cool. The incident did not escalate. A few fires were set and a few arrests made but Detroit remained relatively quiet. Police—black relations, never overly good, began to deteriorate.[30]

In 1967 Mary Beck ran a campaign for the office of Mayor based on a "crime in the street" campaign. *The Detroit News* constantly featured crime news in a way that seemed to emphasize or exaggerate black participation. Blacks had little representation in the Detroit police department, constituting only 5 percent of the force and being almost totally limited to the lower ranks. On June 24, 1967, a black man was killed by a group of whites when trying to protect his pregnant wife from their sexual advances. She later lost the baby. Detroit's major news media did not even report the incident until after it was reported in the *Michigan Chronicle*. A week later a black prostitute was killed. The black community felt that there was reason to believe that she was killed by a member of the vice squad. The police denied this but were not able to present any other plausible account of the events. Fifteen blacks had been shot by whites during the term of office of the incumbent prosecutor. All had been ruled as justifiable shootings despite strange sets of circumstances. Blacks in Detroit had no reason to believe that their official representatives were persons concerned with the welfare of all citizens.

On July 22, 1967, Detroit police officers raided a blind pig — the local term for an illegal drinking place — and found a party in progress for some black servicemen.[31] They arrested the 82 persons present. A crowd gathered as they operated a shuttle to the local jail. The crowd grew and became increasingly hostile. Before the police had completed the transportation of their prisoners to jail the crowd had begun throwing stones. This developed into a six-day insurrection during which 43 people died (9 white, 34 black), 347 were injured, 3,800 arrested, 5,000 were left homeless, 1,300 buildings were destroyed, 2,700 buildings were looted, and over $500 million in damages resulted.

This was not a race riot. There was no fighting between blacks and whites other than that involving police or other symbols of constituted authority. One of the nine whites who died was killed by blacks when he tried to stop them from looting his place. A second may have been killed by a sniper. Two were killed by police allegedly while looting, one was killed as an alleged sniper, one was a fireman accidently killed by a member of the National Guard, one was a police officer accidently killed by another police officer, one was a fireman who accidently died while fighting a fire, and the final victim was killed when she chose the wrong time to look out of her motel window and apparently was mistaken for a sniper. A *Detroit Free Press* examination of the deaths concluded:

Eighteen of the 43 riot victims were shot and killed by Detroit police, and of that number, 14 have been confirmed as looters in the *Free Press* investigation. The other four are a sniper, a possible but unconfirmed arsonist and two of the three men shot and killed in the Algiers Motel. At least six victims were killed by the National Guard, five of them innocent, the victims of what now seem to be tragic accidents. In five more cases both police and National guardsmen were involved and it is impossible to say definitely whose bullets were fatal. Four of these five victims were innocent of any wrongdoing. Two more persons, both looters, were shot and killed by store-owners. Three more were killed by private citizens . . . two looters died when fire swept the store from which they were stealing. Two victims, one a fireman, the other a civilian, were killed by electric power lines. Five deaths remain. They are a 19-year old boy killed accidentally by an army paratrooper; a 23-year old white woman shot by an unknown gunman; a Detroit fireman killed by either a hidden sniper or a stray National Guard bullet, a policeman shot as a fellow officer struggled with a prisoner; and the third victim of the Algiers Motel incident whose assailant is not known.[32]

The above report was compiled by a team of newspaper reporters who gave the law enforcement agencies every possible benefit of doubt. Thus the picture that they paint is much better than the reality. Even at that, they note the frequent use of lethal force against looters. Eyewitness accounts have suggested that several of those shootings amounted to deliberate executions of looters. In one case witnesses observed a man being ordered to run and then being shot down by police and left lying in an alley as the police drove away. It is clear in the case of the Algiers Motel incident that three blacks were executed because they were found in a motel with white women. There is other evidence that the law enforcement agencies frequently panicked and acted irresponsibly. A four-year-old girl was killed when a tank sprayed the room she was in because someone lit a cigarette and spooked the guardsmen.

While an important segment of the black community either participated in or supported the events of the insurrection, actual participation was disproportionately clustered among the more deprived segments of the black working class (i.e., the segment of the black working class that had less stable employment).[33] Insurrection participants were less well educated than nonparticipants on an age-controlled basis, had lower-status jobs and less income, and were more frequently unem-

ployed over the year preceding the insurrection. At each educational level the participants had lower-status jobs and less income, and at each
occupational level they earned less money than nonparticipants. They
were also more frequently unemployed at each educational and occupational level. Thus the insurrection appears to have been conducted by
the segment of the black working class that suffered most from systematic racism in the Detroit industrial structure.

The postinsurrection period

Detroit's black community displayed mixed feelings after the insurrection. There was a certain amount of pride in having stood up and
fought back. This was mixed with anger at the police for the brutality
of the repression and hope that the insurrection would finally wake up
the white community and begin to bring some changes. The hope was
further stimulated by the formation of the New Detroit Committee, by
the Ford Motor Company announcement that they would open up
hiring offices in the ghetto in which they would waive normal job requirements if the requirements were not found to be directly related to
job performance, and by the operation of a Chrysler and UAW federal-
ly supported job-training program. A series of experiences soon led to
an erosion of hope and an increase in bitterness.[34]

Numerous Detroit police officers joined the National Rifle Association (NRA) and purchased rifles. It was widely believed that these were
purchased for use in future riots. White suburban housewives took training on the use of pistols. Guns were purchased in large numbers by both
blacks and whites. The New Detroit Committee never really got the financial or political backing that it needed for a successful program.
Martin Luther King was assassinated April 4, 1968. A curfew was im-
posed on Detroit but was only enforced in black residential neighborhoods. The governor mobilized 9,000 National Guardsmen despite their
poor performance during the insurrection of 1967. Two months later
the Detroit police launched an unprovoked mounted attack against the
Poor People's March and *two* police officers were disciplined. The attack was reported live over local television stations. That November a
number of off-duty Detroit policemen beat up several middle-class
black high school students who had been attending a social function in
the same building where the Detroit Police Officers' Association was
holding a dance. Nine police officers were suspended and charges

brought against two of them. About a month later a Detroit police officer was suspended for pistol whipping a young black. The black community felt that the Detroit police department was trying to trigger another riot so they could really come down hard. The Detroit police department felt that they were harrassed by people who wished to destroy their effectiveness.

This was the milieu that existed in April 1969 when the Republic of New Africa — a black separatist organization headquartered in Detroit — held its national convention in the New Bethel Baptist Church. It is unclear what happened to touch off the initial confrontation, during which one police officer was killed and another wounded, but reinforcements were called in and the church was attacked. The church was riddled with bullets and its 143 inhabitants, men, women, and children, were arrested and held incommunicado. The next morning, Sunday, Judge George Crockett set up court and began processing the prisoners. Most prisoners were released with the consent of the prosecutor but this was not immediately reported in the press. A campaign was begun, supported by the Detroit Police Officers' Association, to have Crockett removed from office.

The campaign focussed on the fact that Crockett, a black man, had served prison time for contempt of court arising out of his spirited defense of the defendents in the infamous Smith Act trials held before Judge Medina.[35] It also focussed on Judge Crockett's belief that while the law may be racially neutral it had been systematically used to repress blacks in America and that he, therefore, intended to reverse the previous situation and use it as a weapon for black liberation. The attacks either charged or implied that he was both a racist and a Communist. The Detroit Commission on Community Relations studied the incident and issued a report condemning the shooting of the police officers, the police response, inaccurate newspaper coverage, and accusing *The Detroit News* of racially biased crime coverage. The Michigan Bar Association and others acknowledged that Crockett's behavior was perfectly proper but this did not reduce the amount of bitterness felt by Detroit police officers and white supporters of "law and order."

The political campaign of 1969 took on both a racial and a "law and order" tone. The three major candidates for mayor in the primary race were Richard Austin (a black), Roman Gribbs (white and the incumbent Wayne County sheriff), and Mary Beck (a white "law and order" candidate). The runoff was between Gribbs and Austin with Gribbs winning a narrow victory by 257,312 to 250,020. Austin had been endorsed by the UAW leadership but the unions could not deliver the votes of their membership for a black mayor during a campaign in which stopping crime was a major issue. The same election found blacks elected to three of the nine Common Council seats — their largest representation in Detroit history.

The economic status of black Detroiters did not improve much more than the quality of Detroit's race relations. Most of the job programs initiated after the insurrection had little payoff for blacks. Table 3.3 presents mean 1969 income figures for black males and for all Detroit males at each level of education with age controlled. An interesting picture emerges if we limit our examination to the prime productive years between 25 and 64. The difference in incomes of blacks and all Detroiters with less than 5 years of schooling for the four age cohorts varies between $1,024 and $1,485. The difference ranges from $1,337 to $1,942 for those with 5 to 7 years of schooling. Detroit males with an eighth grade education earn between $1,723 and $2,234 more than similarly educated black males of the same age cohort. The income differences between black and Detroit males with from 1 and 3 years of high school ranged between $2,262 and $3,164. The differences for high school graduates ranged between $2,582 and $4,532. Detroiters with between 1 and 3 years of college earned from $2,021 to $6,854 more than similarly educated blacks. The difference for college graduates between 25 and 34 years of age was *only* $2,606 but it ranged between $8,722 and $12,126 for those over 35. The difference between black and all Detroit males with five or more years of college was only $1,634 for those between 25 and 34 but it ranged between $3,883 and $10,377 for those over 35. While separate figures are not available on white income it would not appear that blacks had achieved economic equality with whites by 1969. Nor would it appear that the explanation of lower black earnings could be found in lesser education. Economic discrimination against black Detroiters clearly continued at a high level into the decade of the seventies.

Discussion

While Detroit may have provided more jobs and opportunities for blacks than most cities, it certainly was not Mecca. The earliest black Detroit experiences were as slaves. Detroit was characterized by continual racial discrimination and conflict from the first quarter of the nineteenth to the last quarter of the twentieth century. Blacks began at the bottom of Detroit's social structure and remained there as other groups entered at higher points or soon moved past them. There is some evidence that European immigrants, particularly the Poles, learned their racial prejudice after arriving in Detroit (see Chapter 2). It may be the case that racial hostilities were deliberately introduced between blacks and immigrants in order to facilitate the exploitation of both groups just as black—native-white tensions had been exploited earlier in an attempt to prevent or hinder the development of unions. There is little doubt that tension and hostility did develop between blacks and Polish-Americans and that this had an impact upon the subsequent history of the League of Revolutionary Black Workers.

It is also important to note that Detroit blacks had a history of struggle. Their struggles paid off in observable gains but never succeeded in bringing about full racial equality. Their struggles also, at various times, took separatist directions and, at other times, included groups with Marxist orientations. Each of these political inclinations foreshadowed later developments involving the League. The earliest black struggles emerged in the form of the 1833 riot when the black community rose up to prevent some of its members from being carried back to slavery. The next three decades were characterized by continual struggle to achieve the franchise and equal educational opportunities. Black Detroiters fought in the Civil War partially in order to help destroy slavery just as they earlier had participated in the underground railroad and in the abolition movement.

Blacks kept up a constant struggle against housing discrimination and were constantly pushing back residential boundaries. Ossian Sweet demonstrated a willingness to use violence when needed to protect himself, his family, and his property. The hiring of Clarence Darrow by the NAACP to defend Mr. Sweet was a continuation of the same struggle in a different form. The fight for housing rights was continued by the incumbents of the Sojourner Truth housing project and by Mr. and Mrs. Orsel McGhee. The 1943 riot was another indication of the willingness of blacks to take to the streets to defend themselves from white attack.

The struggle took on an economic character during World War II when blacks engaged in strike action first to force the hiring of black workers at the Chrysler Tank Arsenal and then to force the upgrading of blacks at Packard. It was also during World War II that the alliance forged in the 1930's between the Communist Party and many black UAW members was strengthened. The major role played by Communists in building the UAW was described in Chapter 2. They provided

Table 3.3. *Mean male income, by race and education, Detroit, 1970*

Age	Race	Total	Years of Education in: Elementary			High School		College		
			0–4	5–7	8	1–3	4	1–3	4	5+
All	black	6,516	4,685	5,768	6,300	6,292	6,964	7,368	9,099	13,790
	all	9,839	5,136	6,690	7,839	8,528	9,937	10,732	15,830	18,083
	difference	3,323	451	922	1,539	2,236	2,973	3,364	6,731	4,293
18–24	black	4,419	3,225	3,612	4,264	3,829	4,906	4,577	5,645	5,948
	all	4,732	3,592	4,453	4,888	4,036	5,248	4,410	5,246	5,746
	difference	313	367	841	624	207	342	167[a]	399[a]	202[a]
25–34	black	7,226	5,704	5,926	6,676	6,505	7,406	8,150	9,495	11,280
	all	10,174	7,116	7,868	8,399	8,767	9,988	10,771	12,101	12,914
	difference	2,948	1,412	1,942	1,723	2,262	2,582	2,621	2,606	1,634

35–44	black	8,030	6,340	6,821	7,403	7,538	8,270	9,105	9,655	16,878
	all	12,254	7,825	8,686	9,637	10,104	12,018	14,064	18,367	20,761
	difference	4,224	1,485	1,865	2,234	2,566	3,748	4,959	8,712	3,883
45–54	black	7,678	6,139	7,105	7,262	7,559	8,201	9,089	10,832	14,057
	all	12,605	7,307	8,442	9,592	10,436	12,595	15,873	21,404	24,434
	difference	4,927	1,168	1,337	2,330	2,877	4,394	6,784	10,572	10,377
55–64	black	6,633	5,899	6,273	6,488	6,700	7,401	7,715	10,162	13,989
	all	11,014	6,923	7,705	8,757	9,864	11,933	14,569	22,286	22,580
	difference	4,381	1,024	1,432	2,269	3,164	4,532	6,854	12,124	8,591
65+	black	3,303	2,652	2,944	3,193	3,566	6,677	4,086	4,107	10,567
	all	5,368	3,172	3,803	4,552	5,373	6,879	8,620	14,174	16,870
	difference	2,065	520	859	1,359	1,807	202	4,534	10,067	6,303

[a] Mean income is higher for blacks than for all persons in this age and education category.

Source: Constructed from Unites States Department of Commerce, Bureau of the Census: PC(1)-D24, Detailed Characteristics, Michigan, Table 197.

strong support for the black drive to develop a meaningful voice within the UAW and as a result attracted a great deal of black support to their cause. Herbert Hill feels that black Communists were attracted to the party less because of the communist ideology than because they felt that they needed the tactical support of the Communists in the pursuit of their own racial ends.[36] Whatever the reason, black auto workers did come to identify Marxism with people willing to fight for black causes. This identification was spread to the larger community during the late forties when House Un-American Activities Committee (HUAC) hearings continually focussed on Communist—black linkages and directed much of their hostile attention to black Communists.[37]

After World War II much of the black struggle shifted to the political arena. The TULC was formed within the UAW but also played a major role in community politics, especially in the election of Jerome Cavanaugh in 1961. Blacks continued the drive to achieve a voice in Detroit politics but shifted to an attempt to get blacks directly elected to office rather than to elect sympathetic whites. This culminated in the unsuccessful 1969 campaign of Richard Austin for mayor and in the election of three blacks to membership in the Detroit Common Council the same year.

The struggle was mixed and varied. Blacks were exposed to Marxism in a number of forms. The Communist Party was only one of its many advocates. C. L. R. James spent much of World War II in Detroit. He had been active for a long period of time in the Socialist Workers Party under the name of J. R. Johnson, among others, and had been one of the prime movers in the "Johnson—Forest tendency," which argued that one had to combine a class and a race analysis in order to explain the position of blacks in American society. Johnson and Forest eventually left the Socialist Workers Party over the issue of pure class versus combined race and class analysis. A circle of Marxist political theorists and activists centered around James in Detroit. Much of his writing and the writing of his disciples was circulated in the Detroit ghetto.

One of the circle around James was Grace Lee who later became Grace Lee Boggs when she married James Boggs. Both James and Grace Lee Boggs were Marxists. James was a black auto worker and Grace had a Ph.D. in philosophy. Each wrote large numbers of political tracts, which were circulated in the Detroit ghetto as well as nationally. The Socialist Workers Party was also very active in Detroit. Much of their literature was circulated in the ghetto and they had many black members.

Detroit also included a separatist or nationalist tendency within its black community.[38] Detroit had been the birthplace of the Nation of Islam. W. D. Fard started his organizational work in Detroit in 1930. It is here that he came into contact with Elijah Poole, later Elijah Muhammad, and Detroit still has Temple Number 1 of the Nation. Rev. Albert Cleage gave separatism a different twist in developing Black Christian Nationalism centered around his church, The Shrine of the Black Madonna. Separatism took a political direction in the Detroit branches of the Freedom Now Party in 1964 and of the Revolutionary Action Movement. Richard and Milton Henry were among the founders of the Group on Advanced Leadership (GOAL), which was a nationalist political group that sought to militantly push black objectives through traditional political structures. In 1967 they developed beyond GOAL when they founded the Republic of New Africa.

The Republic of New Africa is a separatist organization that seeks an independent black nation to be carved out of the existing United States. It would consist of five states bordering the Gulf (Georgia, Alabama, South Carolina, Mississippi, and Louisiana) and be organized along the lines of African socialism. It was hoped that the Republic would form an umbrella organization that could incorporate all black separatists regardless of religion. They included a diverse group of persons in cabinet posts and executive positions. They range from Robert Williams and Rap Brown to Betty Shabbazz, Malcolm X's widow, and members of the Nation of Islam. The Republic of New Africa attracted a great deal of support in Detroit prior to acquiring farm land in the South and shifting its national headquarters to New Orleans.

Conclusions

The Detroit black community was marked by a history of struggle against exploitation that was partially successful in reducing but not eliminating racial exploitation. The struggle often made gains only to find whites retreating to a different form of exploitation. The struggle took various forms. Detroit always had a strong NAACP chapter and many Detroit blacks never lost their desire and expectation for full integration into American society. Other blacks were less sold on the goal of integration and desired separation from whites. Some blacks, who could otherwise be included in either of the above groups, were receptive to Marxism and saw the need for a socialist revolution. All blacks were united in the desire for change and the willingness to fight for it.

The 1967 insurrection stimulated a new burst of pride and revived belief that blacks could force changes through united efforts. Given the industrial nature of Detroit and the dominance of Detroit by the auto industry, it was to be expected that a major locus of the continuing black struggle would be found among black automobile workers. Nor is it surprising that the struggle would encompass both Marxist and separatist orientations. In Part II these developments will be described by a presentation of the history of the League of Revolutionary Black Workers.

The League of Revolutionary Black Workers

The fall of 1967 arrived in a Detroit black community rife with ferment. It was inevitable that new militant political organizations would develop. Detroit had recently experienced one of the bloodiest and most violent urban insurrections in American history. This had occurred as a part of a nationwide pattern. A new level of pride, anger, and commitment developed in black communities everywhere and especially in Detroit's black community. It was only the political form through which the anger would be manifested that remained to be determined.

Detroit had experienced — as had the nation — an evolution from the quiet forms of civil rights organizational programs through direct action and confrontation civil rights activities to an urban insurrection. The civil rights activities of the first two periods were not believed to have accomplished much beyond "window dressing" changes. Life for black workers was not visibly altered. Changes brought about by the insurrection made it unlikely that the black community — beyond its middle-class component — would be satisfied with returning to "business as usual" or to the traditional form of civil rights struggle. They were on the move and they were searching for new avenues of action.

This search could have led in any number of directions, but the future is always conditioned by the past. The Detroit history of struggle helped to determine the types of struggle that emerged. Many Marxist groups and individuals had been active in Detroit during the preceding forty years. The Socialist Workers Party had a strong chapter in Detroit and oriented much of its literature and political program toward the black community. C. L. R. James, a prominent black Marxist author, spent a great deal of time in the Detroit area on a periodic basis over a number of years. A band of his disciples lived, worked, and organized in Detroit. They published a series of newsletters, pamphlets, leaflets, and small political tracts. Many of these were sold or given away in black neighborhoods. James Boggs, a black auto worker, and Grace Lee Boggs, his wife, were each writing, publishing, and circulating political tracts. The Communist Party, along with various Trotskyists and democratic socialists, played a major role in organizing the auto industry and in forming the UAW. The heart of the Communist Party's strength was Ford Local 600, which was also the local with the highest proportion of black workers.

In view of this political history it was virtually certain that one of Detroit's emerging black political forms would be Marxist. Detroit had a long-term exposure to the language of Marxism and there was a history of socialist and black struggle. The black community had no reason to fear Marxism and every reason to welcome it. The League of Revolutionary Black Workers emerged as a black Marxist—Leninist organization. The League, with its affiliated revolutionary union movements, focussed organizational energies upon black workers in the auto plants. In Part II the history of the League will be presented.

This Part will consist of six chapters. In Chapter 4 the birth of the League will be described and a discussion launched on the development of political consciousness on the part of the League founders, the founding of DRUM, the early period of wildcat strikes, and the establishment of the League of Revolutionary Black Workers. Chapter 5 deals with the history of League involvement in union elections, and Chapter 6 with the death of the League, describing the split of the League into two rival black Marxist—Leninist organizations before fading out of existence. The rationale underlying the split is also considered. In an attempt better to understand the split, a detailed description of the League's ideology and its internal contradictions is presented in Chapter 7. Chapter 8 contains an analysis of the transformation of ideology into practice, examining the League's primary focus on organization — black workers at the point of production — and its relation to the broader community organizational work into which it eventually moved. Those factors contributing to the early growth of the League are analyzed in Chapter 9. The manner in which the ideological contradictions manifested themselves in concrete problems of day-to-day functioning and, combined with strong repressive measures by the establishment forces, destroyed the League is examined in Chapter 10, with an exploration of the concrete accomplishments of the League and its contribution to the Detroit black community's heritage of struggle.

Most of the events are discussed in chronological order but there are exceptions. There is overlap between the events described in Chapters 4, 5, and 7. It was felt that electoral activities were of a qualitatively different nature than wildcat strikes and that they could be more profitably discussed in a separate chapter. Similarly community organizing efforts are analytically of a different order than in-plant activities. This division is organizationally sound but it allows some possibility for confusion. For this reason a chronology of major events is presented. It will be available for the reader's reference at any point if needed to locate any given event within the larger developmental sequence.

Chronology of major events

September, 1967	*Inner City Voice* founded
Fall, 1967	Caucuses of black workers begin at meeting at Dodge Main
May 2, 1968	First wildcat strike at Dodge Main — leads to DRUM
July 7, 1968	DRUM rally
July 8, 1968	DRUM wildcat begins
September 26, 1968	Local 3 election for trustee
October 3, 1968	Local 3 trustee runoff election
October 24, 1968	DRUM rally, Chrysler headquarters
November 10, 1968	ELRUM is formed
November 17, 1968	DRUM rally, raffle, demonstration at Urban League luncheon
January 27, 1969	ELRUM wildcat strike
Early 1969	League of Revolutionary Black Workers established
April 8, 1969	Local 3 election for vice-president
Spring 1969	Detroit branch of The Black Panther Party organized
April 25–27, 1969	National Black Economic Development Conference meets in Detroit
May 17, 1969	Elroy Richardson elected president, Local 961
November 8, 1969	Special UAW convention begins at Cobo Hall
November 9, 1969	League demonstration centering on convention
March 11–12, 1970	Local 961 election for convention delegates
March 17–18, 1970	DRUM runs total slate in Local 3 elections
April 16, 1970	ELRUM wildcat over John Scott firing
May 1, 1970	Delegates fired — ELRUM wildcat strike

May 23, 1970	ELRUM wildcat over Gary Thompson death
Fall, 1970	Control, Conflict and Change book club established
May 28, 1971	Local 961 elections: Jordan Sims fired May 1, 1970, loses disputed election for president
June 12, 1971	Hamlin, Cockrel, and Watson resign from League
July 24, 1971	League expelled from Black Workers' Congress
September, 1971	Black Workers' Congress holds its founding convention in Gary, Indiana
May 23, 1973	Jordan Sims, still not rehired by Chrysler, elected president of Local 961

4. The birth of the League

The 1967 Detroit insurrection and its repression stimulated numerous developments, two of which bear upon the creation of the League. In September 1967 a radical ghetto newspaper called *The Inner City Voice* began publication.[1] It was edited by John Watson. He had previously edited, while in high school, a radical student-oriented paper called *The Black Vanguard* (which ceased publication in 1964). That same fall caucuses of black automobile workers began meeting at Dodge Main (Hamtramck assembly plant).[2] These two events were not totally unrelated as some of the participants in each group had had previous contact through civil rights activities and/or through common membership in Uhuru.[3]

The political development of black students

On October 14, 1963, Luke S. Tripp, Jr., John Williams, John Watson, General G. Baker, Jr., and Gwendlyin Kemp were arrested for disturbing the peace.[4] They were accused of jeering and otherwise creating a disturbance during the playing of the national anthem at a ceremony in which Detroit's Mayor Cavanaugh accepted a cross-country Olympic torch symbolizing Detroit's bid for the 1968 Olympic games. The NAACP picketed the ceremony in order to raise questions regarding the propriety of expending public funds on frills such as the Olympics when Detroit had great needs in the areas of housing and social services. The five Uhuru members had been staging a separate protest over the killing of a black prostitute, Cynthia Scott, when they associated themselves with the Olympic protest. They were finally acquitted of all charges stemming from this incident on February 23, 1966.[5]

This was neither the first nor the last time that these individuals had actively engaged themselves on behalf of the black movement. They had been active in civil rights work since 1961. Perhaps their earliest activities were in a group called The Negro Action Committee (NAC).

The group was interracial and had no well-formed political ideology. Discontent developed over both of these deficiencies, a search for a relevant ideology was launched, and a program of political self-education begun.[6] They were angered by the position of blacks in American society and wished to do something to change it. They realized that effective action must be based upon correct knowledge and analysis.

They read Marx and Lenin; but they also read Mao Tse-Tung, Frantz Fanon, Malcolm X, and Che Guevara among many others. They became acquainted with various black and white radicals in and around Detroit. They listened to what the members of the Socialist Workers Party and the Communist Party had to say. They also gave consideration to the thoughts of the followers of C. L. R. James. Several members participated in a special seminar on *Capital* conducted by Martin Glaberman. In every case they read and/or listened with a critical orientation. They did not believe that any existing ideology could be accepted in rigid dogmatic form if it were to be used in analyzing the situation of black Americans. It was felt that the black experience in America was unique and that any existing system of thought required reshaping to make it applicable. They sought to develop such a political-economic theory. They examined, tested, and reformulated various theoretical orientations until they arrived at a position that enabled them to describe themselves as black Marxist—Leninists.

Over time the group moved in a number of different occupational directions. Some became students at Wayne State University, others took jobs in Detroit's automobile factories and still others found other means of employment. They remained in contact with one another and attracted other like-minded persons. At least one of these had extensive contact with the Republic of New Africa.[7] Thus the parallel orientations of the members of the black workers' caucus at Dodge Main and the editors of *The Inner City Voice* are not unexpected. The manner in which this became translated into the founding of the League is somewhat complex. The first organizational step came in May 1968 when nine black production workers from Dodge Main joined together with the editors of *The Inner City Voice* to create DRUM.[8]

DRUM becomes the first League component

There was a wildcat strike at Dodge Main on May 2, 1968. It is somewhat unclear exactly how the walkout developed. One frequently heard version of events states widespread discontent existed among workers over a speedup in the line.[9] This speedup was only one of many sources of dissatisfaction. There existed a small interacting group of Polish women who worked in the same department, belonged to the same Rosary Society, and generally socialized together both inside and outside the plant. For some unexplained reason their discontent reached a peak on May 2 and they decided to walk off the job. Other persons, who were also dissatisfied over the speedup and otherwise unhappy, joined them and the wildcat was on. While they are not incompatible with this interpretation, there are other versions. Dudnick notes that this wildcat followed a series of five earlier wildcats and that several young blacks helped to organize and lead it.[10] Lee Cain, a black worker who did not join DRUM, admits to having played a major role in the organization of the walkout. Detroit newspapers have generally attributed the wildcat to DRUM leadership. It would appear that the wildcat was somewhat spontaneous and led by a coalition of forces.

Picket lines were established and management is alleged to have used photographs taken of pickets as evidence in disciplinary actions.[11] Punishment was disproportionately administered to blacks despite the fact that the strike and picketing were interracial. Seven persons (five blacks and two whites) were fired but all except two, General G. Baker, Jr. and Bennie Tate (both black) were eventually rehired.[12] The subsequent sequence of events can best be presented through the words of Chuck Wooten, one of the nine workers who founded DRUM, and Mike Hamlin, one of the editors of *The Inner City Voice.* Let us first consider Chuck Wooten's statement:

During the wildcat strike of May, 1968, upon coming to work . . . there were picket lines established . . . manned by all white workers at the time and as a result of this the black workers received the harshest disciplinary actions. A few workers and I went across the street and sat in a bar. . . . It was here that we decided we would do something about organizing black workers to fight the racial discrimination inside the plants and the overall oppression of the black workers. . . . And this was the beginning of DRUM.[13]

Mike Hamlin described the next step:

It happened at a time when many of us who have had a history of radical involvement in this city for some time had just begun to develop a newspaper as a means of getting ourselves together. . . . But we always had an understanding that what was necessary was that we organize black workers. And though we never had a successful entry into the plants with the workers and we really didn't know how to go about it, we attracted to us a group of nine workers from the plant just by virtue of us producing a newspaper and projecting certain ideas. We had certain radical ideas and a certain revolutionary line: That black workers would be the vanguard of the liberation struggle in this country. And we had a series of meetings with these workers to get to know them, for them to get to know us, and to begin to develop a common understanding how to proceed. They came to us because of the objective conditions in the plant . . . that they had tried to deal with in a number of ways. . . . These efforts had been unsuccessful. . . . And we developed a relationship which led to the formation of DRUM. We decided to use the newsletter as a means of organizing the workers. . . . We wrote about incidents, events, conditions of racism, brutality, and other kinds of bad working conditions, which began to build a sense of resentment among the workers and began to develop a sense of unity among them.[14]

Newsletter established

The forces combined to initiate a weekly newsletter entitled *drum* and decorated with drawings of drums.[15] The first issue reviewed the wildcat strike. It stated that it had been caused by a speedup in production from forty-nine to fifty-eight units per hour. It described the harshness of the penalties given out to black strikers, accused the company of racist hiring practices and included a memorial tribute to Malcolm X.

The firings continued to be a point of contention between DRUM, Local 3, and the UAW International.[16] DRUM refused to agree to the Chrysler intention of rehiring only five of the seven discharged workers. They publicly charged that Baker and Tate were being kept out of a job because they were black. Privately they charged that it was because they had played an active role in developing militancy among black workers. Either rationale was unacceptable.

The role of Douglas Fraser, UAW vice-president, is difficult to sort out.[17] He claims that an attempt was made to get all seven back to work. He acknowledges that local union leadership would have been happier if no such attempt were made. He publicly exhorted Local 3 leadership to attempt to understand DRUM's point of view and to make a real attempt to accommodate themselves to DRUM. Yet a letter from the UAW to Local 3 members signed by Liska, Local 3 president, and Fraser, attacked DRUM calling it "a sinister attempt to split the Dodge workers and to make their union ineffective and weak." DRUM newsletters were described as "extremist hate sheets."

There was a fear that DRUM would lead another wildcat strike against Chrysler unless Baker and Tate were rehired. This resulted in the issuance of an injunction naming DRUM, DRUM leaders, and other black workers who were not members of DRUM and enjoining them from picketing Chrysler facilities wherever located.[18] Thus Tate and Baker were left without jobs but as martyrs whom DRUM could use to symbolize the struggle.

The second issue of *drum* carried an "exposé" of a number of blacks in the plant considered by DRUM to be "Uncle Toms." It also included a series of nine questions beginning, "Have you ever wondered why," and continuing:

(1) 95% of all foremen in the plants are white; (2) 99% of all the general foremen are white; (3) 100% of all plant superintendents are white; (4) 90% of all skilled tradesmen are white; (5) 90% of all apprentices are white; (6) That systematically all of the easier jobs are held by whites; (7) Whenever whites are on harder jobs they have helpers; (8) When black workers miss a day from work they are required to bring 2 doctors' excuses as to why they missed work; (9) That seniority is also a racist concept, since black workers were systematically denied employment for years at this plant.[19]

The second issue also included a description of the DRUM program. It justified the separate organization outside the UAW union structure on a number of grounds. The justification stated that 60 percent of the work force at the Hamtramck assembly plant (Dodge Main) were black, that these black workers worked under inhumane conditions, and were exposed to racist practices. It further charged that the UAW leadership was as guilty as management of perpetuating a racist system. It claimed that black workers had consistently addressed grievances to the UAW without receiving any satisfaction. Thus a separate black workers' organization was made necessary. It further argued that black workers had as much, or more, justification than skilled workers for a separate contract and direct negotiation with management.

The third issue continued with its charges and documentations of racist conditions in the plant, but it branched out to include an attack against the UAW for endorsing the annual Detroit police field day. This issue listed a number of black deaths for which responsibility was attributed to the police department and included a description of a violent attack launched by the police against the Poor Peoples March when it visited Detroit. The UAW endorsement of the field day was seen as evidence of an alliance between the UAW leadership and a "racist" police department. Luke Tripp states that an active campaign of proselytizing and recruitment was launched about this time in response to numerous questions from workers as to how they could join DRUM.[20]

Boycott

The next few issues of the newsletter continued with the same general themes. The only major addition was documentation of charges of racism in the administration of medical care in the plant. The level of support and militancy continued to grow. Luke Tripp states:

the more militant workers wanted to go for some concrete action against Chrysler and the UAW. At this point the editors of DRUM decided to test their strength. They called for a one week boycott of two bars outside the gate that were patronized by a large number of brothers. The bars didn't hire blacks and practiced racism in other subtle ways. DRUM achieved about 95% cooperation. This was achieved without the use of pickets or picket signs.[21]

The appeal for the boycott appeared in the eighth issue of the DRUM newsletter. The editors were greatly encouraged by worker response to their appeal. The ninth issue of the newsletter carried a list of fifteen demands. Seven of these were directed towards increased employment of blacks at various levels and in various types of work. Two demanded that black workers cease paying union dues and that these funds be redirected to the black community to aid in developing self-determination. One demanded equal pay for black Chrysler employees in South Africa. The demands were less important than the measures proposed to back them up. The demands were to be supported by legal demonstrations at the Chrysler Corporation headquarters in Highland Park, UAW Local 3 offices, and at Solidarity House (the headquarters of the UAW). These were to be supplemented with a wildcat shutdown of the Hamtramck assembly plant.[22]

Wildcat strike

Thursday, July 7, 1968, DRUM held a rally in the parking lot across from the factory.[23] Different groups from the black community were present. Music was provided by a conga group. The rally culminated in a march to UAW Local 3's offices where an executive board meeting was in progress. The conjunction of the time of the protest and of the executive board meeting was not coincidental. It was the result of good planning on the part of the DRUM leadership. A general meeting in the auditorium was demanded and held but did not produce results satisfactory to anyone. The decision that a wildcat strike should be held the next day was finalized. DRUM and supporting groups arrived at the plant gates at 5:00 A.M. Friday morning in order to be present when workers began to arrive for the 6:00 A.M. shift. Picket lines were set up and manned exclusively by students, intellectuals, and community people. Workers were not allowed on the picket line in order to protect their jobs. White workers were allowed to enter the factory without interference, only blacks were stopped. No force was applied but verbal persuasion was sufficient to keep an estimated 70 percent of the black workers out of the plant. The wildcat lasted for three days and production was crippled. Chrysler lost the production of about 1,900 cars.[24] No one was fired as a result of this action and the DRUM leadership believed that the strike was an overwhelming success.

The wildcat was only a success in political terms. None of the demands were met by either the local union or the company. However, the DRUM leadership felt that it had served two purposes: the creation of solidarity among those black workers who participated and the fostering of a degree of political education. Around noon of the first day of the strike six DRUM members met with President Ed Liska and several other Local 3 officials.[25] Liska agreed to take the grievances to both the International and Chrysler. The delegation reported back to the mass of workers demonstrating outside the plant. Approximately 250 of the demonstrators went by organized car pools approximately five miles to Chrysler headquarters in Highland Park. Chrysler officials refused to meet with the delegation or any set of representatives from it. The workers returned and reported to the main demonstration, which then adjourned.

One consequence of the wildcat was the invitation of several DRUM members to attend that Sunday's meeting of the Detroit Black Caucus, black UAW members from throughout the city. The meeting was not overly satisfactory. The members of the caucus were not entirely happy with conditions in Detroit auto plants but they felt that, all in all, the UAW had done a reasonably good job in improving things. They felt that more could be done but that improvements were most likely to be accomplished by working within the UAW rather than attacking it. Nevertheless there was an agreement that the caucus would support DRUM in its fight against racism at Chrysler.

Meanwhile DRUM continued to hold a series of demonstrations against Chrysler.[26] On October 24, 1968, a mass rally was held at Chrysler's Highland Park headquarters. Several white radical groups lent their support. DRUM began to run short of funds. Dues were not a viable source of funds and contributions were unsteady and unreliable. DRUM decided to hold a combination fund-raising raffle and political rally. A church was obtained from cooperating black ministers and the event was held on November 17, 1968. The first three prizes at the raffle were an M-1 rifle, a shotgun, and a bag of groceries, respectively. These prizes were chosen to symbolize what DRUM saw as the proper perspective on revolutionary change. After the raffle a number of speakers discussed the black liberation struggle and DRUM's place in it.

DRUM did not restrict the targets of its confrontation politics to Chrysler and the UAW. It broadened its attacks to include those members of the black community who lent support to the major enemies. During the same week as the rally and the raffle, the Detroit chapter of the Urban League held a luncheon at the Statler-Hilton Hotel to commemorate the anniversary of Lincoln's Gettysburg address.[27] They intended to present at the luncheon equal opportunity awards to Chrysler, Ford, General Motors, and the U.S. Tank-Automotive Commands. The timing of the luncheon in relationship to the DRUM attack upon Chrysler as a racist concern may have been a coincidence but it certainly did not represent a show of solidarity with DRUM or their black worker supporters. DRUM felt that the occasion could not be allowed to pass without some response on their part. A number of black workers invaded the luncheon dressed in greasy overalls, marched among the tables carrying their protest signs, and then left relatively peacefully.

New League components are formed

The DRUM-sponsored wildcat strike was the stimulus for the creation of two new revolutionary union movements: Ford Revolutionary Union Movement (FRUM) and Eldon Avenue Revolutionary Union Movement (ELRUM).[28] Each of these began their own newsletters. The ELRUM development was especially significant as Eldon Avenue was Chrysler's only gear and axle plant. ELRUM began with a single sheet newsletter passed out on November 5, 1968, and a meeting on Sunday, November 10, in which ELRUM was officially formed.[29]

ELRUM held a demonstration at the UAW Local 961 hall during its eighth week of existence on January 22, 1969.[30] A meeting resulted and lasted sufficiently long that 300 workers on the afternoon shift missed their starting time. When they returned to work the next day, 66 of the 300 were disciplined immediately and more were punished later. Punishments ranged from five days to a month off without pay. Protests against the punishments developed and culminated in a wildcat strike on January 27, 1969.[31]

The Eldon Avenue strike was both more and less successful than the earlier Hamtramck assembly wildcat.[32] A higher proportion of black workers participated. Production was totally shut down because blacks comprised a larger portion of the total labor force than had been the case at Hamtramck assembly. However, twenty-six workers were fired as a result of this strike. They lost their jobs despite the fact that, once again, picket lines were totally manned by support cadres. Twenty-six new martyrs were created to join General G. Baker, Jr. and Bennie Tate from the May 2 wildcat.[33]

Four discharges were altered to suspensions. One of the twenty-two remaining discharged workers was reinstated and twenty-one grievances were filed. Eventually nineteen persons were returned but two workers were not. One of these two workers was Fred Holsey, who had been publicly identified as the president of ELRUM.[34] It is probable that the strength of the management's reaction was, in part, a function of the importance of the Eldon Avenue plant to the Chrysler Corporation. The mildness of the reaction of the union leadership, both local and international, suggests a degree of union approval of the actions. The union approval probably fell short .of the outright conspiracy charged by ELRUM, but there is reason to believe that the union would have liked to see ELRUM out of its hair. The firings and slow processing of grievances might have been designed to dampen enthusiasm among the militantly inclined workers.

The League is formed

More revolutionary union movements began springing up at other factories both in Detroit and elsewhere in the nation. It became increasingly clear that a central organization was needed to give direction to the various separate entities.[35] The League of Revolutionary Black Workers was formed and began a newsletter called *Spear.* When funds later permitted its return to publication, *The Inner City Voice* became the official organ of the League. The League functioned as an integrative body coordinating general policy, political education, and the strategies for its various components. A number of black student groups were formed and directly affiliated with the League. The League acted as a forum for the discussion of ideas and plans but did not issue directives to any of its components.[36]

The League continued the high level of pressure-confrontation tactics directed against both the union and management. An example of the former came in November 1969.[37] Contract negotiation time was drawing near. All estimates were that it would be a long, hard struggle. There was believed to be a high probability that a lengthy strike would be required before a final contract was agreed upon. The UAW wished to build up a large strike fund both in anticipation of the strike and as part of the prebargaining negotiating position. There was a good chance that a dues increase would be part of the overall package of steps involved in establishing the funds. This was, in part, purported to cover an increase in the level of strike benefits. A special UAW convention was called for November 8 and 9 to be held at Cobo Hall in downtown Detroit. The choice of the location may have been dictated by other considerations, but it was a strategic error for the UAW to meet in Detroit. It was a virtual certainty that the League would seize the opportunity to express its views of the UAW in a public and highly embarrassing manner.

The League leadership did perceive the special convention as an opportunity to publicly display their militance, to get good publicity for their grievances against the UAW, to gain increased community support for their cause, and to expand their base among black workers. The League, and its many affiliates, decided to conduct a demonstration at the convention. They put out a special four page (11″ × 15″) newspaper edition calling for a march on Cobo Hall to protest UAW racism. The paper was extremely well written and well constructed. It described a set of conditions — prices increasing at a more rapid rate than wages, speedups in production, unsafe working conditions — that were detrimental for all workers. It asserted that black workers were hit particularly hard. The charge was made that if the UAW was doing its job these conditions would not exist. The issue traced the existence of racism in the auto industry prior to the formation of the UAW, the resistance of white workers to allowing blacks in the union during its formative years, the admission of blacks because it was necessary in order to organize the industry, the continuance of racist practices in the industry after it was unionized, and the "buying off" of militant blacks by finding them posts within the UAW hierarchy. The League demanded that the special convention be held but that its purpose be altered to restructuring the UAW. It claimed the necessity for a complete overhauling of union goals, leadership, strategy, and tactics. The League felt that the convention should particularly consider the special needs of the black auto worker.

The demonstration was scheduled for November 9. It was held, but it did not result in the direct confrontation with the UAW leadership sought by DRUM. The UAW special convention adjourned earlier than anticipated. Early adjournment probably did save the UAW from a certain amount of highly embarrassing publicity, but it did not completely close off the opportunity for the League to gain propaganda mileage from the convention. In fact the early adjournment became the basis for the following item:

U.A.W. RUNS FROM BLACK WORKERS
Once again the League of Revolutionary Black Workers has made its presence felt, and a good feeling it is for the Black community to be assured that at least one black organization is fearless when it comes to confronting the U.A.W.'s racism and its suppressive structure.

On Saturday, November 8, 1969, the U.A.W.'s national delegation convened in Cobo Hall for a two-day session to propose raising the dues of its rank and file membership. This convention was aborted in a very premature stage because of the delegation's knowledge and fear of the demonstration that was to take place the next day, Sunday, November 9th.

This demonstration was highly publicized in advance to the convention by the League of Revolutionary Black Workers (consisting of many well-known groups: DRUM, FRUM, ELRUM, UPRUM, MARUM, JARUM, and other worker based groups).

Aware of the fact that if the convention was still in session on the day of protest, and afraid to be confronted with the questions and issues that the Black worker demands answers for, point-ducking Walter Reuther and his racist delegation hurriedly adjourned and slid back into their plush snakeholes.

Although the U.A.W.'s cowardly run left many black workers angrier than they were when they showed, the demonstration can hardly be called anything but a more startling success than was anticipated. It was successful for a number of reasons:

1. It made black workers more conscious of the fact that if their many grievances are ever to be answered they will have to answer them themselves.
2. It made the entire Black community aware of the fact the power to determine its own destiny is repelled by one of the most Black-built and Black-supported political machines in this country.
3. It showed Black workers the potential of their strength once it has been harnessed in a united war against U.A.W. suppression.
4. It left Walter Reuther trembling with the knowledge that if he constantly refuses to deal with the needs of the Black worker, the League of Revolutionary Black Workers will deal him out.

Black workers are now doing what they have always done on any job, standing up. And as long as Walter Reuther and his flunkies flee to their suburban holes, the League of Revolutionary Black Workers will use the shovel they keep in hand, and they will dig, dig and dig until the snakeism practiced by the U.A.W. is uprooted and beat to death.[38]

The spring of 1970 brought an important series of wildcat strikes to the Eldon Avenue Gear and Axle Plant. The period between June 1968 and January 1970 had been a period of ferment over cleanliness and safety conditions.[39] The early part of the year was marked by continual confrontations between the local union leadership on the one hand and ELRUM and other workers and work groups on the other over the issue of grievances.[40] It was charged that the local union leadership was not overly responsible in its methods of handling grievances. The Local 961 president, Elroy Richardson, accused ELRUM of clogging the grievance procedure by flooding it with unwarranted grievances. The grievance procedure is long and complex at best. The majority of the grievances that go past the first and second stage take months to resolve. Only a small proportion of those are resolved in the worker's favor.

Thus the level of tension was high on April 15, 1970, when a confrontation occurred between a worker, John Scott, and a foreman, Erwin Ashlock.[41] Ashlock apparently threatened Scott with a pinion gear at some point during the confrontation. He claimed that he was acting in self-defense. Whatever the actual state of affairs, Scott was fired as a result of the incident. The workers did not believe Ashlock's claim that he acted in self-defense, felt that John Scott had been fired unjustly, and began a protest wildcat strike on April 16. The work stoppage continued, at least as a slowdown, until April 19.

The wildcat seemed to have three results. John Scott was reinstated on April 20, Erwin Ashlock quietly disappeared from his post as foreman, and twelve Local 961 officials were discharged on May 1 for allegedly leading the April 16 wildcat.[42] Management initially agreed to withhold disciplinary actions stemming from the wildcat until after an upcoming UAW meeting in Atlantic City.[43] On Friday, May 1, management asked to meet with local officers and the Shop Committee. Some of the people made the meeting, others missed it due to the short notice. Management announced its intention to impose discipline for the April 16 wildcat. Richardson asked that it be held off until Monday. The second-shift stewards met later in the day and voted unanimously to shut down the plant if management disciplined anyone that night.

Six second-shift stewards — Johnny Moffett, Tony C. Moore, George Dauer, Clarence Horton, William L. Sparks, and Robert Thomas — and one trustee, J. C. Thomas, were fired later the same night. Five others — Jeremiah Ingram, Donald C. Johnson, Jordan Sims (chief shop committeeman), Leo Oddo, and Howard Willis — were fired by telegram.

This precipitated another wildcat walkout beginning with Friday's second shift. A meeting was held on Sunday, May 3, at the Local 961 union hall. A court order issued the same day enjoined picketing at the Eldon Avenue plant. The role of the Local 961 president, Elroy Richardson, appears to be ambiguous. In one leaflet, ELRUM accuses Richardson of having called the wildcat and then not fully supported it.[44] The League stated in a newspaper article that at the Sunday meeting Richardson told the membership that they would be on strike until further notice.[45] ELRUM stated in a leaflet distributed later that week that Richardson told workers at the union hall Monday afternoon to go home and watch TV for word as to whether or not they should return to work.[46] Later that day he is alleged to have contacted the midnight shift workers to report in Monday night. Homer Jolly states that, to the best of his knowledge, Richardson did call the chief steward on the night of May 1 to warn him of the impending firings and to suggest that the plant be shut down.[47] While it is difficult to determine the actual role played by Richardson, he certainly did not provide strong leadership during the confrontation.

Jordan Sims was among the pickets at the plant on Monday despite having been served with the "no picketing" injunction on Sunday. Work resumed on Tuesday, May 5, and on Wednesday, Chief Steward Frank McKinnon and Jordan Sims were fired for their activities on May 1. This occurred despite the fact that Sims was presumably still fired because of his activities in the earlier wildcat. There are rumors to the effect that Richardson perceived Sims as a possible challenger to his post as union president, knew that McKinnon was one of Sim's main supporters, and caused them to lose their jobs in order to kill Sims off as a challenger. However, despite the fact that one highly placed UAW executive accepts the rumor as true, there is no hard evidence to support it.

Negotiations and grievance proceedings eventually regained the jobs of all of the above except for Jordan Sims. However, it took a great deal of time. The last two, Sparks and Moore, were not allowed to return to work until September 1.[48] While these proceedings were still in an early stage a jitney operator, Gary Thompson, was killed in an accident at the Eldon Avenue plant.The accident took place on May 26. The Eldon Workers Safety Committee, an ad hoc group, voted unanimously in favor of a protest work stoppage. On Wednesday, May 27, pickets were at all Eldon plant gates asking for worker support and suggesting that the plant be shut down.

Jordan Sims was among those picketing and was photographed carrying signs saying, "Death rides a jitney," and "Eldon kills, you will be next." The work stoppage was less successful than the two previous wildcats but a sufficiently large number of people stayed away on the afternoon and night shifts that James Edwards, Alonzo Chandler, Robert McKee, and John Taylor were all fired on May 28.[49] All except Taylor were members of ELRUM. Jordan Sims' grievance over his earlier discharge was finally rejected on December 15, 1970. His participation in the May 27 wildcat was prominently cited by the umpire. Homer Jolly believes that Sims might have gotten his job back if he had not picketed.[50]More will be said about Jordan Sims, never an ELRUM member, in Chapter 10 when the United National Caucus is discussed. The fact that the wildcat may not have been called entirely for capricious reasons may be attested to by the following interoffice communication from Lloyd D. Utter to Art Hughes:

June 3, 1970

To: Art Hughes, Assistant Director, National Chrysler Department
From: Lloyd D. Utter, Safety Director
Subject: Chrysler Corporation, Eldon Axle Plant, Detroit, Michigan LU 961
Complaint: Occupational Safety

On May 26, 1970 we received an emergency telephone request from Art Hughes, Assistant Director, UAW Chrysler Department, to investigate a fatality of the above plant. The deceased was Gary Thompson, 22 years of age – Badge # 252776. Employment date: 7–17–67. This individual became an industrial truck driver on March, 1970 and I made my investigation accompanied by Messrs. Neil McCallum, Corporate Safety Director; George Maxley, Corporate Safety Staff and Homer Jolly, International Representative; Walter Waller, International Representative, Region 1 and Elroy Richardson, President 961.

From the information available, it was determined that this worker was assigned to drive a 10,000 pound, Clark # 2 truck, and to transport chips in a Roura hopper. About 3,000 pounds of chips were loaded into this hopper, and were to be transported and dumped into a railroad car in the scrap yard. It was this driver's first experience assigned to this operation from his usual truck, even though the regular driver usually assigned to this truck was available. He was reported to have been last seen at 6:12 A.M. and was not seen again until he was found crushed at 6:18 A.M. From our observations, this equipment moved a distance of about twenty-seven (27) feet from the location where he was attempting to dump at the railroad car. It could not be determined whether the equipment rolled or whether it was in gear, or slipped into reverse gear. It was reported that the equipment was found to be in reverse gear after the incident. The hopper had not been lowered nor emptied, and Thompson was found under the loaded hopper, only his feet extending. I examined the equipment and found the emergency brake to be broken; as a matter of fact, it was not even connected. The shift lever to the transmission was loose and sloppy. The equipment generally was sadly in need of maintenance, having a loose steering wheel in addition to other general needs.

I also visited the repair area and observed other industrial trucks in this area that were sadly in need of repair, noting: No lights, lack of brakes, horns, broken LP gas tank fasteners, loose steering wheels, leaky hydraulic equipment, etc. I was informed that there is supposed to be a regularly scheduled maintenance procedure for this equipment in this plant. I was also informed that operators are instructed to take trucks to the garage and tag them when they are in need of repair. However, it seems to be the practice of foremen, when equipment is needed, to pull the tags off the equipment in the repair area that badly need corrective maintenance and put them back into service on the floor.

My first reaction to what I observed is that there is a complete neglect of stated maintenance procedures in this plant. The equipment is being operated in an inexcusably dangerous condition.

After the in-plant visit, the entire matter was further discussed with Virgil Anderson, Labor Relations Administrator and Joe Jeffry, Personnel Director and they gave their assurances that immediate attention would be put to my demands that a concerted repair program be instituted at once, to bring this equipment into safe operating condition and they further agreed that they would adhere to a proper and sensible regular scheduled maintenance procedure, giving proper priority to those things on the equipment having the greatest bearing to the safety of the driver and to other employees in the area. Mr. McCallum and I provided Mr. Anderson and Mr. Jeffry with a truck safety priority check list for maintenance. In the course of my tour, I also noted that there were horrible conditions approaching to and on the scrap lot. Proper curbing or dikes should be set up to prevent the dangerous drainage of oil off the scrap onto the aisles and traffic ways used to move people and equipment in and out of the area. Greater safety could also be achieved if truckers deposited loaded Roura hoppers onto surface scrap piles, rather than into railroad cars. The electromagnetic crane could then be used for all of the loading of the railroad cars.

Finally, a general observation as we passed to and from the location of the fatal accident; there seemed to be little attempt to maintain proper housekeeping, except on the main front aisle. Water and grease were observed all along the way, as we proceeded. Every good safety program has as its base good housekeeping procedures. Proper steps should be taken immediately to improve conditions within this plant.

Proper cooperation between Local 961 and the Company could result in bringing about and maintaining decent and safe working conditions.[51]

The League did not limit all of its plant-centered activities to demostrations and strikes. They, through their affiliated revolutionary union movements, participated in a series of local union elections. These will be discussed in Chapter 5.

5. Union electoral politics

The League expanded its activities to include participation in the electoral politics of local unions. This move was made with reluctance and only after a prolonged internal debate. Succumbing to the appeal to engage in reformist activities represents a real danger to any revolutionary movement. It is all too often the case that revolutionary goals are "temporarily" set aside in order to aid in the achievement of important reforms. It is always understood that this is merely a temporary expedient and that the revolutionary goals will be returned to their proper primacy at a later date. However, it is often the case that that later date never arrives. On the other hand, the achievement of reforms is often a means of attracting recruits. Both John Watson and Mike Hamlin were aware of the fact that numerous unsatisfactory conditions could be partially alleviated as a result of the election of militant blacks to union offices (especially as union stewards) and that the elections themselves could serve as vehicles for the recruitment of new members.[1]

DRUM electoral activities

The League's first foray into union electoral politics came in 1968 through DRUM.[2] A trustee at UAW Local 3 died and an election to choose his successor was scheduled for September 26. DRUM was uncertain as to the best course of action. The leadership was divided as to the wisdom of running one of their members for the post. There were three major arguments presented in opposition to direct participation in the election: (1) running a candidate for a UAW office might appear to the workers as compromising with an organization that the League claimed to be corrupt; (2) this might create a situation exposing some DRUM members to temptations toward opportunism; and (3) it might be damaging to DRUM's prospects if it openly entered into a political campaign and lost. Four major arguments were given in response: (1) the election could serve to make the leadership of DRUM more accepta-

103

ble and popular among blacks who were not members; (2) the electoral campaign could serve as a demonstration of black solidarity and strength, with or without a victory; (3) the campaign could serve as a means of raising the consciousness (both political and racial) of workers; and (4) the electoral campaign might contribute to DRUM's membership drive. The DRUM leadership decided after an extended debate to run a candidate for the trustee post and selected Ron March as the candidate.

The campaign was designed to act primarily as a vehicle for the political education of black workers but it was also hoped that it would eventuate in the election of March. Much of the campaign literature emphasized the central importance of the trustee post in controlling the disbursement of union funds. It was argued that the local had not operated in a manner reflecting the interests of its black majority and that the election of March was essential in order to bring about increased accountability.[3] This trustee post took on added importance because the two remaining board members were both black women, one of whom was believed to have militant leanings.[4] Thus the election of March had the potential of creating a local union executive board that would be amenable to a left-oriented program.

The election campaign was hard fought. The DRUM membership expended a large amount of effort in putting up posters and passing out leaflets. They were supported by The Committee for Real Unionism (CRU), which had recently been formed by young white workers.[5] There was also a great deal of effort expended in an attempt to defeat Ron March. It was not unexpected that both the company and the union would perceive DRUM as a threat and want to do everything possible to weaken March's campaign. The UAW magazine, *Battleline,* had previously described DRUM as a racist, communist group, which was attempting to destroy the automobile industry through internal subversion.[6]

BLACK POWER SERVES WARNING TO CHRYSLER CORP.
DODGE ASSEMBLY PLANT IN HAMTRAMCK
Black Power advocates are claiming that "white racist foremen" are "harassing, insulting, driving and snapping the whip over the backs of thousands of black workers at the Dodge plant."

Using these lies as their base for creating discontent they have formed the *"Dodge Revolutionary Union Movement."* (D.R.U.M.). The theory behind the movement is pure marxism (divide and conquer), and they even quote from the works of a noted communist, W. E. B. DuBois, in their newsletter (DRUM).

It appears to us that the communist-inspired black power movement has shifted from looting and burning to leading campus revolts and attempting to bring the black workers into the revolution.

It was exactly this combination of events which the Reds used — almost success-fully — to bring the iron curtain down on France recently. With only a handful they spearheaded the student strike while communist goons kept the French workers from returning to their jobs.

We know the communists look upon Detroit's automobile plants as the economic bellweather of the country. And to bring their production to a screeching halt through internal revolution would better serve the enemy's purpose than if they were bombed out by enemy aircraft.

The content of the leaflet, especially its linking of communism to black activism, is a continuation of the anticommunist, antiindependent black attitudes on the part of the UAW leadership that were discussed in Chapter 2. There is some evidence that Hamtramck police were also concerned with the DRUM threat and that they also did what they could to insure the defeat of March, as illustrated in the following account:

The candidacy of Ron March was obviously a threat, and not only to the established union leadership. Hamtramck police cooperated cheerfully in the effort to suppress DRUM. All candidates were permitted to put up posters and pass out leaflets in the plant — except DRUM's candidate. Some candidates had helpers, who drove workers to the polls at the local, and used "no standing" zones in which to drop off voters; only cars with DRUM posters got tickets, and the cops took as long as a half hour to write them — thus tying up a car that might have brought another DRUM vote.[7]

There may be differences in interpretation as to the motivation of the police, but there is general agreement that police treated DRUM cars differently from those representing other candidates. Similarly there is agreement among a number of observers that Ron March posters were seen being torn down inside the plant by supporters of the incumbent local union leadership and outside the plant by various people including Hamtramck policemen. Further clues to the attitudes of the Hamtramck police might be gathered from their actions after the results of the day's balloting were announced.

Ron March led the balloting with 563 votes. His nearest competitor received 521. This was not sufficient for election as UAW rules require a majority vote for the winning candidate rather than a mere plurality. The two top candidates, including Ron March, had to face a runoff election. The following account provides one description of what happened subsequent to the announcement of the election results:

On September 26 at 5:30 p.m., the election booths were closed. Forty-five minutes later, it was announced that out of a field of 27 candidates, Ron March had won, with a fifty vote lead over his nearest contender. Two Hamtramck pigs (police) stationed at the union hall, greeted the election victory with a spate of profanities. They and other pigs then went over to a bar across from the plant where the black workers hung out. The cops began to verbally harass workers in and around the bar. The black workers responded in a verbal fashion. After a brief moment, the pigs then attacked the workers with axe handles. They arrested one black worker and took him back to the police station, which was right around the corner from the union hall. The black workers immediately gathered into a group and went over to the station. An officer told the workers to go to the union hall where the Mayor of Hamtramck and the Chief of Police would explain what had happened.

About 50 black workers, including Ron March, gathered in the hall. When the mayor and the police chief arrived, one of the union bureaucrats immediately began to lock all the doors. The bureaucratic dog then proceeded to lead a contingent of pigs into the room, whereupon they began to attack the black workers with axe handles and mace. The mayor and Chief of Pigs just stood by and observed.[8]

Again, there may be differences in interpretation of the motivations of various participants in the events described above. There are also minor differences in the descriptions of the events provided by various observers. However, all accounts agree on the basic outline of events. There was a clash between Hamtramck police and black workers who were awaiting the election results. This clash did take place in the vicinity of a number of bars in and around Jos. Campeau Blvd. and one black worker was arrested. A number of black workers did go to the police station to protest and they were directed to the union hall. The Hamtramck mayor and chief of police did come to the union hall; there was a discussion that approached the nature of a shouting match. An official of the local union, Cannonball Silepski, did rush outside and return leading a contingent of police, and axe handles and mace were used on the black workers. The events were such that many people could, and did, see them as evidence of a conspiracy among union, management, and local police to destroy DRUM.

In many ways the runoff election provided a truer test of the strength of DRUM among workers than did the original election. It is one thing to marshall sufficient voting strength behind a militant candidate to get him into a runoff when he is one of twenty-seven candidates, but it is quite another thing for him to make a good showing when the field is reduced to two. Many persons believed that Ron March would not greatly expand his support over the 563 votes he had received in the first election. The bulk of the supporters of other candidates were expected to shift their votes to his opposition. Nevertheless his opposition did not become apathetic and ignore the election as a result of that expectation.[9]

Retired workers have the right to vote in UAW elections but they do not usually exercise that right in large numbers. Local 3 had changed in its composition over recent years so that 63 percent of the active work force was black while the overwhelming majority of the retired members was white. Most of them were Polish-Americans. The union leadership sent the retired workers a letter strongly urging them to participate in the election. It was charged that a victory for March could mean the termination of retirement benefits.

The fear was also created that his victory might have other economic results detrimental to the members of Local 3. Perhaps by coincidence the October 1, 1968, issue of the *Michigan Chronicle* (Detroit's black newspaper) included an article and a headline discussing the possibility that the Dodge plant might be moved to the suburbs. The implication was clear that a Ron March victory might increase that probability and have the net impact of reducing the number of jobs available to black workers.

This was the climate of opinion that existed when the membership of Local 3 went to the polls on October 3, 1968. Ron March was defeated in the runoff by a vote of 2,091 to 1,386. It is not surprising that he lost. It would rather appear that his ability to muster almost 40 percent of the vote under these circumstances is an amazing show of strength. It suggests that the black workers largely interpreted the previous week's events as supporting the general line put forth by DRUM. DRUM leadership was not entirely satisfied with the election results as indicated by the following article, which appeared in the DRUM newsletter:

RON MARCH D.R.U.M. TRUSTEE!
What happened in last Thursday's election should come as no surprise to the overwhelming majority of enlightened black workers here at the Hamtramck Assembly plant. In the preliminary election the week before it became quite evident that there was a conspiracy by Chrysler Corp., Hamtramck city officials, and the U.A.W. to crush D.R.U.M. and the just demands of black workers. In the election last week black workers greeted the election with overwhelming and heretobefore unknown enthusiasm. Our black brothers drove, rode in cars, and many even ran a good 440 to the election hall all day long to cash their vote for brother Ron March from 7 o'clock a.m. on Thursday, Oct. 3; it was the black workers' show. Why? Never before have black people really had a candidate and a program with which they could really identify. D.R.U.M.'s program calls for truth and black unity and such we shall have even if it means shedding our blood to achieve it.

What did the conspirators do in the election? The white reactionary forces issued 15 traffic tickets to Ron March supporters' cars. They tore and ripped down Ron March posters. They launched vicious attacks with axe handles on our black brothers peacefully assembled in the parking lot off Jos. Campeau and Clay. They rampaged the union hall spraying mace in the eyes of our black brothers and beat them with axe handles. They even solicited the aid of the notorious Michigan Chronicle to write a headline story to frighten the black workers at Hamtramck Assembly plant. They then waited until after the election to come out and say that the rumor of moving was a lie. And then they finally stole the election from black workers. It is ridiculous for anyone who saw the election to even harbor the notion that Ron March was not the victor; but to say that he had lost by 700 votes is perfidy, it is outrageous outcry, and an insult to the basic intelligence of black people. . . .

Therefore D.R.U.M. declares that Ron March duly and honestly won in the election for trustee and in light of that we and the black workers here shall recognize him as such. Even according to the fraudulent figures which the thieves at the election counted that Ron March received 1386 votes — we state that on that basis, on the beast's figures Bro. Ron carried over a third of the vote. And that would of necessity be the most militant, the most progressive and aware segment of the black workers at Dodge. We therefore declare that Ron March is the duly and honest elected trustee of the black workers at Hamtramck Assembly plant and we shall recognize him as such. Forward with March. JOIN D.R.U.M. SUPPORT D.R.U.M. Down with the thieving honkies who run Local 3 and their black Henchmen Andy Hardy and Charlie Brooks.

Long Live D.R.U.M.[10]

The article also carries within it the implication that the DRUM leadership was not too unhappy either. They believed that it was a great accomplishment for Ron March to draw approximately two out of every five votes cast under the circumstances described above. The leadership believed that the educational function of the campaign was far more important than the size of the vote for March. The article reproduced above is simply one additional stage of the political education process, as was the charge — apparently true by all reports — that retired workers were allowed to vote without showing proper identification. DRUM alleged that this was done in order to enable Hamtramck Poles who were not members of the local to vote against March. However, it is equally plausible to assume that it was done to accommodate retired workers who may have forgotten to bring proper identification. It is unlikely that black supporters of March would have been so accommodated if they forgot to bring proper identification.

DRUM's political education program was further enhanced by the fact that the leadership of Local 3 had to rely upon the votes of retired workers (a legal but manifestly improper act). The tactic allowed DRUM a propaganda opening that enabled them to link the election loss to the history of black auto workers and continuing white racism:

Down With The Hamtramck Retirees

In the election last week, the Joe Elliot supporters relied heavily upon the retiree vote. The U.A.W. bigots along with Hamtramck city officials went around the entire city of Hamtramck scraping the back streets and searching the cracks in the walls for old retired polish pigs. There are something like 1300 old retired Pollacks who were former employees at Hamtramck Assembly Plant, and are still members of local 3. These Pollacks were stomp down racists while they worked at the plant and continue to be so until they die.

They were part of the white racist walk-out that took place in the early 1950's here at Old Dodge Main, because they refused to work next to black people. Let us never forget the harassment and insults our black brothers suffered at the hands of these racist pollacks. They were the same white workers who reaped the benefits of the segregated park that once stood on Jos. Campeau facing the plant. We shall not be so naive to think that their attitudes have changed. We suffered too long merely having to work with these racists. And now we are still made to bear the brunt of their racism by contending with their voting power. We must therefore seek to put an end to this gross misjustice in the same manner that we shall deal with all injustice at this plant. Prepare to strike a blow at the right of these white racist retirees to be able to continue to have a voice in the decisions of the work force which now is a majority of black brothers. Down with the white racist retirees.[11]

The election and its surrounding events went a long way toward convincing many black workers that the UAW was a corrupt organization that would do anything to prevent black workers from achieving their proper voice in decision making. The article in the *Michigan Chronicle*, the acts of the Hamtramck police, and the company — which implicitly supported the regular union candidate — reinforced and provided illustrations for DRUM's charges of collusion among the company, the union, the law enforcement agencies, and segments of the black elite. All appeared to be united in the drive to destroy DRUM and to crush militancy among black workers. The DRUM leadership believed that the election try was a great propaganda victory even though it resulted in the defeat at the polls.

DRUM's second attempt

The second venture into a local union election came in early 1969.[12] A DRUM newsletter warned that a vacancy was probably going to be created in the office of vice-president of Local 3. The newsletter stated that DRUM would run an as yet unselected candidate for the office. The statement was repeated in the following issue, which was circulated on or about March 7. Perhaps there was no relationship between this statement and the newsletter dated March 10 sent by the UAW International executive board to all UAW members. It recounted a version of UAW history that portrayed the union as a perpetual battler for justice and equality, attacked the rise of a tiny handful of black revolutionaries who are racists and separatists, and charged them with carrying on a campaign of terror and intimidation against democratically elected union leaders. The newsletter continued with a description of the structure of union safeguards against discrimination practiced by either company or union and it claimed the existence of a high degree of black representational strength in "threatened" locals. The newsletter (a copy of which was provided by Douglas Fraser) concluded with a plea for brotherhood and integration.

March 10, 1969

Greetings:

These are difficult and trying times — times that test the common sense of the American people and their commitment to democratic values.

As a nation and a people, we face deep crisis on many fronts — education, housing, health care, transportation, air and water pollution. Our major cities face financial crisis and most serious is the crisis in race relations for this is a crisis of the human spirit, of man's relationship with his fellow man.

The UAW came into being in the 1930's in a period of great economic crisis in our nation. To win recognition and the right to help shape their own destiny in the plants, the auto workers had to fight to overcome the opposition of wealthy and powerful corporations. We succeeded because we were united — black and white, foreign born and American born workers, skilled and production workers — dedicated to the achievement of common goals in a common bond of solidarity and brotherhood and true to a common belief in the worth and dignity of every person.

The UAW has from its very beginning fought for equal rights and equal opportunities for all people regardless of race, creed and color. We work for these principles in the plants, in the community and in the nation for as a matter of justice and morality every person must be judged by the quality of his character and not by the color of his skin.

We in the UAW believe there can be no separate answers. No white answers. No black answers. We believe there can only be common answers which we must find together in our common humanity.

We believe that the violence of extremism — whether white or black — can only create more bitterness, more misunderstanding, more division.

Each of us must work with greater courage and compassion to help right the grievous wrongs of the past. For centuries, the black man in America has suffered exploitation and discrimination everywhere he has turned. He has been robbed of his dignity as an individual. He has been denied his natural right to participate fully in the society in which he lives. Many times the hiring office was closed to him completely. When it was open, he generally was offered work that no one else would take, the hard, dirty, low-paying job.

These are shameful and tragic historical facts.

During the last 33 years, the UAW has worked and fought hard at the bargaining table and when necessary on the picket line to help provide all workers and their families a fuller measure of economic and social justice. Because of the solidarity and support of all workers standing and marching together, UAW members are the highest paid, best-protected industrial workers in the world.

UAW members have won solid safeguards against the ancient enemies of all workers — illness, accident, unemployment, old age. They have won a greater measure of job security. They have a workable and rational grievance procedure to assure justice on the job and a greater sense of dignity.

But our task is not completed, for ours is a continuing struggle to make life in the plants more humane and to add to the dignity and security of every worker and his family.

The revolutionary changes in technology confront us with new problems and new opportunities. We shall be equal to solving these new problems and realizing these new opportunities only as we remain united and strong in finding responsible and satisfactory answers together.

We must not permit any group within our Union to divide that strength and unity since such a division will only weaken our Union and hobble our efforts to find adequate solutions. The UAW has always fought against the bigotry and prejudice of white racism because we have understood that separation along racial lines, whether by white people or black people, serves only to weaken our Union and is therefore intolerable.

A group now exists in a few plants where UAW represents the workers which calls itself a black revolutionary movement and whose goals are the complete separation of the races in the shop and the destruction of our Union through the tactics of violence, fear and intimidation.

In recent weeks, a tiny handful of people, not all of them auto workers or members of the UAW, attempted to shut down the Eldon Ave. Axle plant of Chrysler Corp. by picketing the gates, carrying picket signs with racist slogans. They were unsuccessful in shutting the plant down, but hundreds of workers lost wages as a result of this illegal and unwarranted picket line.

Incidents of violence, including knifings and physical assaults have occurred in both the Hamtramck Assembly and Eldon Axle plants of Chrysler, perpetrated by members of this so-called revolutionary group.

Fires have been started inside the plants which, had they not been brought under control, could have meant the loss of workers' lives and the loss of jobs.

This group of extremists and racial separatists has sought to spread terror in the plants among both black and white workers and to undermine the unity and solidarity among all the workers, which are essential if the UAW members are to continue to make economic and social progress for themselves and their families. They have sought to intimidate local union leaders who have been democratically· elected to serve all the workers.

The weapons of fear, violence and intimidation have been used in the past in attempts to divide and weaken our Union. We have had to struggle against company goons, company police, gangsters, the underworld and the communists in order to survive and grow strong. But we did survive and we did grow strong — because we were together.

The UAW has a legal and moral responsibility to represent all workers in plants in which we have been democratically chosen by the workers as their collective bargaining agent. We are determined to carry out these responsibilities and we condemn all efforts of racial division and separatism both in the plants and in our society.

The UAW will continue to fight all forms of discrimination and will provide the fullest protection to workers who have legitimate grievances.

The UAW, however, will not protect workers who resort to violence and intimidation with the conscious purpose of dividing our Union along racial lines; for these workers would undermine our Union, the principles upon which our Union was founded and put in jeopardy the jobs which our members hold.

A worker with a problem has access to the grievance procedure. Any worker who feels his grievance requires action beyond this procedure may appeal to the International Union.

And there is an additional, impartial safeguard which UAW members have.

Unlike any other organization in the United States, the UAW has made provision for appeal to an authority outside the UAW by any member who feels he is treated unjustly by his Union.

He can appeal to the UAW Public Review Board, an independent, impartial agency which has the constitutional authority to change or set aside decisions of the International Executive Board.

The existence of the Public Review Board is an assurance of the UAW's desire and determination that every member be treated fairly and entitled to justice.

The UAW, moreover, has a National Fair Practices Dept. whose staff members devote their efforts to assist workers whenever valid claims of discrimination are made either against the company or against the union.

The many steps taken by UAW to safeguard the individual's rights have provided workable alternatives to violence and other criminal acts.

Through the democratic procedures of our Union, the workers elect their union leaders.

In the Dodge and Eldon Avenue plants, black workers are solidly in the leadership of those UAW locals. At the Dodge plant in Hamtramck (UAW Local 3), four out of the six full-time officials are black and 56 percent of the elected stewards in the shop are black. At Eldon Axle (Local 961), 65 percent of all elected stewards and committeemen in the local are black. Both black and white workers have shared in and helped make possible the historic progress accomplished by the UAW.

The establishment of black organizations to influence the destiny of black people in American society is a sound concept. Separatism, dividing society, instilling fear and hatred, using violence and intimidation, however, are divisive, harmful to the workers and their welfare and damaging to the basic democratic values of society.

The UAW throughout its history has taken its stand firmly in support of the struggle for justice, for equal rights and equal opportunity to all people. UAW leaders and members have been in the vanguard of the legislative fight for civil rights. We have marched in Detroit, in Washington, D.C., Selma, Alabama, Jackson, Mississippi, Memphis, Tennessee, for justice and equity.

We have been in the leadership in the crusade against poverty. We have worked to help provide housing for low income families, to improve police—community relations, to establish community unions, to create job training programs and pre-apprenticeship programs for the disadvantaged, to improve our educational system particularly in the inner-city area, to insure equal rights and equal opportunity in the factories and also to bring to fruition the freedom, the self-respect, the dignity and the good life to all people which a democratic society can provide.

The UAW has built its progress in behalf of its members and their families and the community-at-large on the principles of human brotherhood and solidarity.

"Brotherhood", not "hatred", is the cornerstone on which to build a society in which each person lives and works in dignity and security with his neighbor. We in the UAW believe in brotherhood and in Union solidarity. We shall continue to dedicate ourselves and our efforts to the cause of justice and human brotherhood.

We call upon all UAW members to unite in this spirit. This is a time when men and women of good will must reject hatred and violence and must stand together for only as we join together can we build a better tomorrow for ourselves and our children.

Sincerely and fraternally,
The UAW International Executive Board

The following issue of the DRUM newsletter was largely devoted to a response to the UAW newsletter.[13] It began with a summary of the UAW newsletter and asserted that DRUM, rather than dividing workers along racial lines, was responding to a situation in which the UAW had always been so divided. It described a strike conducted by white workers at Dodge Main in 1937. Black workers, excluded from the union, decided to cross the picket line. The UAW then decided to admit black workers in order to strengthen the strike. The newsletter also noted the failure of the union to attempt to do anything to make it possible for black workers to eat at segregated restaurants across from the plant despite the absence of any nearby places that would serve blacks. It further cited a walkout of white workers as recently as the 1950s protesting compulsion to work with blacks. The charge of a racist UAW was brought up to date by citing a relative absence of blacks among the skilled trades and the weaknesses of the grievance procedures in rectifying grievances brought by blacks. It concluded with a plea for black workers to vote for the as yet unidentified DRUM candidate for vice-president.

An interview with Emil Mazey, secretary-treasurer of the UAW International, appeared in the Sunday issue of the *Detroit News*.[14] No reference was made to an upcoming local union election. The following series of quotes were included:

violence by black militants in Detroit's auto factories poses a greater peril to the UAW now than Communist infiltration did in the 1930's. . . . We can no longer tolerate the tactics of these young militants. . . . They are a group of fanatics who don't know where they are going, but whose actions are an attempt to destroy this union. . . . [The militants are] a handful of fanatics who are nothing but black fascists, using the same tactics of coercion and intimidation that Hitler and Mussolini used in Germany and Italy.

The interview went on to suggest that the union would not protect these militants against company actions and that the union itself might feel that it was necessary to call in the police in case of future demonstrations.

It is not possible to demonstrate conclusively that the UAW newsletter and the Mazey interview were designed to influence the outcome of the forthcoming election but the interview demonstrated that anticommunism and the fear of independent blacks continued to be exhibited by the UAW leadership. Nor is there any hard evidence that links the UAW leadership (either International or that of Local 3) to the appearance of a counterfeit DRUM newsletter about the same time. The counterfeit appeared under the general heading "drum" and the subheading "election special." It endorsed Willie (Bill) Fowler as the DRUM candidate for vice-president. The endorsement was made in pseudomilitant language that exceeded even the high level of anger and invective normally included in the DRUM newsletters. There were other signs of its lack of authenticity. The heading (drum) had the same size and shape letters as those appearing on the genuine newsletters but they remained in silhouette rather than solidly filled in. Similarly the volume and issue numbers were missing as was the subheading DODGE REVOLUTIONARY UNION MOVEMENT and the drawing of drums, which were part of the regulation heading.

Later the same week (on March 21) the actual candidate was announced in a DRUM newsletter.[15] He was Don Jackson. Jackson ran a campaign focussing upon the need for union leadership responsive to the mass of black workers rather than to the UAW International leadership. Don Jackson and Andy Hardy each received enough votes on April 8 to proceed to the runoff. Jackson did not receive as much support in the runoff as March had earlier. He lost by a tally of 1,600 to 2,600.[16]

This election also had its share of controversy. DRUM election challengers were not allowed the opportunity to inspect the voting machines prior to the beginning of the election. DRUM charged that the voting machines were taken out of the local the day following the election in violation of UAW rules requiring a 72-hour waiting period, and DRUM leadership charged that retired workers were allowed to vote without showing proper identification thus "allowing any old Pollack" to vote as many times as he chose.[17] It was also charged that police again played a partisan role in the election:

Just as DRUM's trustee and support were harassed, ticketed and beaten by the Hamtramck police dept., last Sept. DRUM's Vice President, Don Jackson was harassed the morning of the election by the Hamtramck Police Dept's. comrades in arms the notorious Detroit Police Dept. The Detroit Police came to Don Jackson's house and confiscated his license plates from his car under the pretense that they were stolen even though he produced his registration. They held his plates for a couple of hours and returned them stating that it was a mistake. The play was successful in holding up a badly needed car to carry voters to the polls. On Wed. the day after the election, DRUM challengers Ray Johnson, Raymon Ramous, and DRUM Trustee Ron March, went to the Union Hall and filed a formal protest of the election. Upon leaving they were followed by the Hamtramck Police and then picked up by the Detroit Police, who continued to follow them. They were stopped at Lawton and Pasadena, taken out of the car at shot-gun point and arrested for allegedly assaulting an officer and resisting arrest. This is purely and simply harassment by the oppressive forces against black people and it clearly illustrates the extent of the forces arrayed against us.[18]

While Jackson did not win the election he made a strong showing in receiving over one-third of the vote. What is more to the point the election campaign provided an additional opportunity for political education. The series of events surrounding Jackson's defeat must have been disquieting for those black workers who had been unconvinced by the DRUM interpretation of the events surrounding the March election defeat. It requires great faith in the neutrality of the UAW executive board to view the UAW newsletter and the Mazey interview as anything other than an attempt to influence illegally the outcome of an election in a union local. Similarly the charge that the auto companies, the UAW, the city government, and the police were all in collusion to repress the legitimate aspirations of black workers seemed to receive support from the problems surrounding the conduct of the election and from the actions of the police.

DRUM tries again

DRUM's next and final open move into union electoral politics came on March 17 and 18, 1970, when Local 3 elected all of its major officers and twenty-five delegates and alternate delegates to the forthcoming

UAW International convention in Atlantic City. DRUM prepared for the election by holding a special convention at St. Joseph's Episcopal Church in Detroit on Saturday, February 28.[19] At the meeting approximately 100 delegates voted to run a slate of candidates on the platform of fifteen demands approved by DRUM the previous November. Three new demands were added, one of which directly related to the electoral process:

The U.A.W. must prevent retired workers from controlling in-plant union politics. In every U.A.W. election the Reuther machine buses in retired U.A.W. members, who are neither familiar with, or concerned about, conditions inside the plant. These workers, the vast majority of them reactionary, anti-black, white racist, inevitably vote for reactionary, anti-black, white racist candidates, who do not represent the black workers in the plant. The U.A.W. must establish a special department for retired workers, which relates directly to the U.A.W. International in pressing their economic demands, so that they cannot hinder the struggle of rank and file workers inside the plants.[20]

This appears to have been a reasonable demand that would solve most of the problems associated with the rather complex issue. It is clear that retired workers have a legitimate concern with union operation insofar as they affect retirement funds, and so on. However, it is also true that the interests and concerns of young black workers are different from those of white retired workers. It is an inherently conflict-producing situation to have the votes of retired workers affecting the lives of young active workers. Resulting strains are greatly exacerbated when complicated by existing racial differences and the history of racial conflict. The UAW International leadership perceived the situation differently and saw no reason to alter the pattern of retiree voting.

The DRUM slate of candidates running on this platform was as follows:

President: Ron March
Vice-President: Don Jackson
Financial Secretary: Raymond Johnson
Recording Secretary: Gerald Wooten
Treasurer: Carlos Williams
Trustees: Betty Griffith
            Charles Roberts
            Grover Douglas
Sergeant-At-Arms: Don Gaitor
Guide: Lafayette Philyaw

Delegates: Albert Hicks
Don Jackson
Sam Powe
Jerome Harvard
Grover Douglas
Raymond Johnson
Aaron Pitts
George Smith
Mitch McClellan
Leon Picket
Lula Hoskins
Portia Redman
James Ware
Irvin Bostic
Mary Allen
Joyce Bivens
Walter Harris
Ann Jordan
Charles Grant
Walter Barnett
Earl Robinson
Ron March
Richard Jackson
Lafayette Philyaw
Eugene Watkins

This election campaign was less successful than previous ones in that only Carlos Williams (treasurer) and Betty Griffith (trustee) made it into the runoff elections where both were soundly beaten. This election was also not without its controversial aspects. DRUM charged that the election was again stolen through a series of irregularities. It is probably best to place the major charges in the words used by DRUM. In reading the following one should keep in mind that Ed Liska was both the incumbent president and a candidate for the office:

LISKA WON AT THE POINT OF A GUN!
How could Ed Liska beat out two Black men for the office of President? Anybody who saw the turn out of Black workers, to vote on March 18th and 19th, knows damn well that Liska could not have possibly won with a clear cut majority or even ran a good third. Ed Liska knew this. Helen Borner who was chairman of the Election Committee knew this, and together they decided to use the Hamtramck

Pig Department to insure Ed Liska victory. Never before have they had so much trouble trying to cheat in an election. The DRUM challengers, Lewis Zachery, Tyrone Travis, Robert Fields, Zeke Benion and Hersche Figgs challenged any and all discrepancy in the election. They had the Election Committee working overtime trying to figure out ways to cheat without getting caught. On Thursday the 19th, they had a new set of rules drafted just for the DRUM challengers. This did not stop them, they tried to slip a bunch of old dried up Pollocks, who had never worked at Dodge Main, by our challengers but they got caught. The brothers had these almost dead racist old pollocks standing in line for two and three hours trying to vote for some already dead pollocks.

After not being able to use the long standing secret weapon of using any old pollock in Hamtramck to vote in Local 3 elections, Liska knew he could not win! Left with no other recourse Liska came in the local at 12:33 A.M. with two thirds of the Hamtramck Police Department, and read some unwritten never before heard of rule and then evicted all of the challengers from the local. This left Ed Liska and the Election Committee and the Hamtramck pigs and last but not least 15 unsealed voting machines. We contend that they voted for Liska the rest of the night, what do you think? Later that day Geo. Merrille, racist director of region No. 1, came to the local with his entire staff, all of them armed, and said that they would now supervise the counting of the ballots. You know the rest. What have they told us, the Black worker at Dodge Local No. 3, they have said that we are not going to let you "Niggers" have this Local if it means keeping it at gunpoint. Blacks pay the majority of union dues at this plant and are not going to continue to sit back and let these low level ignorant thugs take our money and our right to duly elect any-one we choose to head up this local. There can be only one answer if we are going to have any pride and dignity, and that has to be NO — CUT OFF — CHECK OFF. If anyone ever asks you how did Liska win, tell 'em "Liska won at the point of a gun!"

Local 3 workers have been robbed. The "stick-up" by Ed Liska began Wednesday, 3-18-70, with the help of Helen Borner, Election Chairman.

The "stick-up" began, Wednesday, 3-18-70. Voting began with only 3 machines out of 30 in working condition. Because there were only 3 machines out of 30 in working condition, many workers were leaving the election hall without voting — not to be late for work. DRUM challengers made a protest to the Election Chairman, Helen Borner, to re-date the election based on the fact that workers were being cheated out of their opportunity to vote for representatives. The membership pays the expense of the election, it is their right to have all machines in proper order. This challenge in behalf of workers voting rights, was totally ignored.

Other negligent acts and/or violations of election rules include:

1. Throughout the election; machines were going on and off. There was sup-posed to be an electrical problem with the wall sockets. Wires from the machines were connected to extension cords. These extension cords were laying all across the floor. They were being knocked out of their sockets stopping the machines and cutting off lights in the voting booths. DRUM made another protest to the Election Chairman, Helen Borner.

2. Jerry Howell, supposedly a repairman, was allowed by the Election Committee Chairman, to conduct illegal duties.
3. "Retirees" voted a whole day without proper identification. Because of this, DRUM protested to the Election Chairman to re-date the election. At first, Helen Borner wouldn't consider the challenge. However, she was forced to come up with a written ruling regarding retirees. According to the written rules, every retiree must show membership cards and secure an OK slip from the Local Office. This rule was only enforced on the last day of the election. Who were the people that voted as "retirees" Wed., 3-18-70?
4. About 5:30 p.m. Thursday, 3-19-70, a voter, Lewis Zachery, entered a voting booth. After a few minutes, he called for the Election Chairman, Helen Borner, and the C.P.A. He complained that everytime he tried to pull a lever under one of the DRUM candidates, the lever for number 13, under Recording Secretary, "Edith Fox", would go down. The election Chairman told Zachery to push all levers up and start over. Zachery did, however, the same thing happened again. Challenger, Tyrone Travis, protested to have the machine void from the election. This machine had cheated the unaware voters of their choice of candidates.

   The election chairman had a meeting with her committee and the C.P.A. man about 7:00 p.m. Then, she called for all challengers and Mr. Zachery. Borner told Zachery to cast a paper ballot. The only time a person is given a paper ballot is when they do not show proper identification. Zachery had proper identification − he would not have been allowed into the voting booth without it! The challenger protested that the machine was questionable − not Zachery.
5. According to by-laws of Dodge Local 3, UAW, under election rule (25)
   "After the polls are closed, the building shall be closed to all members, except Election Committee, Flying Squadron, Challengers, and C.P.A. personnel."
   Anthony Waluk, however, was handling machines and making decisions in secret with the election committee. This is against election rules!
6. Ed Liska, violated election rules, by coming into the hall after polls had closed. Liska ordered all challengers out of the hall. The election committee − not defending the challengers right to stay inside the hall − violated election rules.
   By-laws of Dodge Local 3 UAW Election rules, under Article 5: "The election committee shall be responsible to the Local membership and shall not be interfered with by any officer, by the Executive Board or by any other division of the Local."
   Section (25) − "After the polls are closed, the building shall be closed to all members, except election committee, Flying Squadron, Challengers, and C.P.A. personnel."

Ed Liska, as President of the Union, is a part of the division of the local. As an officer and candidate, he had no business interfering with the election. Furthermore, the police (brought by Liska), without a warrant, illegally occupied the hall, attacked a challenger and membership owner of Local 3. It was the responsibility of the Election Committee to order police without warrants, as well as Liska, out of the Election Hall.

We charge Ed Liska of the biggest armed robbery in the history of Hamtramck, Michigan. He robbed every worker of a fair election with his armed police guns. We have been robbed by the criminals, Ed Liska and his accomplice Helen Borner. As Election Chairman, Helen Borner is guilty of negligence and deliberate deviation from election rules. Let's throw these robbers out of the Union Hall.[21]

None of the foregoing discussion should be interpreted as suggesting that all charges of election improprieties are valid. The degree of truth in the charges is, in many ways, less relevant than the fact that the charges were made, were sufficiently compatible with observed fact to be plausible, and that they were believed by enough people to serve as useful organizing propaganda. The degree to which any set of charges can serve as effective propaganda is a function of their plausibility. Thus it is worth digressing to an examination of the charges as such.

There is little question that the incumbent officials in Local 3 considered the DRUM organization a threat. The rhetoric of revolutionaries may be well designed to recruit support for the angry masses but it is not as well suited to gaining acceptance by the representatives of the established order. Terms like "racist," "honky," "Polack," "pig," "Uncle-Tom," "sell-out" and "house-nigger" are not terms likely to create endearment in the hearts of those toward whom they are directed. Thus the natural tendency toward the preservation of positions of status, power, and privilege was reinforced by hostility directed at the challengers as well as the perception of the challengers as irresponsible.

Chrysler, as is the case with all private enterprise manufacturers, is primarily concerned with maintaining production at a profitable rate. DRUM had already exhibited its willingness and ability to disrupt production. It also exhibited a level of militancy that was likely to cause further problems, especially in the areas of black upgrading and safety conditions. What is more to the point, the League was always open in describing itself as Marxist–Leninist, revolutionary, and committed to the destruction of capitalism. The International Union has a need for credibility if it is to conduct effective contract negotiations. It must be able to demonstrate to the company that its contract will be kept. Thus it also had reason to fear the existence of an organization such as DRUM among its membership. Its opposition to the League was well demonstrated by the *Battleline* article and the UAW executive board newsletter of March 10 quoted in this chapter.

The company and union had reason to join in common cause against DRUM and the League. Similarly the police, even ignoring the impact of prejudice on the part of individual officers, have a commitment to law and order. They must be opposed to militant, revolutionary, or other groups likely to disrupt the normal functioning of the community. The extent to which the police viewed the League as a threat and reacted hostilely toward it is evidenced from testimony presented before a congressional investigating committee.[22] The Detroit police observed and investigated the League, engaged in covert surveillance, and concluded that the League was subversive.

Therefore it is plausible to expect that union, company, and police would all act to hinder the growth and development of DRUM. This would be likely regardless of the presence or absence of a conscious conspiracy. The events surrounding the elections did show a pattern of opposition but fall short of showing a conscious conspiracy, *per se.* There is little question that the company, the police, the local union leadership, and the international leadership all went beyond the bounds of strictly correct and neutral behavior during the elections. In doing so, they opened the gates for effective utilization of the "conspiracy" charge as a propaganda weapon in recruiting support for the League.

It is probably the case that such opposition was stronger and better organized than it had been for the two previous DRUM elections. However, this fact cannot, by itself, account for the decline in voting support for DRUM candidates. This election took place at a time (March 1970) when the League was already beginning to show visible signs of internal strain. The relevant events will be described in more detail in Chapter 6 and analyzed in terms of the growing strain in Chapter 10, so only a brief discussion will be presented at this point. John Watson returned to college for the academic year 1968–9. Much of his time was taken up by events surrounding his editorship of the student paper and in defending himself against an assault charge growing out of an incident related to that activity.

Various members of the League became increasingly involved in community activities. League activists organized a Detroit chapter of the Black Panther Party in spring 1969. The National Black Economic Development Conference (NBEDC later simply called BEDC) met in Detroit in April 1969. This stimulated a debate within the League as to whether it should become a national organization and/or whether it should affiliate itself as a part of a new and different national black workers' organization. League members were involved in the founding of the International Black Appeal. Increasing amounts of time were expended upon collaborative activities with white radicals. Plans were discussed for the establishment of a racially mixed, predominantly white book club as a vehicle for propaganda, political education, and the generation of community support. This club was established in the fall of 1970.

All of these activities diminished the amount of time and energy that could be expended on in-plant organizational efforts. There was increasing discontent among workers with the League focus on community efforts at the expense of factory efforts.[23] This discontent was shared by some members of the League cadre. There is also some evidence that the revolutionary union movements in the plants were becoming weaker. Chuck Wooten was fired from Dodge Main in February 1969 for hitting a supervisor and Sidney Lewis, very active in League affairs, was fired in August 1969. No successful protests of these activities were conducted. It would appear that the League was so weakened by internal tensions and by diversions of resources to community activities that it was unable to wage an effective electoral campaign. DRUM was unable to take up the slack due to a loss of leadership and some increased discontent with general League policies and priorities. Consequently the election went badly.

The League withdraws from direct participation

The results of this election led the League to abandon all direct participation in future union elections in favor of a policy of lending support to black candidates who exhibited a high level of militancy and a basic commitment to at least a nationalist perspective. Candidates with a fully developed class perspective were preferred when, and if, available. They made this decision fully cognizant that by so doing they were sacrificing a potentially valuable means of propaganda and political education. It is not entirely clear why this policy shift was made. It may be the case that the League cadre did not wish to risk the possible negative consequences of further election defeats. It is also possible that they were concerned with the seductive nature of reformist activity. Once one enters into reformist activities as recruiting devices there is a real temptation to attempt to make actual reforms even if, by so doing, the broader revolutionary program is set back. In other words there may have developed the belief that real changes could be made if only honest, militant blacks were elected to responsible posts in the unions. On the other hand, there may have been the longer view taken in which it was felt that the shortsightedness of the reform position could best be proven by electing honest, militant blacks to responsible positions and then allowing circumstances to demonstrate that they were powerless to bring about significant change.

Regardless of the intent, the actual practice of the "united-front" position allowed for the latter form of political education. However, this opportunity was largely lost. The concentration upon candidates, personalities, and local issues left the larger role of capitalism, imperialism, and racism largely undiscussed. There was no concentrated discussion of the need for revolutionary change and the role of black workers in bringing it about. This can be best illustrated by three ventures of ELRUM into united-front type electoral activities. ELRUM backed a slate of black candidates during the May 1969 elections for offices in Local 961. Three of the candidates that they backed made it all the way through the electoral process and won office in runoff elections on May 17, 1969. Elroy Richardson was elected president over incumbent Ed Rickard by a vote of 1,480 to 966.[24] However, just two years later in the May 1971 elections ELRUM backed a slate of candidates that ran Jordan Sims for president against Elroy Richardson.[25] Richardson finished third in the original balloting and did not make it into the runoff. The election was marked by red-baiting and the use of armed guards, both the responsibility of Richardson as evidenced in the following citation from the *Detroit Free Press:*

Sims has denied he is a member of any radical group. But Richardson said Sims was endorsed in leaflets distributed by the Eldon Revolutionary Union Movement (ELRUM), an affiliate of the militant League of Revolutionary Black Workers. The armed guards were hired by Richardson. He defended the decision saying that it assured a fair election. He said that the guards prevented "extremists and outsiders from disrupting the electoral process."[26]

Sims lost a close and highly disputed election runoff. This will be discussed more extensively in that portion of Chapter 10 dealing with the United National Caucus. What is particularly relevant at this point is that the attack directed against Richardson by ELRUM was largely personalized rather than structural. Richardson was called a Tom and accused of being "controlled by the honkies down at Solidarity House."[27] He was also accused of being a sell out:

UNION SELL OUT

It has been 8 months now and Robert McKee, James Edwards, Alonzo Chandler and John Taylor along with committeeman Jordan Sims are still on discharge status from Eldon Avenue. These heroic workers who staged a worker's safety protest of the inhumane, degrading, and hazardous to life and limb working conditions practiced on black workers in particular and all workers in general are still fighting the same two-fold battle against management and the union.

Committeeman Jordan Sims while participating in the safety protest had already been discharged during the time the original stewards were discharged as a result of Elroy's wildcats. We make this point because now Jordan Sim's case has moved through all the proper channels of our irrelevant grievance procedure and has been thrown out at the last stage (umpire decision).

With all the factual information Sims had on union—company activities at Eldon he lost his case in the end on a sell-out by our main sell-out artist Elroy Richardson, whose attempts of sell-out have not ceased. As you know Elroy called for the two wildcats at Eldon last year that resulted in a rash of discharges of his officials who he didn't back. At Sims' umpire hearing this traitor Elroy denied any part in the walkouts and stated that Sims and the other stewards were acting on their own while he simply told people to go back to work. Athough this is in contradiction to what we know as being fact it was enough to convince the umpire that Sims was just a troublemaker and should not be returned to work. Sims must now pursue the legal courts to get his job back. Elroy Beware![28]

Other names directed at him include "lard-belly," "faggot-ass," and "jive punk." This further illustrates the dilemma of reform versus revolution. Both revolutionaries and reformers must believe that change is possible but revolutionaries believe that local limited changes will be inconsequential unless accompanied by sweeping alterations in the total system. Thus the election of responsible, honest, black officials should be a major step toward resolving grievances and bringing about significant improvement in conditions. However, a revolutionary would see the local plant in a context that includes the place of the plant in a larger company, the local union as located in a larger international union, and both as imbedded in a system of monopoly capitalism operating on an international scale. In the latter case events on the local level take on prime significance in terms of their relation to the processes of political education, consciousness raising, and political mobilization.

This dilemma is further illustrated by the claim by UAW Vice-President Douglas Fraser that after several League members had been elected to local union office the responsibility of the position transformed them into good, serious, union functionaries.[29] Their concern for revolution was replaced with a concern for day-to-day operating problems of the union. Occupation of positions of responsibility may have just such a coopting function. Yet the failure to occupy such positions prevents the achievement of any changes. In the absence of change and progress, worker optimism and support may wither away. The personalized attacks launched by the League against individuals are more consistent with a reform orientation than with the political education associated with a revolutionary movement. But it is problematic whether black workers would have responded to a reform-free revolutionary organizing drive. This dilemma haunted the League as long as it existed.

In between the two presidential elections delegates were elected to attend the 1970 UAW convention.[30] ELRUM cooperated with others to field the Voice of the Black Worker slate. Unfortunately there was a foul-up in the selection process and two black slates wound up running for office. It was originally believed that union members could vote for the six delegates plus four alternates so the coalition nominated persons for all posts. When it was later determined that members would only be allowed to vote for six candidates, alternates being those with the next highest number of votes after six had been elected, the slate had to be pared to six. The final Voice of the Black Worker slate consisted of James Edwards, Robert McKee, Jordan Sims, Nathanial Smith, William L. Sparks, and Alonzo Chandler. Some of those pared off the original slate then became part of a second slate of black workers. It has been charged that the shift in procedure (ten to six votes) was consciously designed to accomplish exactly this result.

It appears that there was also an unannounced slate of white workers running for the posts. The split between the two black slates partially accounts for the fact that five of the six delegates elected in the March 11 and 12 voting were white. Jordan Sims was the lone member of the Voice of the Black Worker slate to be elected. The election results were challenged on the grounds that: (1) a large number of members were only allowed to vote "challenged" ballots because of an alleged nonpayment of dues during an earlier strike period; (2) allegedly 53 known ELRUM ballots were deliberately voided; (3) the ballot boxes were stored at the same police station that five days earlier had mistakenly picked up James Edwards and Robert McKee (candidates) on invalid armed robbery charges; and (4) Gordon Francis, a candidate, allegedly played a role in voiding 320 ballots for nonpayment of dues. The protests did not alter the outcome of the election.

One major lesson did emerge from that election — or at least it should have. The need for unity among black workers, especially militant black workers, was clearly demonstrated. However, while the League consistently pushed the black unity line, it was not always as ready to cooperate with blacks possessing different lines of political analysis. The duality of the League orientation toward elections — viewing them primarily as vehicles for political education but also seeking concrete reforms — may be illustrated with the following quote from Brooks:

As Hamlin told me, "Our thrust is not toward getting workers to vote in union elections, per se." Both Watson and Hamlin, however, possess a pragmatic as well as a chiliastic bent. They readily concede the necessity of obtaining "relief" for black workers. And, in this instance, Hamlin quickly added, "We participated (in elections) as an organizational technique, and as a possible way of having some impact because there are things stewards can do that benefit workers on the line."[31]

The League participated in wildcat strikes, elections, and demonstrations primarily as organizational vehicles. In every case the prime intent was to build a revolutionary organization with a solid base rooted among black workers. In Chapter 6 the League's ideology will be discussed and in Chapter 7 its organizational activities and their underlying rationale.

6. Ideology

In preceding chapters some aspects of the League's ideology have been briefly discussed (e.g., its self-designation as a black Marxist—Leninist organization, its concentration upon black workers at the point of production, and its support for other revolutionary groups) but the major focus was directed toward other topics with only an incidental treatment of ideology. In this chapter a more systematic examination will be attempted, commencing with a relatively detailed presentation of the League's own ideological statements. No single statement exists that presents the League's ideology in a unified concise form. There are three documents that may be combined to arrive at a reasonably complete understanding of the position developed by the League: a 38-page pamphlet incorporating the League's general policy statement and labor program, an initial publication of a portion of this document in the *Inner City Voice*, and a republication of a revised version.[1] Part of the League leadership felt that the initial formulation was inadequate because it failed to include sufficient labor history to provide a complete understanding of the relationship between blacks and capitalism and between blacks and organized labor. This discontent surfaced after a portion of the original statement was published in the newspaper and led to the publication of a revised version.

Basic premises

This presentation of League ideology is a summary description of the document that would result from an integration of the separate statements. The introductory section is titled, "Here's Where We're Coming From," and begins:

The League of Revolutionary Black Workers is dedicated to waging a relentless struggle against racism, capitalism, and imperialism. We are struggling for the liberation of black people in the confines of the United States as well as to play a major revolutionary role in the liberation of all oppressed people in the world.[2]

127

A small all-white capitalist class owns the basic means of production in the United States. Most whites and virtually all blacks are workers. All Americans gain from imperialism and all whites gain from racism. The dual set of privileges gives white workers an investment in the status quo and encourages them to collaborate with the United States government to perpetuate imperialism abroad and racism at home. These systems of privilege were expected to create the environment in which the League would grow and attract members inspired by internal struggles for black liberation and international revolutionary struggles and aid all struggles against imperialism. These efforts would be guided by the principles of Marxism—Leninism and led by a Marxist—Leninist political party. The League program for building a party included: organizing black workers on a broad scale; politicizing and educating blacks to the nature of racism, capitalism, and imperialism; supporting black efforts to develop a broad economic base in the community; developing a community self-defense organization; conducting struggles on behalf of black workers and the total community; and forming principled alliances and coalitions with others who struggle against racism, capitalism, and imperialism.[3]

Labor history

The League analysis of American labor history interpreted slavery as both a set of economic relations and a set of social relations. The restriction of slave status to black Africans transformed class into race. Labor was divided between free whites and unfree blacks. Both were exploited but whites retained white skin privilege. This difference prevented either white or black labor from becoming fully proletarianized.

League analysis concluded that white working-class struggles historically have been a mixture of race and class struggles. White workers opposed slavery because they did not wish to compete with slave labor but they did not favor abolition because they were opposed to racial equality. White workers fought for workers' rights but they also fought to restrict black civil and work rights. White skin privilege sometimes hurt the white worker when blacks were used as strikebreakers but organized labor, including many of the early socialists, did not sympathize with the black struggles. Organized labor often supported American imperialism. The League concluded that the organized labor movement was the enemy of black freedom and that white labor had to be considered hostile because of the support that it gave to American imperialism.[4]

The League presentation of labor history was less hostile toward the white worker than toward organized labor. White skin privilege accrued from the development of imperialism during the late nineteenth century but was eroded during its decline in the twentieth century. The erosion of privilege removed the major motivation for white workers to be racist. Capitalism has been, and is currently, under attack from revolutionary groups around the world but organized labor has consistently rallied to its defense. It is at this point that the role of the white worker was viewed as significant but problematic:

as long as white workers think of themselves as white workers or white middle or lower class, they will be counter to the struggle, and will retain white consciousness as opposed to class consciousness. To think in those terms means a struggle for the decaying privileges that buttress the system of racism and exploitation instead of for the liberation of all working people. It is without question that white labor will be forced to shift gears. Currently, however, the liberation struggle of blacks is moving at a quickening pace. It is our contention that the key to the black liberation struggles lies with the black workers.[5]

The League argued that the black liberation struggle is part of a worldwide struggle of oppressed against oppressor but that not all elements are strategically located to exert leverage toward change. The black worker was singled out as the most crucial element in the coming struggle but not all black workers occupy equally strategic positions. It was primarily black workers in mines and factories who were expected to form the nucleus of the revolutionary struggle. This results from the high proportion of blacks in these occupational locations, the high proportion of persons in these locations who are black, and the key position of factories and mines in the capitalist extraction of profit.

Position of black workers

The League noted that, when compared to whites, blacks had higher rates of labor force participation, were overrepresented in blue-collar and service occupations and underrepresented in craftsmen, foremen, and upper white-collar occupations. It asserted that blacks were also disproportionately concentrated in the harder, dirtier, less desirable jobs within occupational categories. The virtual exclusion of blacks from decision-making posts in American society was stressed.

Economic situation of black workers

The League demonstrated that black workers are concentrated in occupations receiving the lowest pay rates. It argued that the American economy requires poverty in order to discipline the work force and inhibit the development of revolutionary political movements. The spiral of low wages, inflationary prices, and increased taxes was portrayed as keeping many black families hungry despite having one or more employed members.

Working conditions for blacks

Black workers work in the sector of the economy characterized by the most dangerous jobs. The jobs are dangerous both in terms of the possibility of industrial accidents and in terms of exposure to disease-producing and debilitating conditions. Accidents result from speedups in pursuit of higher profits. Industries with a high proportion of blacks have a high degree of regimentation and control over the worker. The League viewed struggle over these conditions as especially significant:

The struggle of black workers in industry over working conditions, organized and consciously led, or unorganized and undirected, is primarily the struggle to control the process of production. It is the responsibility of the revolutionary workers movement to provide leadership to this struggle and to clearly demonstrate to the masses of workers that to control and improve conditions, to control the process of production, we must control the instruments of production themselves. It is the transformation of the struggle against the excesses of production into a movement to seize control of these instruments which will lead to the organized, consciously led struggle of all people to own and control the instruments of power in this society up to and including the state.[6]

The position of black workers in organized labor

It was charged that organized labor is corrupt and racist. The League chronicled the long battle for black representation at decision-making levels in the UAW and the exclusion of blacks from the skilled trades. Management and the UAW claimed that DRUM, FRUM, ELRUM, and so on constituted racist attempts to divide racially a labor force that the League claimed was already so divided. The UAW was charged with using a number of subterfuges including retiree voting in order to exclude blacks from power even in those areas where they had large numerical concentrations. The UAW was perceived as opposing the revolutionary union movements because they had the potential to disrupt the union's pattern of influence over the social, political, and economic life of black communities.

Unorganized black workers

Large numbers of black workers are employed in sectors of the economy that are not yet organized and have even worse conditions of employment than those existing in the organized sector. The League believed that it was their task to reach out to unorganized black workers and aid in the creation of a new militant organization. Unorganized workers were seen as constituting a potentially potent revolutionary force.

Black women workers

Black women constitute a significant segment of the reserve labor force that is called upon in times of need. They are subject to both sexual and economic exploitation when active in the labor force and are the producers of the next generation of workers when not directly in the labor force. The League did not do much to organize black women *qua* women but it recognized a special need and believed that a special program was required. They placed highest priority upon the organization of workers. Black women were recruited as black workers and did play a significant role in League activities.

Economic conditions

Black workers occupy a precarious position in which slight economic fluctuations have a major impact in the black community. The speedup often remains despite unemployment. It is not unusual to find some black automobile workers required to work a 56-hour week while many of their co-workers are unemployed. High unemployment rates do not diminish management's desire to "rationalize" production and increase output per man-hour of labor.

Blacks in auto

The League argued that an internal revolution was needed in the UAW. It had been involved in civil rights activities but it also tolerated racist conditions in the plants. The League charged that the UAW had only token integration at decision-making levels. The UAW collected dues from black workers subject to unsafe working conditions. The League demanded that dues collected from black workers be turned over to them so that they could establish a black "United Foundation."

The union as a political force

The League recognized that a large labor union is a major political force controlling large numbers of workers who can strike and who pay dues that may be used to influence societal affairs. It charged that the UAW failed to do all that it could to improve conditions of life for blacks, end the Vietnam war, improve working conditions, slow down the pace of production (end the speedup), prevent harassment of black workers — particularly those of either a nationalist or revolutionary inclination — and help end unemployment by reducing the work week.

Revolutionary organization in organized industry (the DRUM) experience)

This is the most important section of the League's position statement because it incorporated self-criticism of past practice as well as the development of the correct line for the future. Struggles against racism were seen as contributing to the development of class consciousness among black workers. This was often expressed in the development of black caucuses within unions, which were doomed to fail as long as they restricted their activities because of loyalty to the dominant union leadership. DRUM-type structures (i.e., independent groups capable of waging a revolutionary struggle unhampered by loyalties to existing capitalist structures) are needed because they are free to wage an unlimited struggle against both management and the union. Struggles for DRUM-type organizations have had both important successes and important failures. Strike actions produced some worker political education and improved some working conditions. The League felt that its challenges forced the union leadership "to expose its basic racist, class collaborationist nature in the most open and brutal manner to the masses of black workers."[7]

Past struggles were not seen as having eliminated racism and exploitation in the plants but as having pointed the direction for future struggles. The basic lessons emerging out of past struggle were seen to be:

1. In-plant organizations must be well organized and disciplined. We must have a division of labor within the organization. Decisions of the organization must be carried out in accordance with the rules of the League. . . . The organization must hold its loyalty to the League particularly and black workers in general, and must be free from political and financial ties to the union hierarchy which prevents independent action on the part of the rank and file.

2. Isolation of workers in a single plant is a major cause of failure of strike or other actions on a local level. The struggle is not an individual struggle for higher wages and better working conditions for workers in a particular plant, it is a class struggle to free all workers. . . . When workers engage a corporation in a struggle for power, the ruling class inevitably brings in outside forces such as the police and courts to repress the workers' struggle. In such instances, we must be able to meet increasing force with equal or greater power. This may mean expanding the struggle to other plants, eventually to the point of general strike. . . .

3. To prevent isolation and solidify the black working class, the League of Revolutionary Black Workers must be developed as a broadly based labor organization. The League must unite black workers from all plants and in the common struggle to overcome the drawbacks of isolation, lack of skilled organizers and resources . . . any members of the League must aid and defend the struggles of any other member or any other organization when called upon to do so. . . .

4. The League must increase its capacity to educate, organize and lead workers in industries where we are already active, and must develop new DRUM-type movements throughout the ranks of organized labor. . . . The organization of workers is not a one-shot affair. . . . It requires fortitude, determination, planning, discipline, correct political direction, sophisticated administration, material resources and capable, unselfish, educated and experienced leadership. These qualities can only come from a thoroughly organized base within the black working class itself. . . .

5. The DRUM experience indicates the necessity of engaging workers inside the plants in constant struggle with the company and union leadership. Struggle is necessary to increase the unity, strength and level of consciousness of the workers. The process of struggle itself unites workers as a powerful force against their enemies. . . .

6. The involvement of workers in protracted struggles inevitably leads to serious mass action such as wildcat strikes. The DRUM experience shows that we must protect and provide for workers engaged in open conflict with the company. We must be able to support the families of striking workers, to provide for workers who are fired, lawyers when necessary, etc. To provide the supportive base for struggles in which workers face economic or legal reprisal, the League of Revolutionary Black Workers must develop the National Black Labor Strike and Defense Fund [LSDF]. Workers and the community will be asked to contribute to the LSDF. . . .

7. To win struggles, leaders must be familiar with labor laws, union contracts, history of blacks in labor, the internal policies of the union, history of

union leadership, union procedure, etc. — for instance, few workers in organized labor know that safety strikes are legal.

8. Attempts to seize control of unions at the local level are concrete means of engaging workers in struggle against local union tyrants. It is theoretically possible in many cases to win local elections. Often victory is lost only when union bureaucrats are willing to totally and openly expose the corrupt and undemocratic nature of the union to its rank and file. The DRUM experience shows that even when elections are stolen, the bureaucrats still lose. The consciousness of the workers is raised, their aggressiveness is heightened and their determination to join DRUM-type organizations and resolutely fight the union pirates is strengthened. . . .

9. The League will struggle to win rank and file union positions of stewards, committeemen, convention delegates, etc. Where union cheating prevents assumption of such positions we will use every available method to struggle (i.e., appointment of blue ribbon [blue button] stewards).

10. The League and its membership shall struggle against union leadership at union conventions, conferences and meetings.

11. The League will regularly hold local, regional and national level conferences, conventions and congresses for the purpose of expansion of the organization of black workers.

12. The League organizers shall use public denunciation and demonstrations against racist union bureaucrats and corporation, using community and student support in these efforts.

13. The League will use the courts, NLRB [National Labor Relations Board], and other "legal" devices as offensive tools of struggle wherever possible. This is "legal" struggle against election cheating, violations of workers' rights under NLRB, etc.

14. The League will oppose the influence of the racist labor bureaucrats and corporations in the black community.

15. The League organization will organize workers for self-defense against the white racist corporations and unions.

16. The League organization will conduct social and cultural activities for the recreation of black workers as respite from the total alienation of work (i.e., rallies, raffles, cabarets, dances, picnics, parties, etc.).

17. League organizations will develop programmatic demands based on the general League program and the specific problems of local workers. These demands must relate in such a manner as to rally the support of black workers in terms of their general and specific characteristics.[8]

Strains in the ideology

League ideology incorporated internal contradictions, which produced strain and tactical inconsistencies. League ideologues implicitly attempted to merge two models of racial stratification without full articulation and development of strategic and tactical implications. Part of the League's ideology was derived from the capitalist exploitation model. The model begins with the exploitation of all workers under capitalism. Race prejudice develops to justify the exploitation of entire racial groups and is used to divide the work force into mutually distrustful and hostile camps. This prevents the development of solidarity and class consciousness and keeps the proletariat weak and exploitable. Race prejudice harms both majority and minority segments of the proletariat. No claim is made that race prejudice always has an immediate economic explanation. Once it is introduced into a society it takes on a meaning and a life independent of its original cause.

The League accepted most premises of the capitalist exploitation model and believed capitalism to be the major source of the exploitation of blacks in America and imperialism to be the major source of exploitation of blacks in the third world. The League recognized that the capitalist class was primarily white and that it had been quite successful in selling racism to the white worker, partially by insuring a skin color advantage. The League believed that white skin privilege was a capitalist ploy designed to split the working class but that many white workers bought it hook, line, and sinker. The only hope for the black American was seen to be a socialist revolution, which could only be brought about by workers. A multiracial workers' revolution was made unlikely by white racism and the role of revolutionary vanguard had to be assumed by black workers.

The League saw the role to be played by black workers as more active than had Cox.[9] Cox thought that socialism could only be achieved by a white-led worker revolution. Black gains would be a byproduct of worker gains. The League saw the black worker as the most significant element in that revolution. Black workers are more responsive than white workers to organizational attempts because of their superexploited position in American society. Organizing attempts would initially have to be along national (racial) lines and focussed on racism and concrete working conditions. Successes should stimulate further organizational efforts and facilitate political education. Political education will not be effective in a vacuum but must be combined with meaningful action. White radicals could be accepted as allies providing that they could relate to the political orientations and objectives of the League. It was believed that white workers would become radicalized by the black workers' example of successful class action on behalf of proletarian objectives. The populist movement of the late ninteenth century demonstrated that white workers can overcome their racism when they perceive it in their interest to do so but it also demonstrated that latent racism is a weak point, which may be exploited to destroy such movements.[10] One League spokesman cited the experience of the Populist Party as the basis for the League decision to restrict its membership to blacks.[11]

The League also derived a portion of its ideology from the colonial model (see Chapter 1). Five major aspects of the colonization process may be applicable to the black experience in America: (1) black entrance into America was involuntary; (2) whites control black institutions; (3) black culture was destroyed; (4) white racism persists; and (5) cultural nationalism and ghetto revolts parallel the early stages of colonial revolutions. Blauner believes that this model must be modified to account for a shift in exports from raw materials in traditional colonies to labor power in the black internal colony.[12] However, it is not the case that raw materials were the major export in all external colonies. The major export of Upper Volta, Malawi, and Mozambique was labor power.[13]

The League attempted to merge the colonial model with the capitalist exploitation model. It accepted as a basic premise the nature of capitalism as an intrinsically exploitative system, which used race prejudice to justify the exploitation of an entire race and as a tool to divide the proletariat. Capitalists were believed to create the perception of opportunities for individual mobility in order to hinder the development of class consciousness. The League believed that encouragement for black capitalism was designed to introduce a cleavage into the black community analogous to the split in the proletariat. Their two programs for domination combine to produce a small black bourgeoisie incorporating minor capitalists and individual blacks who have been placed in visible but minor positions in the establishment. This black bourgeoisie may be expected by the capitalists to act as agents of indirect rule — a role corresponding to that of the bourgeoisie of the colonies as described by Fanon.[14]

Ideological implications for strategy

Different racial stratification models imply different lines of tactical endeavor. The capitalist exploitation model suggests the pursuit of a socialist revolution. The colonial model implies cultural and revolutionary nationalism aimed at establishing a separate black state. A combined capitalist—colonial exploitation model contains internal contradictions. Black workers are unlikely to be able to carry out a socialist revolution without white allies but white workers are seen as enemies. Wars of national liberation require the unified actions of all blacks but a socialist revolution requires that black workers overthrow black along with white capitalists.[15]

The contradictions in the League version of the capitalist—colonial exploitation model suggested incompatible tactical lines, which were a constant source of strain in the organization. It is difficult to engage in principled cooperation with white radicals if all whites are defined as exploiters and enemies. It is also difficult to build a community support movement if all members of the black bourgeoisie are also defined as exploiters and enemies. These contradictions are resolvable but the League did not succeed in resolving them. In Chapter 7 the manner in which League ideology — complete with contradictions — was translated into practice will be explored, and the question of the validity of the various racial stratification models will be pursued in greater detail in Chapter 12.

7. League organizational activities

In previous chapters the birth of the League was reviewed, its activities and ideology examined. The League and its affiliated revolutionary union movements organized demonstrations, conducted wildcat strikes, and mounted challenges in local union elections. None of these activities was pursued because of its intrinsic value. All were designed to be steps toward building a revolutionary black Marxist—Leninist organization. It is, therefore, important to examine the organizational theory that provided the underpinnings for League organizational activities and to contrast the theory with actual practice.

The workplace is the focus for organization

The prime focus of the League's organizing activities was always the black worker at the point of production. All other organization practices were secondary and designed, at least in principle, to stimulate support for worker organizations and worker-organizing activities. John Watson states the theoretical rationale for this focus as follows:

We have a certain program, a certain understanding of the dynamics of American capitalist society and we're acting on the results of our analysis. This doesn't mean that we're against those people who are involved in community organization. Our analysis tells us that the basic power of black people lies at the point of production, that the basic power we have is the power as workers.

As workers, as black workers, we have historically been and are now an essential element in the American economic scene. Without black slaves to pick the cotton on the Southern plantations, the primitive accumulation of capital which was necessary to develop industry in both Europe and America would never have been accomplished. Without black workers slaving on the assembly lines in automobile plants in the city of Detroit, the automobile companies would not be able to produce cars in the first place, and therefore, wouldn't be able to make the tremendous profits which they have been making.

Therefore, we feel that the best way to organize black people into a powerful unit is to organize them in the factories in which they are working. We feel that black workers, especially, have the power to completely close down the American economic system. In order to implement that power, we have to become organized.[1]

138

Our program clearly demonstrates in our analysis of American society that the white workers enjoy a privileged position within the proletariat. They have time and time again chosen to defend their position of privilege rather than to move in conjunction with black workers to overthrow all inequities. This has demonstrated to us the necessity of developing a strong independent black organization. At the same time, we clearly understand white workers are oppressed and exploited. They face many of the same problems and contradictions that black workers face. We feel that as revolutionary development takes place within the white proletariat, and as white workers begin to move to overthrow racism, capitalism, and imperialism, then principled alliances are possible. We call for such alliances and coalitions in our program, but we accept them only on principled grounds. We have encouraged some of the smaller but more positive elements of the white Left, some of whom are located in Detroit, to attempt to work with the white proletariat. So far, there have only been meager results.[2]

Its theoretical analysis led the League to conclude that its main thrust had to be toward the worker at the point of production. However, the dual nature of black oppression in America — as members of the working class and as members of a race — could not be ignored. Organization of blacks *qua* blacks as well as blacks *qua* black workers was conceivable. Numerous groups all over the United States were pursuing a variety of programs aimed at the black community. The League believed that its major organizing thrust should be aimed at the factories for reasons of pragmatic effectiveness as well as for reasons derived from theory. They believed that the best way to organize the community was first to organize the factory:

In one factory we have 10,000 people who are faced with the same brutal conditions . . . When you go out into the community, the interests of the people . . . are going to be much more greatly dispersed . . . Just in terms of expediency there are greater possibilities in the organization of the plant . . . The kinds of actions which can be taken (in the community) are not as effectively damaging to the ruling class as the kinds of actions which can be taken in the plant . . . When you close down Hamtramck assembly plant . . . for a day you cost Chrysler corporation 1,000 cars . . . also . . . you automatically can mobilize the people in the streets, 5,000 or 10,000 at a single blow. Whereas when you go house to house . . . it is much more difficult to gather that many people . . . Finally . . . workers are not people who live in the factories 24 hours a day. They all go home and live somewhere . . . It's almost an inevitable and simultaneous development that as factory workers begin to get organized, support elements within the community are also organized.[3]

The League and community organizing

However, the League did not confine its activities to the work place.[4] It branched out into the community. As previously stated many League members had histories of participation in the civil rights movement. Many had also been active in community organizing. John Watson had been a staff organizer for the West Central Organization (WCO) and later became its director. John Williams was formerly a community organizer for the North Woodward Interfaith Organization and later headed the Santa Maria Schools. Ken Cockrel successfully participated in the legal defense of the members of the Republic of New Africa charged in the shootout with police at the Bethel Baptist Church.[5] He also participated in the successful defense of a black automobile worker charged with murdering his foreman and shooting two others.[6] The latter defense was based primarily upon the claim that the conditions of work in the automobile plant were responsible for causing a state of temporary insanity. Subsequent court action won workmen's compensation rights, back pay, and medical costs. Ken Cockrel had previously worked as research director for the North Woodward Interfaith Organization.

The organization of the Detroit branch of the Black Panther Party

The notion that community organization should primarily be designed as a vehicle for generating support for the black workers' activities also played a role in the establishment of a Detroit branch of the Black Panther Party.[7] The same period of ferment and struggle that produced the League in Detroit also produced the Black Panther Party in Oakland.[8] The Black Panthers had a great deal of romantic appeal for black youth. The national media gave them extensive publicity as a result of their confrontations with the police. There was a great deal to the style of confrontation, to the "machismo" involved in carrying guns, "policing the police," dressing in berets and leather jackets, that was likely to attract imitators and recruits.

The League was aware of this appeal and felt a certain degree of empathy with the Panthers as fellow black revolutionaries, fellow self-identified Marxists—Leninists. However, the League officers were concerned with what they believed to be fundamental errors in the Panther's theoretical analysis, particularly as it related to organizing the lumpen elements of the black community. The League was convinced that no successful revolutionary movement could be built with the lumpen as its base. The League believed that the lumpen lacked a basic source of power, whereas black workers had potential power through their relation to production. John Watson believed that some of the problem resulted from a failure to distinguish between the role of the lumpen in the type of society analyzed by Fanon and the role of the lumpen in the United States:

In Fanon's case he was describing the landless peasants, the peasants in Algeria who were kicked off the land and forced to come to the cities. These peasants presented a certain kind of militant rebellious class – as opposed to the lumpen proletariat as it exists in America. Now even the lumpen proletariat . . . as it exists in the third world countries is a class which many times does go over to the side of the oppressors. It is a class in which there is that capacity, if the ruling class is willing to pay out enough, to buy mercenaries to buy agents, etc. from that class. On the other hand, it was Fanon's position that this particular class would be willing to fight with the liberation forces. However, they would only be willing to fight if they were properly politically educated, if they were properly engaged in struggle, if they were constantly involved in the process of reevaluation of study. For a while in this country, that was a point of great debate within the black movement; that is, especially when the development of the League began to take place at the same time the Panthers came into national prominence. The Panthers actually switched their line and changed their line a number of times, but we know they were being pushed by *Tele-Star*, *Life Magazine*, etc. When they developed the line that the lumpen proletariat is the vanguard of the revolution, it became a line which was being espoused on a tremendous level throughout the country by all kinds of elements which described themselves as political revolutionaries. It was a question with which we had to struggle. From our experience and our struggle, we could emphasize that the working class is the vanguard of the major force within the revolutionary struggle, and that the lumpen proletariat is in and of itself a class which generally splits. Whole sections of the lumpen proletariat go over to the other side, whole sections are totally undisciplined and cannot be disciplined, and will engage in that "Go for yourself" thing regardless of the political situation. There are other sectors of that class which can become revolutionaries and which can also become the greatest, the most courageous of revolutionaries. However, in terms of that latter class, I guarantee you that you will never find that happening if you don't have a very intensive program of political education, if you don't have a very intensive program to redeem them from the sordid bourgeois values which have been saturated into their brains for so many years. I think in many ways that a lot of the experience of the Panthers has come precisely from that analysis – the analysis that the lumpen proletariat, which isn't a stable class, is going to be in the vanguard of the revolution. That is precisely why the Panthers have been led into so many adventuristic actions over the past three years, and have been engaged in so many of these shoot-outs in which they essentially came out on the losing end. It's precisely why the Panthers have been unable to prevent their organization from being infiltrated with agents. In the first place, a dude who's a lumpen cat can go into an organization, saying "Yeah, Brother, what are we going to do?" Then somebody comes along and says, "What we're going to do is I'm going to give you $5,000 to turn these dudes in." . . . The lumpen says, "Yeah, cool!" That happens. Agents are sent in there, and time and time again it is impossible to discipline them either in a military sense or in a political sense. We could go on and on in terms of that particular experience. It's a clear example of the need for political education, the need for rationality, the need for a clear and logical assessment of the condition which we're facing.[9]

The League officials recognized that it was inevitable that there would be a Detroit branch of the Black Panther Party. They also recognized that it would be highly successful in attracting members, including many potential League members. They were afraid that the romantic appeal of the Black Panther Party would lead to the dissipation of youthful enthusiasm and energy in unproductive directions. The League wished to prevent this and sought to harness such enthusiasm for more viable programs. League members hit upon the strategy of being the first to organize a Detroit branch of the Panthers. Several League members were involved in this attempt, but the prime role was carried out by Luke Tripp aided by John Williams. A chapter was organized and its activities were directed toward supporting worker organizations, that is, toward carrying out the League program. The degree to which the League was successful in this attempt may be seen in the April 24, 1969, statement by Panther Chief of Staff David Hilliard that the majority of DRUM and FRUM members were Panthers.[10] Hilliard meant to imply that the League of Revolutionary Black Workers was an offshoot of the Detroit branch of the Black Panther Party. It is probably more correct to state that the Detroit branch of the Black Panther Party constituted an organizing vehicle for the League.

Community organizing and black workers

It was noted above that a revolutionary group may enter into reformist activities as a vehicle for attracting recruits to their revolutionary program. It was also noted that those reformist activities may become ends in themselves and ultimately hinder the development of a revolutionary program. It is equally true that community-organizing programs may be initiated as a means of generating support for worker-centered activities. It is also possible that these community programs may have value in themselves and may become sufficiently attractive that energies will be distracted from the prime focus — workers — to more peripheral concerns. Both the revolutionary rationale for community organizing and its seductive nature may be seen in the following statements made by Cockrel and Hamlin:

when you talk about the League expanding into what is called community work . . . it simply recognized . . . a broader political definition of . . . workers. And it was also an objective understanding of the fact that workers leave the plant and have to go somewhere. They live where we live so it become [s] eminently sensible, as well as objectively desirable, to have organizations that relate to workers within a context outside of the plant so that we can generate the kind of support that we need in order to support the struggles inside the plant.[11]

. . . most of the organizing areas that we have gotten into we were kind of dragged into reluctantly. We always had an impulse to stay with the plants and organize the plants because that's where the power was. That's where the blacks have power, they are the producers, they can close down the economy. And so our impulse was to stay there. But after we recognized that we had to involve all our people in supporting the struggles in the plants, we began to look beyond factories. Plus certain situations became so critical that we had to move in to begin, to begin to organize to avert disaster, and to try to provide some kind of help and leadership. The most obvious one was the schools. What had happened was that the League represents a merger of various elements in the black community and students . . . The reason we first got involved with students and the lumpen proletariat, the brothers from the street, was because the workers themselves could not go out to the plant to pass out literature. If they did, they obviously would get fired. And so to protect them from that, we allowed them to remain anonymous when we first began. And we now do that in every new place we go into.[12]

Thus all community activity was primarily designed to support the main thrust, organizing black workers at the point of production. It was sometimes the case that this paid off in somewhat unexpected ways. An influential interdenominational organization of black ministers announced its support of DRUM during its battle with Chrysler in August 1968.[13] They announced their support of black workers at Dodge Main, sympathy with the goals of DRUM, and called for an investigation of both the plant medical practices and the grievance procedures. While the ministers did not have any direct power base to use as a lever with Chrysler, their appeal lent respectability to DRUM's cause and made it more difficult for Chrysler to write off their problems as the result of irresponsible agitators.

The National Black Economic Development Conference

An important turning point in the history of the League came in 1969. The National Black Economic Development Conference met in Detroit

April 25 to April 27, 1969.[14] The conference was funded by a grant
from the Inter-Religious Foundation for Community Organization
(IFCO) and seemed to be originally conceived of as a means of encouraging black self-help on the order of "black capitalism." However, the
conference was infiltrated and taken over by persons more interested in
establishing a program for black socialism. It was determined that BEDC
should be a permanent organization with a 24-person steering committee. All seven members of the executive board of the League of Revolutionary Black Workers were included on the steering committee. Several
League members cooperated with James Forman in the preparation of
the Black Manifesto calling for reparations to be largely raised through
white churches and synagogues. Forman presented the manifesto to
BEDC where it was adopted on April 26. Selections from his introductory address are illuminating:

We have heard the rhetoric, but we have not heard the rhetoric which says that
black people in this country must understand that we are the Vanguard Force. We
shall liberate all the people in the U.S. and we will be instrumental in the liberation
of colored people the world around. We must understand this point very clearly so
that we are not trapped into diversionary and reactionary movements. Any class
analysis of the U.S. shows very clearly that black people are the most oppressed
group of people inside the United States. We have suffered the most from racism
and exploitation, cultural degradation and lack of political power. It follows from
the laws of revolution that the most oppressed will make the revolution, but we are
not talking about just making the revolution. All the parties on the left who consider themselves revolutionary will say that blacks are the Vanguard, but we are saying that not only are we the Vanguard, but we must assume leadership, total control and we must exercise the humanity which is inherent in us. . . . We no longer
can just get by with the use of the word capitalism to describe the U.S., for it is an
imperial power. . . .

But while we talk of revolution, which will be an armed confrontation and long
years of sustained guerilla warfare inside this country, we must also talk of the type
of world we want to live in. We must commit ourselves to a society where the total
means of production are taken from the rich people and placed into the hands of
the state for the welfare of all the people. This is what we mean when we say total
control. And we mean that black people who have suffered the most from exploitation and racism must move to protect their black interest by assuming leadership
inside of the United States of everything that exists. The time has passed when we
are second in command and the white boy stands on top. This is especially true of
the Welfare Agencies in this country, but it is not enough to say that a black man is
on top. He must be committed to building the new society, to taking the wealth
away from the rich people such as General Motors, Ford, Chrysler, the DuPonts,
the Rockefellers, the Mellons, and all the other rich white exploiters and racists
who run this world.

Where do we begin? We have already started. We started the moment we were brought to this country. In fact, we started on the shores of Africa, for we have always resisted attempts to make us slaves and now we must resist the attempts to make us capitalists. It is in the financial interest of the U.S. to make us capitalists, for this will be the same line as that of integration into the main-stream of American life. Therefore, brothers and sisters, there is no need to fall into the trap that we have to get an ideology. We HAVE an ideology. Our fight is against racism, capitalism and imperialism and we are dedicated to building a socialist society inside the United States where the total means of production and distribution are in the hands of the State and that must be led by black people, by revolutionary blacks who are concerned about the total humanity of this world. And, therefore, we obviously are different from some of those who seek a black nation in the United States, for there is no way for that nation to be viable, if in fact the United States remains in the hands of white racists. Then too, let us deal with some arguments that we should share power with whites. We say that there must be a revolutionary black Vanguard and that white people in this country must be willing to accept black leadership, for that is the only protection that black people have to protect ourselves from racism rising again in this country.

Racism in the U.S. is so pervasive in the mentality of whites that only an armed, well-disciplined, black-controlled government can insure the stamping out of racism in this country. . . . We say . . . think in terms of total control of the U.S. Prepare ourselves to seize state power . . . and all around the world, the forces of liberation are directing their attacks against the U.S. It is a powerful country, but that power is not greater than that of black people. We work the chief industries in this country and we could cripple the economy while the brothers fought guerilla warfare in the streets. This will take some long range planning, but whether it happens in a thousand years is of no consequence. It cannot happen unless we start.[15]

The manifesto and fund raising

The manifesto, backed by the militant demands of BEDC members, resulted in the raising of a relatively large amount of funds in Detroit and nationwide. Some of these funds were made available to The League of Revolutionary Black Workers and were used to facilitate getting their message to a larger audience. Many of the funds raised were routed through IFCO who, in turn, disbursed various grants. BEDC received an initial grant of $80,000 with an additional $79,000 going to its associated research agency. Many local organizations received grants from IFCO after receiving approval from BEDC. DRUM received $8,000 with additional amounts going to other Detroit groups. The WCO, with John Watson as director, received $30,000. IFCO later earmarked an additional $200,000 for use by BEDC in 1969 but it is unclear how much of that money was ever delivered. League participation in, and on behalf of, BEDC had a major economic payoff.

These funds were put to effective use. The League established its own print shop (The Black Star Press), its own publishing concern (Black Star Publishing), established its own film production unit (Black Star Productions), and set up its own bookstore (Black Star Book Store). These facilities enabled the League to print and distribute their own materials thus reducing the need to rely on the good will of outsiders. It had previously had difficulty in getting material published because of reactions of some white printers. The ability to publish material freed them from the restrictions that this caused, reduced the degree of their vulnerability to outside pressures, and enabled them to expand their political education program. Other significant accomplishments included the making of a movie on the League history, *Finally Got the News*, a second movie dealing with drugs in the ghetto, and the distribution of films produced on other revolutionary groups such as El Fatah. They also published an important theoretical pamphlet by Ernie M. Kalimoto and a significant book presenting the political perspective of James Forman, by that time a League officer.[16]

The International Black Appeal

Another outgrowth of BEDC with great potential significance was the establishment of The International Black Appeal (IBA) with John Williams at its head.[17] This was a fund modeled after the United Jewish Appeal, Catholic Charities, and the Community Chest. All funds raised by the IBA were to be dispersed within the black community. A series of programs were planned: (1) emergency food and health centers were to be established; (2) a labor strike and defense fund was to be established; (3) legal defense services were to be provided; (4) a black-controlled welfare system was to be organized; and (5) housing and recreation programs were to be established. The labor defense fund was given an especially high priority because of the experiences of the ELRUM strike:

It happened that in that particular strike twenty-six workers were discharged. Many of them were not members of ELRUM but were people that management wanted to get rid of. But we felt a degree of responsibility to all the men because what happened was that naturally management and UAW was trying to make us the villains in this case: they wanted to make us the ones responsible for those workers losing their jobs. So we tried to do what we could to support them in terms of raising funds and we tried to arrange jobs for them. A number of them got back to work some six or seven months later without back pay.

But that strike taught us a lot. We knew at that point that what we had to do was to begin to organize workers in more plants and begin to organize the black community to relate to the struggle in the plants, in the city, in the state, and eventually around the country. That led to the formation of the League. Now the reason that that was necessary was because it became clear that no one group of workers in a single plant can win a struggle for control of a plant, even a struggle for justice in a plant, in an isolated situation. The only way that these struggles can be won is through the support from workers in other plants. And through support of the black community too. So we decided after the Eldon situation to set about organizing toward that end. And immediately after that, the League was created and we began to gather resources. We went into a long stage of getting resources for that organizational thrust.[18]

It was generally acknowledged that one could not ask workers, especially family men, to risk their jobs unless some alternative source of support was insured. The defense fund could provide that insurance and strengthen the League in the factories. The fund was designed to be supported entirely by black donations. Campaigns were conducted throughout the black community and attempts were made to get the IBA established as a "check-off" charitable contribution in the factories. It is not surprising that the auto companies and the union noted the association between the League and the IBA and viewed the fund with a jaundiced eye.

The IBA was unsuccessful in its attempt to get accepted as a regular part of the check-off contribution system in the factories. This greatly curtailed its fund-raising ability. Nevertheless, some funds were raised and a very limited start was made on some of the programs. This occurred primarily in the realm of sponsoring social events, athletic competitions, and providing limited support to blacks who had lost their jobs through militant activities.

Nonworker-oriented activities

Some activities deviated from the general League policy of concentrating major efforts on the work place and limiting community activities to the development of support. It is true that one intended function of the IBA was to provide financial security for persons losing their jobs as a result of militancy in the work place, but the fund also supported other types of community activities. There were two other occasions when the activities of the League appeared to be in conflict with the stated objective of organizing black workers at the point of production.

Watson brings the revolution to college

The first of these came in the academic year 1968–9. The *Inner City Voice* was short of operational funds. John Watson, an irregular student at Wayne State University, wished to retain a newspaper outlet so he ran for and was elected editor of *The South End,* the Wayne State University student newspaper.[19] The previous editor, Arthur Johnston, had changed the paper's name to *The South End* from the *Wayne Collegian.* The name change was done for the expressed purpose of attempting to relate the university community to the community located at the south end of the campus, which was poor, transient, and a mix of blacks, Indians, and southern whites. Under Johnston's editorship the paper took on a "counter-culture" cast. John Watson transformed the newspaper into a political organ. It represented the ideas of all revolutionary groups but gave prime focus to the black liberation struggle. It was possible to see the League's influence in the content of the paper. Mike Hamlin was senior editor and Luke Tripp edited a special issue on the history of the League. The masthead was changed in fall 1968 to read, "The Year of the Heroic Guerilla," and in the spring to read "one class-conscious worker is worth a hundred students." Both mastheads were flanked by a black panther at either end of the slogan facing each other.

This changed orientation caused dissatisfaction among many students, faculty, and alumni. Charges were levied by Wayne State University President Keast, among others, that the paper printed articles that were anti-Semitic and anti-Polish. Part of the charge was based upon the fact that the paper published articles that supported the Palestine Liberation Movement. The paper was more anti-Zionist than anti-Semitic. The anti-Polish charge was based on the free use of the word "pollack," usually in reference to white auto workers or Hamtramck police. The paper also reported that John Watson, Mike Hamlin, news editor Nick Medvecky, and international affairs editor Nikos Boyias met with two representatives of the National Liberation Front of South Vietnam in Windsor, Ontario. Both groups expressed solidarity with each other's revolutionary struggles.

The furor reached a peak on February 10, 1969, when Joe Weaver, a television newscaster of WJBK-TV — one of Detroit's more conservative media outlets — attempted to interview John Watson in his *South End* office regarding the controversy. Watson refused to be interviewed and ordered Weaver out of his office. Weaver refused to leave. One version of subsequent events states that John Watson attempted to leave the office, Weaver blocked his way, and then attacked Watson when he brushed past. A second version states that Watson attacked Weaver while attempting to throw him out of the office. Weaver brought assault charges against Watson. Watson was acquitted in a jury trial in which the TV-tapes of the confrontation were shown to the jury and Ken Cockrel served as one of the defense attorneys. Watson continued as editor and *The South End* continued to function as an organ of the black movement, reflecting League ideology during the remainder of the academic year. However, it broadened its coverage to include more of the traditional type of items normally published in student newspapers.

Watson's activities as editor of *The South End* undoubtedly helped to build student support for the League. However, *The Inner City Voice* ceased publication during this period. It is doubtful if the student paper reached as large a segment of the black community as had the *Voice,* despite regular distribution outside factory gates. It certainly could not relate to the black worker in the same manner as a newspaper that was clearly designated as a black paper for black workers.

Public schools and black students

Another League venture into community organizing came when the Detroit school board announced during the 1969–70 school year that it intended to decentralize control of the public schools.[20]. John Watson, acting as director of WCO called a conference attended by approximately 300 representatives from various community organizations. This conference formed a coalition group aimed at achieving community control of the schools: Parents and Students for Community Control (PASCC). At about the same time a Black Student United Front (BSUF) was formed with Mike Hamlin as its adviser. BSUF remained organizationally independent of PASCC but cooperated in the drive for community control as well as organizing student activities and propaganda programs in support of the League.

Three PASCC offices were set up. Workers ran for offices on school boards in an attempt to make community control mean workers' control. The UAW already had a major voice in the existing Detroit school board, which it did not wish to have weakened by power shifting to local community groups that were heavily influenced by the League. Consequently the UAW and the Detroit school board joined hands in opposing PASCC. PASCC did develop a great deal of community support. Its slates received upwards of 70,000 votes. However, it ultimately failed in its efforts to establish any significant degree of worker or community control over the schools in Detroit.

Control, Conflict, and Change Book Club

The second major deviation from a concentration of energy upon the black worker came in the fall of 1970 when the Control, Conflict and Change Book Club was organized by the Motor City Labor League.[21] Its membership included white middle-class liberals with a sprinkling of radicals. The club was quite successful and grew very large. However less than 2 percent of its approximately 700 members were black. The intent of the book club was to expose this population to radical literature with the hope of socializing the membership to a radical perspective. Members of the League cooperated with the book club by helping select books, lending speakers, and providing discussion leaders. The book club was justified in terms of principled cooperation with white radicals and by the hope that it might generate increased community-wide support for League activities. Whatever the justification, this sphere of activity remains inconsistent with the stated objective of organizing black workers at the point of production. It caused the diversion of much time and energy away from factory organizing.

Discussion

The League had an ideological view that stressed the importance of organizing black workers at the point of production, viewed community organizing as relatively less productive except as a vehicle to develop support for worker-centered activities, and downgraded the value of organizing members of the lumpen. Despite these orientations the League experienced an evolution in which community organizing became increasingly important and occupied increasing amounts of time. This change was a result of both tactical and latent ideological concerns.

The most obvious reason for the change in organizational focus was the growing realization that a black worker movement could not survive entirely on its own. It needed community support. If workers strike or otherwise damage either company or union they are subject to suspension and firing. A strong degree of community support makes it more difficult for either company or union to retaliate without at least a pretense of due process and cause. The *Michigan Chronicle* and black clergymen could publicize an issue so that it would both reach a larger audience and have greater respectability than if the League were the sole source of propaganda and education.

The League also needed money and the black community was the most likely source. It is expensive to put out a newspaper and print leaflets on a continuing basis. An ongoing organization needs to be able to rent space, have access to a printing press, typewriters, paper, newsprint, vehicles for distribution purposes, and occasionally a little food for those persons who dedicate so much of their time to the organization that they have no time to earn a living. There also has to be a certain amount of funds available to support workers who lose their jobs or are suspended because of militance in behalf of the revolution. Nothing is better calculated to inhibit direct action than the sight of co-activists unemployed and hungry as a consequence of fighting for the cause.

Thus it became necessary for League members to attempt to form alliances with the very elements in the community whom they perceived as class enemies. Black businessmen and clergymen are not normally those to whom revolutionaries turn for allies. This does not occur unless the revolutionaries perceive the struggle in terms of a war of national liberation rather than a class-based struggle to end capitalist exploitation. There were many nationalistically inclined members of the League who were quite ready to accept such an orientation. They were ideologically prepared to accept a program of community organizing because it would help to further the black struggle even if it did little for the proletariat.

Thus there were two tendencies within the League that contributed to the drift toward community organizing. There were those who supported it out of concern with pragmatic considerations and those who supported it because of their ideological orientations. Regardless of the initial attraction toward community organizational activities, it had a detrimental effect upon in-plant organizing. There was a limited number of cadre. They had a limited amount of time and energy. Any expenditure of these scarce resources upon community activities left less for in-plant work. It is true that the cadre could draw upon other League or revolutionary union members to help them but, as will be seen in

Chapter 10, the latter were the very group that was initially most likely to possess a nationalist perspective.

Despite these organizational problems the League continued to expand its base. Units of hospital and newspaper workers were formed. In addition to expanding its strength and membership in Detroit, the League moved to develop revolutionary union movements in steel and other nonautomobile industries located in industrial centers across the nation. Cooperation was given to, and aid provided for the organization of, black workers' caucuses in several cities across the nation. The League exhibited a real potential for organizational success wherever a sizable concentration of black workers was located in a metropolitan center possessing heavy industry. This potential for organizational success was not borne out by the subsequent history of the League. The decline of the League will be described in Chapter 8, and analysis made in subsequent chapters of the reasons for early League advances and subsequent League decline.

8. The League splits and dies

For a while the League continued to expand its base. Units of hospital and newspaper workers were formed. In addition to growth in Detroit, the League helped develop revolutionary union movements in steel and other nonautomobile industries located elsewhere. It cooperated with and helped to organize independent black worker caucuses in several cities across the nation. There appeared to be a potential for organizational success in all metropolitan centers possessing heavy industry and a sizable concentration of black workers.

Despite this apparently strong showing the League was racked with internal tensions, which eventually produced an organizational split.[1] Three of the seven-member executive board (John Watson, Ken Cockrel, and Mike Hamlin) resigned from the League on June 12, 1971, to work for another black Marxist–Leninist organization, the Black Workers' Congress. The public announcement of the resignations was withheld until after the August convention of the Black Workers' Congress. The remainder of the executive board continued to work for the League until it faded from the Detroit scene.

The split in the League resulted from ideological differences over a number of issues, including national consciousness, principled cooperation with white radicals, and the scope of the struggle. There was disagreement as to whether the struggle should be narrowly limited to an attack against racism and capitalism or broadened to include sexism and imperialism. Most disagreements can be traced to differential points of ideological emphasis in interpreting the cause of black exploitation. These differences in emphasis, in part, reflected a social division. The League included both workers and intellectuals who had different life experiences leading them to see the world differently. Thus they tended to analyze black exploitation in terms of different conceptual schemes. The split and the demise of the League may be best understood by examining the rationale given for the resignations and the League responses. The latent tensions manifested themselves in a split at this par-

153

ticular point in time because of the additional strains created by the establishment of the Black Workers' Congress.

The Black Workers' Congress

The League cadre had always been cognizant of the undefined nature of their relation to the national black struggle.[2] There was a great deal of discussion over alternative lines of development. One option, that which had been followed in the early years of the League, was to build a strong base in one key city (Detroit) that could be used as a model to be emulated by black worker groups in other cities. The second option was to "go national" in the sense of creating affiliated revolutionary union movements in various cities around the nation.

BEDC brought the League to national prominence in April 1969. The League cadre was forced to confront and resolve the issue of their relation to a national movement whether or not they were ready to make such a decision. There were several factors to be considered. The League cadre shared with many black Marxists a belief that there was a vacuum on the national level. No strong organization existed to provide a viable Marxist–Leninist leadership direction to the national black movement. It was argued that some organization had to fill that vacuum or the entire black struggle was in danger of being effectively wiped out or coopted. It was suggested that the League was the appropriate organization to take on this task.

It was generally agreed that the black Marxist–Leninist worker organization of the League was the proper one for the national black struggle but there was disagreement as to whether the League was in a position to take on the task. Expansion was questioned at a time when many revolutionary union movements appeared to be in danger of being destroyed in Detroit.

One position proposed for consideration was that the League had no option — time and circumstance dictated that they move without further delay. It was recognized that there were serious problems associated with franchising League affiliates around the country. The experiences of other national groups indicated that there was often a problem of national control over local affiliates. A local organization might act in direct contradiction to national policy but, by acting in the name of the national, create legal and other problems for the members of the national cadre.

The final decision was that a Black Workers' Congress was to be formed. A national convention was scheduled to be held in Gary, Indiana, in September 1971, after a year of planning. It was understood that the League of Revolutionary Black Workers was to be its key unit, its national showcase of a successful affiliated structure. The Congress itself would be a federation including the League, other similar worker organizations, student and community groups. The debate over the formation of the Congress and its relation to the League intensified the latent conflicts within the League cadre and provided the occasion for a split that had long been developing.

Motivations for the resignations

Cockrel, Hamlin, and Watson presented the rationale for their resignations in a thirty-page manuscript.[3] The best method of understanding their motivations is to closely examine the document. It begins by presenting a brief history of the League, which is more or less paralleled in Chapters 4 through 6 of this book. This was followed by the assertion that there had always been three tendencies within the organizational leadership, each of which had different ideological lines resulting in differences in social practice. These internal differences produced a constant struggle over questions of ideology, policy, programs, strategy, and tactics.

Those three tendencies can best be described as follows:

A. The proletarian revolutionaries, striving to function as socialist political leaders and workers in the struggle to build socialism and hasten the defeat of imperialism in the world.

B. The petty bourgeois opportunists who, while continually parading their "knowledge and understanding" of the principles of Marxism–Leninism, practiced revolution in a way that showed their disdain for not only the working class but every other stratum of the population that did not instantly recognize their "superior theoretical virtues" and anoint them with the title of leader of the masses which they so obviously coveted. The basic fear and disdain of the people that characterized their style of practice had the organizational effect of producing carefully studied stagnation.

C. The backward reactionary-nationalist lumpen-proletarians whose view of revolutionary struggle was one of equating such struggle to a popularity contest, in which the judges were the most reactionary, least conscious sections of the population and the prize was to be viewed by all as a "basic brother."[4]

The authors, considering themselves the proletarian revolutionaries, saw their political positions as reflecting a Marxist—Leninist view of the United States and the world:

We saw the fundamental contradiction in the world and the U.S. as existing between capital and labor, nonetheless recognizing that the color-caste nature of U.S. society gives a national character to the oppression of blacks within this society. Consequently, we feel that of all the forces in the U.S. proletariat, the black working class constitutes, by dint of its peculiarly acute oppression and a conscious history of relentless opposition to this oppression, the objective vanguard of the proletarian-led struggle to defeat imperialism and build socialism as a necessary step in creating a new world free of imperialist aggression and the degradation of the masses that accompanies the maintenance of the imperialist system.[5]

The authors stated that the petty bourgeois opportunists had no problems in accepting the political position outlined above but that they failed to translate their theory into practice. It was charged that this second group was not actively engaged in the hard day-to-day work necessary to build a movement. The document listed the major accomplishments of the League and asserted that these were primarily achieved by the proletarian revolutionaries. This was not done in order to glorify themselves as persons but to demonstrate that various ideological orientations lead to lines of behavior having predictable consequences.

The accomplishments fell into a number of separate areas. The first area included the establishment and structuring of the Labor Defense Coalition, the defense provided to James Johnson and the defendents in the Republic of New Africa shoot-out with police, and the education of the general public as to the class nature of justice in America. Other areas of accomplishment included the establishment of the League newspaper along with establishing publishing and film-making facilities that functioned as organs of political education. Not only were the other two tendencies accused of not aiding in these activities but it was charged that they actively opposed BEDC until after it had raised a certain amount of financial resources. They then were accused of attempting to seize control over these resources in order to use them for their own purposes.

One of the major points of contention discussed in the document was the question of principled cooperation with white radicals who were willing to accept the notion that black workers constituted the vanguard of the revolution. The proletarian revolutionaries believed that the necessity for such cooperation was derived both from theory and from the practical realities. It is not possible for unaided black workers to carry out a successful revolution against world capitalism. They need allies both within and without the United States. Thus it is essential for blacks to form alliances with white workers in the United States, with European workers, and with revolutionaries around the world.

It was in this light that participation in the Control, Conflict, and Change Book Club was justified:

This program served a two-fold purpose; one, the development of an organizational structure of whites committed to increasing their understanding of Marxism—Leninism so as to function as discussion leaders and staff for the book club, and two, the establishment of a forum wherein less highly developed whites can make contact with Marxist—Leninist revolutionaries and their programs free of the condescension so often characteristic of such meetings.[6]

The value of such programs of principled cooperation with white radicals is seen as having been demonstrated by the formation of organizations like the Motor City Labor League and the Labor Defense Coalition. It was felt that these groups had made concrete contributions to the League and to the black revolutionary struggle. It was charged that the other two tendencies within the League either grudgingly accepted such cooperation or greeted it with outright hostility.

A portion of the document was devoted to the specific discussion of the reactionary-nationalist tendency:

In discussing the reactionary nationalist section of the organization, it must be observed that it was present from the beginning of the League. The history of the leadership of this tendency was well known at the time, but this section "agreed" that Marxist—Leninist ideology and practice were correct, and expressed a willingness to struggle against the bourgeois and cultural nationalist tendencies.

Moreover, we observe that the history of reactionary nationalism, which precedes the history of the League, is a history of bankrupt politics and policies, laced with such idealistic perversities as astrology, mysticism, infantile militarism and adventurism. For years past such elements around the country and locally were continually involved in "clandestine plots" to "get it on" or to start the revolution through some dramatic act of violence. . . .

The record of disaster flowing from such elements is much too long to chronicle in this paper.

The nationalist elements attempted to disguise their reactionary line while using the organization as a "front" for various kinds of clandestine activity.

Nationalism was injected into the workers organizations through gossip and behind the back conversation rather than through the vehicle of open political discussion. In those instances when the question was openly discussed the left position was always accepted by the general membership of the organization. . . .

They did minimal organizational work, they refused to study, complaining that the material used in political education was too hard, too abstract, boring, etc.

They refused to seriously push the newspaper, the official organ of the League.

They lived in League facilities, but maintained them in a way that was not consistent with the minimum standards of a serious organization.

Non-black persons who were cooperating with the League were insulted and alienated by non-serious reactionary elements repeatedly.

The low standards of discipline resulted in numerous instances of petty offenses that drained legal and material resources from the struggle.

They received free legal service and medical service, and used their positions in the League as a basis for arrogant condescending parade inside the black community.

Such conditions are obviously intolerable inside a serious political organization guided by Marxist—Leninist principles.

It must be stated that we were guilty of gross liberalism in not pressing more vigorously for a resolution of such problems in a forward way. However, it must be stated that this kind of conduct was protected by the right wing [petty bourgeois opportunists] of the leadership.[7]

It was argued that the internal contradictions within the League made it impossible to maintain any semblance of democratic centralism. Violations of League rules rarely, and only in the most flagrant cases, met with disciplinary action. Political education was rendered almost totally ineffective. Concrete achievements were impeded. It was finally concluded that the League had to be superseded by another organization:

As a result of the inability of the League to solve its internal contradictions, at a time when black workers across the country were increasingly engaging in militant action against imperialism at the point of production, the left forces in the League were compelled by historical necessity to try and assist in building, with other proletarian forces around the country, an organizational form to unite such forces and carry the struggle to a higher stage. The new organizational form is the Black Workers' Congress. Initially, it was projected that the League, by dint of its experience, would be a key foundation stone in the new form.[8]

Other segments of the League spoke out in opposition to the Black Workers' Congress. They did not wish to expand beyond the Detroit auto plants. It was charged that they were parochial and that they took a narrow economistic position. The proletarian revolutionaries concluded that it was impossible for the League to close ranks and place all of its energies behind a move to build the Congress. Thus Ken Cockrel, Mike Hamlin, and John Watson felt it necessary to resign from the League and become full-time workers for the Congress.

The League response

The League response to these resignations and its own ultimate expulsion from the Black Workers' Congress on July 24, 1971, is presented in a series of documents put together by John Williams, Rufus Burke, and Clint Marbury.[9] Their analysis of League history and constituency differs from that presented above. They saw the League membership as comprising five groups:

Firstly there were the workers who comprised a substantial majority of the League. Their orientation was basically off of the racism that ran rampant in the plants. In addition the national consciousness of Black people given the revolts in Watts, California, Newark, New Jersey, Detroit, etc. had risen along racial lines predominantly. With the advent of the general consciousness of Blacks the plant struggles emerged led by the contact with some members who had political development. Basically this group was nationalist activist or Blacks whose consciousness had risen along racial lines and the subsequent tactics basically revolved around replacing white management and union personnel with Black. The overriding and binding factor of our group was getting the honkies off of our backs.

Secondly there were a few community people who attempted to provide us with resources based on their favoritism to one person or another. This group was inconsistent in its assistance and related basically in the aforementioned manner. Its political direction was not developed and the form of their assistance was to help some Black people who appeared to be doing something.

Thirdly there were elements who were jobless, on the run, etc. who had to be taken care of. It was via a few of our members that some of them were provided for and this became a strong motive for their allegiance. This group varied as few had political direction — most of them had none but all had strong nationalist tendencies. This group also characterized our greatest problem segment in terms of discipline, etc. However they were not educated to levels of understanding and thus they performed tasks of leafleting, getting the paper passed out, etc., as more of a payment for their being provided for in addition to their allegiance to certain people.

Fourthly there were the students who had begun to organize and relate to the League. As national consciousness grew in general, the specific form it had taken among students was enhanced by the student boycott of 1966 at Northern High School epitomizing the worsening conditions in Black schools. Our students were basically nationalistically oriented and moving to organize around and on that basis.

Fifthly there were the Black Marxist—Leninists. This group is the most crucial in terms of the direction of the organization and the manifestations of the split. Basically this group was comprised of about seven or eight people and there were different historical backgrounds that led to certain differences. One segment of the group had a long history of struggle together (Watson, Williams, Tripp, Baker — back to '61—'62) whereas the other sector came at varying points subsequent to and around '67.[10]

The executive board of the League is seen as having consisted of three elements: (1) black workers primarily oriented toward national consciousness; (2) a wing of the black Marxist—Leninists (the authors of this packet of documents) primarily oriented toward a national consciousness form of analysis; and (3) another segment of the black Marxist—Leninists primarily oriented toward class analysis (Hamlin, Cockrel, and Watson). This produced continual strife. Constant meetings were held to resolve the conflicts. Workers gradually quit coming to executive board meetings. The situation was seen as deteriorating as problems got worse rather than solved. The cadre that remained with the League after the split describes the problem as follows:

the major and fundamental problem in the leadership of the Marxist—Leninist group was the national question. This was the problem that had not been discussed. Some of us saw the form that Black people were taking obviously led to the recognition of independent nationhood. We also recognized this as a necessary struggle and that capitalism et al. must be liquidated in order to achieve this. The other sector viewed the Black struggle as a present form becoming subsumed at a later stage in a multi-racial party ruling America. At one point this faction saw the multi-racial party subsequent to the dictatorship of the Black proletariat ruling America until whites proved themselves by their practice and entered the multi-racial party. However, this position has been voted out in favor of the involvement of third world peoples, poor whites, and Blacks making up the multi-racial party in America. This faction also saw that nationalism was in essence reactionary and Ken Cockrel, Mike Hamlin and John Watson . . . indicated that they would purge themselves of all nationalism.[11]

Those using the class analysis were attacked for broadening the struggle to such an extent that it was diffuse, weak, and lacking in central focus. They were charged with wishing "to elevate the problems of women on par with capitalism by calling it sexism."[12] BEDC, the book club, and the Congress were seen as slaps at nationalism and the color-caste form of struggle. The call for a struggle against imperialism was seen as subsuming the black struggle to that of the majority. The ultimate outcome was viewed as antiwar demonstrations rather than struggles relating to the concrete conditions of blacks.

Watson, Hamlin, and Cockrel were accused of attempting to flood the masses with what they perceived as purely a class form of struggle. This was rejected as a fundamental error and the following alternative was proposed:

Our sector sees the revolutionary right to self determination and secession after capitalism is smashed. The Black liberation struggle in general and the Black workers' struggle in particular are definitely moves along these lines. The cry by Black people in general and Black workers in particular is "Black control of the Black community" as well as independence for Black people. We do not believe that Blacks can run America because the removal of capitalism does not stamp out racists. Our emphasis is on building the mass base of Black workers around proletarian consciousness relating to all groups principally who fight against racism, capitalism and imperialism while establishing a strong political, economic and military base.

On the other hand, our sector was erroneous in our application of Marxism–Leninism. The organization should have been organized around mass lines with corresponding measures and structures persons could have passed through to elevate themselves . . . The segment of Marxist–Leninists who believed in the right of self-determination and nationhood made the mistake of not using Marxist–Leninist methods correctly to guide the major concrete struggle.[13]

The resignations appear to have been welcomed by the League as a means of strengthening itself through the unification of its ideological position. A line was adopted stressing the organization of black workers around the issue of national consciousness, a black vanguard leading a socialist revolution to be followed by establishment of a separate black socialist state, and a party in which the leadership is elected by the mass membership.

For a brief period of time both Marxist–Leninist groups continued to function in Detroit.[14] Each attempted to draw its supporters from essentially the same population of black workers. A great deal of personal hostility developed between persons involved with each of the organizations. There was a battle for control over League-owned facilities (Black Star Publishing, Black Star Productions, Black Star Book Store, etc.). Gradually activities within the League slowed down. Overt Marxist–Leninist activities virtually disappeared from factories where DRUM, FRUM, and ELRUM had once flourished. The League faded out of existence and some of its cadre moved into the Communist League. The Black Workers' Congress continues but Ken Cockrel, John Watson, and James Forman are no longer with it. Mike Hamlin remains as a major figure. More will be said about the Black Workers' Congress in Chapter 11. In Chapter 9 factors contributing to the early League growth will be analyzed and the reasons for its demise explored in Chapter 10.

9. Why was the League initially so successful?

It is appropriate to pause at this point and examine the reasons for the initially high degree of receptivity among black workers to the League and its program. There are several factors that contributed to the initial League advances. These include national, local, and industrial developments in addition to characteristics of the League leadership cadre. The subject of this chapter is an examination of the impact of the civil rights movement, urban insurrections, development of a separatist rhetoric, national mood of protest, development of a Marxist rhetoric, racial segregation, changing composition of the work force, history of the auto industry and the UAW, weakness of the TULC, and characteristics of the leadership cadre of the League.

The civil rights movement

The civil rights movement emerged as a mass movement in the mid-fifties as a result of a coming together of several developments affecting black aspirations, expectations, perceived deprivations, and perceptions of viability of protest. The 1954 Supreme Court school desegregation decision combined with a long-term economic improvement to stimulate black aspirations at the same time that the growing gap between black and white standards of living increased black perceptions of relative deprivation.[1] The example of gains resulting from black militance during and immediately after World War II had demonstrated the potential effectiveness of black protest activities.[2] This was the societal context existing on December 1, 1955, when Mrs. Rosa Parks refused the order of a Montgomery bus driver to give up her seat and was consequently arrested.

This incident provided the spark that led to the formation of the Montgomery Improvement Association, the conduct of an extended boycott of Montgomery buses by black patrons, the desegregation of the bus system, and the launching of Martin Luther King and his program of nonviolent resistance to national prominence. This provided further evidence

162

of the viability of a program of black protest as a weapon to achieve social change and it stimulated a series of similar boycotts throughout the South.[3] In 1960 four black college students escalated the level of confrontation tactics by sitting-in at a Greensboro lunch counter. This action stimulated both a wave of imitators and violent resistance.[4] White violence brought forth both anger from the black community and support from sympathetic white liberals. Northern support was manifested in picketing of northern chain affiliates of stores under attack in the South.

This combination did achieve a significant degree of desegregation, which further stimulated black aspirations and confidence in the potential utility of protest activities. The civil rights movement evolved throughout the early sixties. Tactics escalated in militancy as boycotts and sit-ins were supplemented by hit-and-runs, mass marches, the blocking of streets, the impeding of construction vehicles, and voter registration drives. These tactics aroused continued white resistance in the South, which often was expressed in violence stimulating increased liberal support for the black cause. This support eventually manifested itself in federal intervention and in limited black progress.[5]

Civil rights victories further stimulated black aspirations and contributed to a growing optimism among blacks that black liberation could indeed be achieved by blacks willing to fight for their rights. Consequently the civil rights movement, initially largely comprised of middle-class blacks and white allies, recruited increasing numbers of working-class blacks into its ranks. This brought into the movement an increased number of less well-disciplined participants at the same time that there was growing dissatisfaction with the rate and scope of change. All of this contributed to an increased militance of tactics, decreased commitment to nonviolence, increased advocacy of self-defense, and the first appearance of violence on the part of blacks.[6]

Urban insurrections

By 1964 it was becoming increasingly obvious to blacks that the civil rights movement was not able to accomplish a basic change in the life situation of black Americans — especially not in the North. The civil rights movement demonstrated that blacks could organize themselves and collectively exert sufficient pressure upon whites so as to coerce concessions but these concessions were largely symbolic in nature. A certain amount of desegregation was achieved in the South and there was an increase in the number of blacks who could exercise the franchise but there was little real increase in the extent to which blacks could control their own lives and little real improvement in economic opportunities or standard of living.

Thus increased aspirations and increased perception of power existed in combination with increased anger and bitterness. Black ghetto residents had neither a moral nor a strategic commitment to nonviolence. They admired the example of southern black demonstrators who had stood their ground in the face of police opposition. Harlem, Rochester, and Philadelphia all experienced urban disorders in 1964. Each of these stimulated a response on the part of governmental officials, which demonstrated to many blacks that urban insurrections could prove to be a viable tactic for black advancement.[7] A riot ideology emerged and the four years between 1964 and 1968 were characterized by the extensive tactical use of urban insurrections as part of the evolving black revolt.

This assertion requires some clarification. I do not mean to imply that any of the insurrections were planned or deliberately instigated. I do mean to suggest that in every black ghetto in America numerous black activists developed the belief that urban insurrections invariably had two important consequences: violent police repression stimulated increased black solidarity and anger; and civil and governmental agencies responded with moves that increased the number of jobs for blacks and generally improved social and economic opportunities in those cities where there were insurrections. This stimulated an increased sense of efficacy and pride in black Americans. The Detroit insurrection of July 1967 was the largest and the most brutally repressed of any during the four-year period of insurrectionary activity. Consequently the fall of 1967 found Detroit blacks exhibiting a contradictory combination of anger, frustration, pride, and sense of collective efficacy.

The growth of a separatist rhetoric

The Nation of Islam had long been advocating the establishment of a separate black nation to be created out of a portion of the United States.[8] Malcolm X was suspended from the Nation in December 1963. He founded the Organization for Afro-American Unity in 1964. He continued to advocate a program of black separatism although he seems to have abandoned the goal of a separate black nation. Malcolm X was assassinated in February 1965 but his influence did not end. Many young blacks read and were influenced by his autobiography and his speeches.[9]

James Meredith organized what he called "A March Against Fear" in the summer of 1966. The march was designed to go through Mississippi. It attracted relatively little attention until Meredith was shot. Stokely Carmichael was part of the group that carried on. As the march wore on Carmichael began attracting increasing attention and support by shouting out the slogan "Black Power." The slogan attracted increased attention and stimulated much debate.

Supporters of black power increasingly gave it a separatist interpretation. This was embodied in a book that Carmichael co-authored with Charles V. Hamilton.[10] Both the Congress of Racial Equality (CORE) and the Student Non-violent Coordinating Committee (SNCC) gradually shifted toward a separatist orientation. Blacks increasingly took charge of their own movement. Whites either left voluntarily or were asked to leave. There was little support in the black community for the establishment of a separate black nation – possibly only because this was believed to be an unrealistic objective – but there was a strong and growing belief among blacks that integration was not working and that blacks had to take charge of their own future. This belief took many forms, ranging from the drive for community control over black schools, to separate black occupational and professional organizations, and to a drive for black capitalism.

The national mood of protest

The national mood in the fall of 1967 was one of strife and ferment. The black protest had continually escalated but blacks were not alone in their willingness to engage in collective protest action. The Mexican-American fight for equality began at Delano, California, in 1965 and escalated over the next few years.[11] The Puerto Rican community was also on the move. The Young Lords had been formed in Chicago in 1965. There was also a rising tide of militancy in the Indian community although most of their more dramatic acts of protest did not come until later. The sixties had been marked by a continual wave of protests by activists. The gay liberation movement was beginning to take shape. The women's liberation movement was strong and growing more and more militant with every passing day.

The free speech movement was born during an extended controversy that ripped through the Berkeley campus from September 10, 1964, to January 4, 1965.[12] This was the beginning of a student movement that disrupted campuses all across the nation for several years.

The student revolt was complex and involved many different issues. Free speech was a major concern at Berkeley but the issue surfaced primarily because there was an attempt to restrict student attempts to bring about significant changes in the community around them. The student movement encompassed a drive for expanded civil rights along with counter-cultural elements seeking freer life-styles. But perhaps the most important element in the student movement was that which sought to bring an end to the war in Vietnam. The antiwar drive started with students but it soon spread far beyond the college campuses. Important elements drawn from all segments of American society joined in a massive protest against the war. The ambiance of the entire nation was one of militance and protest against the establishment as 1967 drew to a close.

The rise of a Marxist rhetoric

The period of the mid to late sixties saw an increasing espousal of a rhetoric and ideology that incorporated Marxist concepts and revolutionary yearnings.[13] This was found among both black and white segments of the protest movements. Students for a Democratic Society (SDS) increasingly included in their ranks persons advocating programs of action that were closely allied to the programs of the old left. The Young Socialist Alliance (YSA) was very active in the student and peace movements. The YSA was the student affiliate of the Socialist Workers Party. Marxist rhetoric was being espoused by black activists — sometimes in a relatively pure form and other times mixed with separatist notions. The Black Panther Party was formed in 1966. SNCC members increasingly advocated a version of a Marxist program as did many members of CORE. Carmichael and Hamilton published *Black Power* in 1967. Malcolm X increasingly incorporated Marxist notions in his analysis shortly before he was killed. It was very difficult for young politically involved blacks to remain unexposed to a Marxist form of analysis.

Ghetto segregation

The transformation of Detroit into a black city was described in Chapter 3. The black population was constantly increasing while the white population was decreasing. Detroit areas of black residence constantly expanded but there was little if any reduction in the extent of segregation. Blacks struggled against residential segregation and succeeded in desegregating neighborhood after neighborhood. One by one Russell

Woods, Fitzgerald, Bagley, and other neighborhoods would have their all-white character violated.[14] However, each neighborhood seemed to follow the same pattern. The neighborhood aged and became less desirable. Eventually someone moving away would be unable to find a white buyer who could, or would, meet his price. Being physically removed from community pressures and needing money, the departing homeowner would sell his home to a black family.

Initially the neighborhood community would rally together and vow to stand firm. They stressed the positive aspects of integration and assured each other of their commitment to remain an integrated neighborhood. However the residents in these neighborhoods tended to be older than the typical Detroiters. Death created some vacancies. Contracting family size as children moved away led other persons to seek smaller homes. The general tendency was that only blacks could be found to purchase houses in the neighborhood once it began to change racially. The proportion of blacks continually increased until the "tipping point" was reached and a panic flight of whites ensued. Gradually the racial composition changed from all white to predominantly black. The black area of residence expanded but no significant desegregation occurred.

Changing composition of the work force in Detroit auto plants

In Chapter 2 the changing racial composition of the labor force involved in auto production was discussed and data cited revealing that black auto workers were disproportionately concentrated in Detroit. Chrysler plants had as high as 60 to 80 percent of their work force comprised of black workers. Other Detroit area plants had similar proportions. Blacks comprised an even higher proportion of workers on the least desirable shifts and in those departments that had the hardest, dirtiest, most dangerous, and generally least desirable jobs. Thus it was possible to find specific departments on certain shifts that were left virtually without a white face. Those few workers who were not black often were Arab. The second half of the decade of the sixties brought even more basic and fundamental changes in the work force composition, which helped to lay the groundwork for the emergence of the League.

The recessions of 1957–8 and 1960–1 greatly retarded the expansion of the work force engaged in auto production.[15] Rapid economic growth returned in 1963 and was accelerated during the escalation of the war in Vietnam in 1964. This brought about a great increase in auto production. All automobile plants increased their rates of hiring and greatly altered the social composition of their labor force. Not only did the number of black workers increase but the proportion of young workers greatly expanded. The UAW estimated that as of 1969 approximately 36 percent of auto workers employed by Chrysler were under thirty years of age. It was similarly estimated that one-third of the General Motors work force and 30 percent of Ford's workers were also under thirty. Besides being young the workers had little seniority. The proportion of workers with under five years of seniority was 51 percent at Chrysler, 41 percent at Ford, and 40 percent at General Motors.

Thus the economic upswing had an impact upon the composition of the work force but so did the insurrection of July 1967.[16] While the first wave of studies of the Detroit insurrection tended to show that the majority of participants were currently employed, it was nevertheless believed in Detroit that unemployment was somehow related to the propensity toward violent insurrection. Consequently the New Detroit Committee undertook a program in cooperation with local industry to increase employment opportunities for blacks — especially those who had previously been considered to be the hard-core unemployed, that is, virtually unemployable.

Some efforts had been begun in this direction even before the July uprising. They were largely in response to urban uprisings in other ghettos across the country and were designed to prevent a similar occurrence in Detroit. The Greater Detroit Board of Commerce created a Manpower Committee in May 1967. It was designed to act as a coordinating body for some 175 job placement agencies in Detroit. One of its initial tasks was to find jobs for 10,000 hard-core unemployed members of the black community. Little progress had been made in this direction when the July rebellion broke out.

The New Detroit Committee was established after the insurrection was crushed. It joined forces with the Manpower Development Committee of the Greater Detroit Board of Commerce. They set up a center for the recruitment of unemployed workers, which eventually located at the corner of Twelfth and Clairmont — next door to the "blind pig" that was raided to ignite the rebellion. The center placed more than 1,700 persons in jobs, of which approximately 800 were still employed in April 1968. The same two organizations cooperated with CORE, NAACP, and the Franklin-Wright Settlement to establish job centers, which were initially manned by Chrysler representatives. Approximately 645 job applicants were referred to Chrysler during the month that its representatives manned the centers. Approximately half of this original group was still employed by Chrysler in April 1968. This group was supplemented by additional hirings of persons referred by the centers after Chrysler representatives ceased to man them. Ford Motor Company also followed a policy of hiring the hard-core unemployed. They used the former Total Action Against Poverty centers and hired 4,600 persons. The Ford retention rate as of April 1968 was higher than their normal experience — almost 80 percent of those hired from this hard-core group remained on the job.

The campaign to hire the hard-core unemployed was not motivated by altruism. It was designed to reduce the chance that Detroit would have a repeat of the July violence. Nevertheless there was a change in hiring practices by the automobile companies. Many of the traditional criteria for employment were either reduced or waived. Many persons who were previously considered unemployable now had jobs. The program did not operate totally without rancor. It was charged — with some validity — that Ford set up many of its hiring locations sufficiently far from the ghetto that it was assured that a significant proportion of those hired would be white. Nevertheless the net result was a basic change in the composition of the work force in auto plants. This was especially true of Chrysler. The work force was becoming increasingly black, increasingly young, and was beginning to include significant numbers of those previously considered to be unemployable. In other words the work force in the auto plants was increasingly beginning to resemble those elements of the black community who waged the July insurrection.

History of the auto industry and the UAW

In Chapter 2 a brief history of blacks in the auto industry and in the UAW was presented. Blacks had largely been excluded from jobs in the auto industry until war-induced labor shortages, combined with expanded production for defense purposes, forced the companies to open their doors to black workers. The one exception to this pattern was Henry Ford, who hired workers for his River Rouge plant as an insurance policy against unionization. The unions similarly tended to exclude blacks from membership until the exigencies of a strike situation forced them to bring in black members rather than lose the strike.

The opening of factory doors to black employment and union doors to black membership in no way insured black workers of equality either on the job or in the union hall. Black workers tended to be concentrated in the least desirable jobs and consistently earned less than their white co-workers because of their disproportionate occupational distribution. Race continued to be a factor in hiring, upgrading, and especially in admission to craft occupations. Black unionists often found social barriers within the unions. Perhaps of even greater importance is the fact that they found the local unions to be dominated by those whites who had preceded them in the occupations that they currently held. Polish-Americans, who were not known for an exceptionally high level of racial tolerance, occupied the leadership posts in many local unions.

The weakness of TULC

Black workers had little voice in controlling decisions either on the job or in their unions. Local unions and the International leadership were both dominated by whites. Blacks had had a certain amount of influence as long as the union leadership had been split between competing factions. The Communist-led faction had consistently championed black rights and supported the black position on many issues. The Reuther faction virtually destroyed the Communist faction between 1946 and 1948. In doing so they also destroyed any viable independent black voice in the UAW. Almost a decade later a caucus of black unionists formed the TULC, which did manage to develop a degree of black power within the union largely as a consequence of their influence in the larger black community. However, they never organized the rank-and-file workers to the degree of earlier caucuses. They gradually weakened themselves with internal dissension and were further weakened by the development of competing community groups who were able to wield influence with Detroit blacks. The TULC had declined to relative ineffectiveness by the late 1960s.

The composition of the League leadership cadre

The leadership cadre of the League of Revolutionary Black Workers was a mixed group but one that was able to communicate with the workers in the automobile plants. The cadre developed a theoretical syncretism. They had a basic Marxist—Leninist orientation, blended with various elements of nationalist thought. There is always a possibility that the cadre of any such movement will become so abstract and abstruse in its patterns of thought that it becomes totally incapable of reaching or communicating with workers. There were elements in the social background and experiences of the League leadership cadre that militated against this. Thus it may prove valuable to examine briefly some characteristics of the leadership cadre.

The executive board of the League consisted of seven persons: General Baker, Ken Cockrel, Mike Hamlin, Luke Tripp, John Watson, John Williams, and Chuck Wooten.[17] Four of these (Baker, Tripp, Watson, and Williams) had had extended contact with one another over a period of years. They had all been members of the special seminar on capital conducted by Martin Glaberman and had all been part of the group arrested in the Olympic protest. John Watson met and became close friends with Ken Cockrel and Mike Hamlin during a period when he worked for the *Detroit News*.[18] Mike Hamlin was a driver distributing the *News*, Ken Cockrel was his assistant, and John Watson worked in the distribution area. General Baker became acquainted with Chuck Wooten while employed at Dodge Main.

John Watson was born and raised in Detroit. His father worked as a janitor until John left home but he gradually moved up through the hierarchy at the Post Office until he occupied a supervisory post. Watson's mother began as a postal clerk but also advanced to a supervisory post. Watson graduated from high school and went to Wayne State University, which he attended off and on over a number of years. He only lacked a few credit hours for graduation as of spring 1976. He was always active in political groups.[19] He worked with CORE in 1960 but found it to be too conservative. He moved on to SNCC but was expelled along with the entire Detroit chapter for trying to bring direct action to the North. Then over the course of time he worked with NAC, the Freedom Now Party, and Uhuru.

John Williams was born in Louisiana and raised in Detroit. His mother was a domestic and his father worked as a cook. Williams graduated from high school and Wayne State University. He was active in most of the same political organizations as John Watson. General Baker was born and raised in Detroit. His father was an operative at Dodge Main as was Baker himself after graduation from high school. He had been a member of Uhuru, the Revolutionary Action Movement (RAM), and had been to Cuba in 1964.[20] Luke Tripp was born in Tennessee and raised in Detroit. His parents were on welfare for a good part of his youth but his father eventually found work as an elevator operator and his mother as a domestic. Tripp was educated in the Catholic school system and is a high school graduate. He was a member of Uhuru.

Ken Cockrel was born in Royal Oak Township just outside the Detroit city limits.[21] Both of his parents were from the deep South. His father worked at Ford Motor Company in Highland Park. Cockrel's parents died when he was twelve years of age and he went to live with an aunt and uncle. His uncle was a factory worker and his aunt a cashier in a supermarket. Cockrel quit high school in eleventh grade and joined the Air Force. After discharge he attended Wayne State University as part of a program for adults who had not completed high school. He then attended Wayne State University Law School and graduated in 1967.

Mike Hamlin was born in Mississippi and raised in Detroit. His father was a factory worker. He did not go beyond high school and I am uncertain as to whether he graduated. Hamlin held a series of jobs in and around Detroit. He worked briefly in the auto plants before finally becoming a truck driver for the *Detroit News*. Hamlin had been actively associated with a variety of radical and nationalist groups in Detroit including the Communist Party, the Socialist Workers Party, NAACP, CORE, and the Republic of New Africa. I have much less information on Chuck Wooten. He was born and raised in Detroit. His father was a blue-collar factory worker and Wooten himself was an operative at Dodge Main. I am uncertain as to his level of education. Wooten is the only one of the executive board who did not have an extensive history of political activism and who does not appear to have developed a sophisticated political understanding prior to the founding of the League.

Summary discussion and conclusions

Thus the year following the July insurrection saw the confluence of many forces favoring the rise of the League of Revolutionary Black Workers. The black revolt had evolved from nonviolent protests of middle-class blacks and liberal white allies. Tactics escalated in degree of militance. The base broadened to include increasing numbers of working-class and marginal working-class blacks. Increasingly, whites either voluntarily left the movement or were driven out. The movement increasingly took on a separatist and/or Marxist rhetoric. The culmination of the black revolt was the wave of urban insurrections beginning in 1964 and peaking in 1967. The Detroit insurrection was brutally repressed, leaving many members of the Detroit black community both proud for having fought back and angry over the repression.

The growing level of militance in the black community was paralleled by the increased ambiance favoring protest and confrontation on the national level. The civil rights movement had given way to the student and antiwar movements as vehicles for the involvement of militant white youth. The antiwar movement kept expanding to take in more and more persons and escalating the militancy of its tactics. These trends were supplemented by the rise of the women's and gay liberation movements.

Meanwhile the composition of the Detroit labor force in Detroit's auto plants was altered by the expansion of the economy combined with deliberate postinsurrection attempts by the auto companies to hire the hard-core unemployed. The work force was becoming increasingly black, increasingly young, and included more and more members of the marginal working class. These were the very societal elements that had previously been most exposed, and most responsive, to the growing mood of militance and revolt. Their inclinations in this direction set the context within which the cadre of League leadership could operate.

The leadership cadre were readily able to communicate with workers because they shared the same backgrounds. Some members of the cadre were southern-born as were many of the workers. Most members of the cadre were either from working-class backgrounds and/or had extensive work experiences. They were not intellectuals who were so removed from the culture and experiences of black workers as to be unable to communicate. The nature of the ghetto is such that class differences are less likely to result in physical and social isolation for blacks than for whites. But even that degree of isolation normally found between middle- and working-class blacks was missing in the case of the League leadership cadre and auto workers.

The leadership cadre had also had a history of political activism and education. In most cases they were able to convey to workers a rudimentary form of this radical ideology in understandable language and with a content that was closely tied into the history of workers in Detroit and particularly in the auto industry. It was not hard for League members to point to the racial distribution of jobs in the plants, to the white domination of local unions, to white control over the UAW at the International level and link these conditions to the racism experienced in Detroit and the society at large. It was relatively easy to educate workers to the history of the UAW and the industry and convince them that they had no friends other than themselves. Workers were unlikely to resist a Marxist rhetoric both because of its increased prominence among protesters nationally, its increased prominence in the black revolt, and the memory of the Communist Party as virtually the only group that had consistently fought for black rights within the UAW. The League of Revolutionary Black Workers had an ideal context in which to develop and grow and initially had the quality of leadership to make maximal use of this opportunity. However, while this opportunity was used to stimulate an initial growth spurt, the impetus could not be sustained. The reasons for this will be discussed in Chapter 10.

10. Why did the League die?

There are always a multiplicity of factors involved in the death of any organization and the destruction of the League of Revolutionary Black Workers is no different in this respect. Some of the causes were external to the League and some were internal. One would have to include among the external causes the actions of the various automobile manufacturing companies, the leadership of the various local unions within which the respective revolutionary union movements were organizing, the International UAW leadership, and several law enforcement agencies. Most of the internal causes may be traced, directly or indirectly, to strains in the ideology evolved by the League. In many ways the internal weaknesses were probably more significant than the external attacks. However, the external attacks cannot be ignored.

External enemies

In Chapter 2 the evolution of the auto industry and the UAW were described revealing the fact that blacks were relative latecomers to the industry. The River Rouge Ford plant was the only one that employed significant numbers of blacks prior to World World II. The proportion of black auto workers grew after the war until it constituted a majority on certain shifts and in a number of plants. This historical pattern produced a situation in which the majority of high-seniority and retired workers were white while the majority of younger workers, especially on the least attractive shifts and in the least desirable departments, were black. In many, if not most, cases the political structure of the local union was dominated by whites.

This created the situation in which black workers could look around them, observe the pattern, and conclude that they were victims of racism. This conclusion was reinforced as black workers developed an increased knowledge of UAW and auto industry history. Black workers sent out a demand for an end to racism. This demand was made more

174

strident by safety conditions that resulted in a large number of injuries disproportionately concentrated among blacks due to their disproportionate concentration in the more dangerous jobs.

White workers did not empathize with the call to end racism because they did not believe that racism existed. They felt that their higher concentration in better jobs, the greater likelihood of holding a post as a foreman or a union steward, and their domination of local union offices were the result of their greater seniority. They could not accept the charge that seniority was a "racist" concept. They did not believe that they should be held accountable for the fact that blacks had been excluded from the industry at earlier periods in history. This had nothing to do with them or their seniority. They had worked long and hard to get it and they were not about to let anyone erode its value. Their advice to blacks was simply to wait: if blacks waited long enough they would develop seniority and would gradually move into better jobs, become foremen, become union stewards, and take over control of union locals.

When the revolutionary union movements began to organize in the plants and the rhetoric began to take on a more strident tone, the lack of sympathy of the whites turned into outright hostility. In many cases this did not require much of a change inasmuch as many white auto workers had initially high levels of racial prejudice. It was not a pleasant experience especially for those who thought of themselves as relatively unprejudiced, to be referred to as a "racist pig," a "honkey," a "pollack," or a "devil." It was particularly unpleasant to hear those terms coming from someone who was a "Communist," a "revolutionary," and a "black nationalist." The white workers had lived through the Detroit insurrection and read newspaper articles describing alleged black plots to invade white neighborhoods and shoot white children playing in the streets.[1] These "un-Americans" supported the Viet Cong and, what was most upsetting of all, they wanted to destroy the system of union rights and prerogatives that protected the job security of long-time union members. This could not be tolerated.

It is not surprising that the local union leadership did everything it could to destroy the various revolutionary union movements. There is little question that the local leadership leaned over backwards to interpret all bylaws and contract provisions in such a way as to hinder the League at every turn. It is not clear from the evidence whether elections were stolen through overtly illegal tactics but it is clear that the union leadership made it considerably more difficult for a member of DRUM or ELRUM to win an election than it did for a nonmember. It is also clear that the union leadership did not "push" as hard as they normally did on a grievance protesting the discharge of a DRUM or ELRUM leader.

A perusal of the evidence suggests that the actions of the UAW International leadership were midway between objective neutrality and the overtly hostile opposition of the local leadership. They clearly felt threatened by the League. Wildcat strikes are a violation of contract that constitute an attack upon both parties to the initial agreement and make later negotiations more difficult. Wildcats enable management to question the value of an agreement with a union that cannot or will not enforce that contract against the wishes of some portion of its rank-and-file membership. Wildcats also cause a great expenditure of time and energy that interferes with the normal conduct of union affairs.

The International leadership and, to a lesser extent, much of the older local union leadership was especially resentful of being called racist, class collaborators. Most of the long-time union activists were veterans of numerous civil rights battles. Many members of the leadership were old-time socialists. All of them had risked a great deal to build the union. It was dangerous to be a union organizer in the thirties. There was much violence. The UAW top leadership felt that they had earned their credentials as radicals and humanitarians. They, along with many of the older members and local union officials, had fought for equality and justice and now they were attacked as racist and establishment.

It is clear that the International wanted to see the League disappear from the Detroit scene. They contributed to that disappearance through a series of public statements that cast aspersions upon the League. They also contributed to that disappearance by attempting to increase black visibility in the UAW leadership. It is — probably, but not clearly — demonstrated that they also were a bit more agreeable than normal when "pressing" grievances regarding management firing or harassing League activists. How much they went beyond this is impossible to tell.

It is hardly necessary to state the rationale for management's opposition to a revolutionary Marxist–Leninist organization in the automobile plants. It is difficult to determine the exact manner in which the company acted out its opposition. Their actions in discriminatory firings of persons believed to be revolutionary union movement activists are only the more obvious form of opposition. It may be the case that the *Michigan Chronicle* report, which implied that the election of Ron

March might trigger the removal of Dodge Main from Detroit, was the result of a "leak" from management. There is no evidence to that effect but it is a plausible way for the company to attempt to influence the outcome of an election. It is also possible (again there is no evidence that it is the case) that police activities directed at League and revolutionary union movement supporters were stimulated by the management of one or more of the various auto companies. However, it is also possible that the police did not require any prodding to behave in such an aggressively hostile manner.

Similarly it should not be necessary to state the reasons why law-enforcement agencies would be hostile to a black Marxist–Leninist revolutionary organization within their jurisdiction. There is little doubt that law enforcement activities hindered the operations of the League. One need only cite police infiltration and observance, the Grand Jury investigations of BEDC, the violent confrontations that took place after the election returns were announced during Ron March's attempt to be elected union trustee, the ticketing of several cars and the seizure of the registration and plates of another, which were used in revolutionary union movement electoral campaigns. The image of harassment damaging to the League is further buttressed by several arrests of League members, which did not result in convictions. This pattern of opposition could be interpreted as harassment but it is not possible conclusively to demonstrate a pattern of *illegal* harassment. It is clear that there was a pattern of conflict that must have damaged League operations.

The combination of management, local union leadership, International UAW leadership, and law enforcement agencies made a powerful coalition of enemies that the League had to combat in order to survive. However, it is possible that, if the League had been internally united, it might have been able to withstand these external attacks. It would not have been able to conduct a successful socialist revolution in the early 1970s but it might have been able to survive as a center of radical ideology and radical organization among black workers. It was not internally sound and much of that unsoundness resulted from internal inconsistencies within the League's ideological stance.

Consequences of ideological strain

The internal ideological split in terms of class versus national orientation caused problems in developing a consistent line of behavior in day-to-day operations. This was especially evident in the making of *Finally*

Got The News. Some of the more racially conscious League members drove white film makers out of League headquarters and away from the plants where they were filming various scenes.[2] This conflict also produced problems in political education as evidenced by the following statement by Mike Hamlin:

We had no meaningful political education program. We tried it a number of times but it was sabotaged by the attitude of reactionary nationalists. They didn't want to study Marxism so they used various tactics to stop the classes. That is not to say that some of our instructors were not dull for workers, but that's another question. The nationalists would say that Marx and Lenin were white and not relevant.[3]

In order to conserve space we will limit ourselves to a few additional examples of problems in relation to white radicals that were caused by the more nationally conscious members of the League. League leadership decided to engage in a legal struggle in an attempt to get the twenty-six persons fired for the ELRUM strike returned to work with full back pay.[4] It was felt that the struggle, whether or not successful, would be a useful organizing activity. If it were to be successful, it would be likely to have a fantastic payoff in increased worker support. The team of lawyers recruited to aid in the effort were white. This drew opposition, undermining the effort. It is difficult to get a lawyer's best work when he feels rejected by those persons for whom he is working.

Another conflict emerged when the League attempted to improve the quality of writing in its newspaper by holding journalism classes conducted by sympathetic white journalists.[5] The classes were attacked and undermined. The nationalistically oriented members of the League accused the instructors of teaching "white journalism." One of the more overt manifestations of hostility toward whites was exhibited by some individuals who distributed League leaflets at plant gates. Hamlin describes it as follows:

We used the *Inner City Voice* office to draw on a reservoir of people from the street to distribute (*drum*). Some were nationalists who had nothing else to do but sit around our offices. Others were students. Others were just off the street. We got them all involved in going out to the plant to leaflet. . . . Some of them went out because they thought that it would be a chance to hit some whites, to jump on some whites.[6]

It is also possible that this internal contradiction hindered the organization of a multiracial worker movement for socialism. It is doubtful if many white workers were at the stage of political consciousness at which they would respond to such an appeal. Some probably were. However, that is a moot point as no real effort in such a direction was made. As Mike Hamlin stated:

from the beginning at Dodge we wrote off any possible mobilization of white workers during that period. That is not to say that some of us did not understand that the working class is multi-national and that there has to be a unity of the entire working class. But during the time, we deliberately and consciously wrote off white workers.[7]

Activities became too diffuse

Not all problems were caused by the nationalists. The class-oriented members of the League established a program of activities that involved them in actively cooperating with white radicals for extended periods of time and a variety of purposes. Some of these activities, such as the Control, Conflict and Change Book Club, took a great deal of time that many felt could not be spared. If there was a shortage of people who were willing to do the hard day-to-day work of putting out leaflets, writing and publishing a newspaper, distributing propaganda, speaking, etc., then any additional tasks should be taken on only after careful consideration of their value. Any activity that had a relatively low pay-off in terms of the League's major thrust, organizing black workers at the point of production, should have been bypassed. The book club may have been an activity with some positive payoff but it also may have spread the League too thinly.

It is possible also that some of the varied concerns with the war, prison conditions, and other general racial issues — while no doubt valuable in and of themselves — might better have been left to others while the League members concentrated on conditions more closely tied to black workers. This appraisal, to a lesser extent, may apply also to those activities centering around the Detroit public school system. It was important to build a base of support in the black community, but a small organization can destroy itself by being involved in so many things that it cannot handle any of them well.

The problems involved in attempting to maintain a revolutionary stance while engaged in reformist activities were discussed in Chapters 6 and 8. The attempt to actually achieve reforms may necessitate downplaying political orientations that create a vulnerability to charges of opportunism and hypocritical behavior. Open statements of political orientations are likely to destroy any chance of achieving reform. This dilemma was never adequately resolved.

The attraction of new recruits should be the major reason why any revolutionary group would wish to work for, and achieve, reforms. New recruits were sought in order to expose them to a program of political education and to turn them into revolutionaries. One difficulty that may result from this approach is the possibility that the organization will attract a large number of supporters who are only interested in re- form and have no desire, or willingness, to expose themselves to a pro- gram of political education. These people often are able to move into positions in which they may coopt the movement and transform a revo- lutionary organization into a reform organization. This appears to have been the case with many of the recruits attracted to the revolutionary union movements.

Problems in relating to other black activists

An additional problem that was never resolved was the proper stance that the League, through its revolutionary union movements, should take toward black militants, black activists, or black caucuses who were willing to cooperate with the League but who did not wish to affiliate themselves as members. Hamlin states that:

One of our problems was that we ended up alienating a lot of workers. We had widespread support among young workers which meant we had almost majority support in some of the plants. But our approach was such that we turned off what I would call the moderate worker, certainly the backward workers, and certainly the white workers. We made the mistake of attacking other workers individually, by name and as a group. We attacked their organizations verbally and in some instances physically. I think that was incorrect. I think we could have led that struggle and gotten their support if we had taken a different approach. I'm referring to other black caucuses, social clubs, individual leaders. We didn't have to alienate these forces. There was an objective base around which we could have united with them on some issues. We foreclosed that possibility from the beginning. As a result, we were less successful than we might have been.[8]

The state of the economy

Each of these factors, by themselves, represented a serious threat to the continued existence of the League. In combination, they became virtually lethal. The final factor that greatly exacerbated the seriousness of the threat posed by all other factors was the deterioration of the state of the economy — especially as it related to the automobile industry.[9] There was a slump in car sales beginning in July 1969. Sales figures fluctuated but continued on a general downward trend for close to a year. The slump caused layoffs. The layoffs disproportionately hit the younger worker, black workers, and the former hard-core unemployed who had only recently been brought into the plants.

Chrysler and the United States Department of Labor terminated the job creation program contract by mutual agreement. This was the contract through which Chrysler was to receive $13.8 million in exchange for training and hiring 4,450 production workers in seven plants. The Detroit news media noted that Chrysler would miss the money but that they would benefit from the reduction in the pool from which DRUM and the other revolutionary union movements were drawing their membership.

It does not stretch the mind to entertain the notion that League and revolutionary union movement supporters were found among those losing their jobs at a rate greater than would be justified by their low level of seniority. Nor does it boggle the mind to entertain the notion that the union "looked the other way" and/or failed to vigorously pursue grievances in such cases. Whether or not they were true, charges were made that the economic cutbacks were manipulated in order to weaken League strength in the plants. This may or may not have happened but there is no question that the layoffs by themselves weakened League strength. This occurred at the same time that increased community activities were diverting more and more League cadre attention to non-worker-related activities. This combination of circumstances renders the subsequent decline in League strength within the factories perfectly understandable.

Discussion and conclusion

Despite the strength of their external enemies, it is possible that the League's internal enemies were stronger. Mistakes were made simply because things happened too fast. The politically sophisticated cadre within the League leadership was small in numbers. When several important developments occurred simultaneously, the cadre was kept constantly on the run. They had little time for thought and reflection. Strategic decisions had to be made without due consideration. Errors resulted that might not have been made if proper planning and discussion had been possible. It is often easy to sit in a living room or classroom far from the field of battle and say, "they should have done this here, that there, etc." However, it is much more difficult to make decisions and map strategy when hotly involved in important events. Decisions had to be made in short-time intervals and, often, with limited information.

To this set of problems must be added the difficulties resulting from the conflict between the class-oriented and the nationalist-oriented Marxist−Leninists and the problems caused by the nationalistic members of the League who rejected Marx and Lenin as "a couple of white cats with nothing to say to us." The League might have been able to survive its external enemies if it had been internally sound. It is doubtful if it could have survived its internal contradictions even in the absence of external enemies. It is simply not possible for an organization to function with its leadership divided into subcadres, each undermining the other's activities. This discussion has not made reference to personalities. However, it would be incomplete if it did not at least state that Watson believed that the personal unwillingness to work and the actually obstructionist activities of many of the nationalist-oriented black Marxist−Leninists were more important than ideological issues in bringing on the split.[10] Nevertheless it is possible that these activities were a consequence of ideological position rather than a function of personality. Similarly it is rumored that some of the nationalist hangers-on (those who were not Marxist−Leninists) were guilty of appropriating for their own use a significant amount of League resources. The latter, if true, certainly contributed to the downfall of the League.

One must approach with caution any exploration of the career of a social movement that is stated primarily in terms of ideological beliefs. Ideology does not emerge independent of material foundations. It is precisely the differentiated class composition of the League that explains its attraction toward apparently contradictory ideological currents.

Class composition and ideological strain

Intellectuals and workers have different life experiences, which lead them to view the world differently. Black intellectuals and workers share the experience of being black in a racist society but do not experience their blackness in an identical manner. They are likely to interpret the cause of black oppression in terms of different conceptual and theoretical schemes. The conditions and organization of their work experiences also differ and, consequently, they are likely to develop different orientations toward the need for, and the value of, political education.

Workers, especially automobile workers, are involved in work situations that have a higher degree of visible correlation between race and job desirability (e.g., pay and working conditions) than is the case for students and intellectuals. Black workers confront racism much more directly than they confront class exploitation. That is, they may suffer more from class than racial exploitation but class exploitation is more difficult to observe and identify and its recognition requires more political sophistication. Black workers have no difficulty in recognizing that they are exploited but they do not as readily recognize the exploitation of their fellow white workers. They see that white workers are better off than black workers. They have better jobs and more income. They do not appear to experience exploitation of the same type or degree. It may be the case that racism must be eliminated before most black workers can develop a sense of their shared exploitation as workers regardless of race. Thus black workers are more inclined to develop national consciousness than class consciousness. They are relatively receptive to the colonial model of racial stratification and are not usually inclined to cooperate with white radicals who may be seen as part of the exploiting group.

Black workers do not tend to be readily attracted into political education programs. Most black workers, especially in the auto industry, work long hours at demanding jobs. They do not have a great deal of energy to spend on political education classes. They are especially unwilling to make the sacrifice when they see political education as unnecessary because it is not directly related to the prime task: "getting the man off their backs." It is not consistent with this orientation to spend a great deal of time and energy attacking peripheral issues such as sexism and imperialism before racism has been destroyed. It may be difficult for many black workers to accept the suggested relationship between capitalism and racism as anything other than a diversionary ploy designed to retain white skin privilege by undermining the fight against racism.

The leadership cadre had different social experiences. Most of them came from working-class backgrounds but, for many, their days as students, either formal or self-taught, altered their perspective to a degree. While many returned to working-class occupations, this was usually on a temporary basis. They had options open to them that were not open to most workers. This removed some of the more intense consequences of racism; consequently, they were able to view things more abstractly and in a longer time perspective. They were more able to comprehend the function that racism plays within capitalism and to see the complex interrelations between imperialism, capitalism, racism, and sexism. They were more prone to accept the need for a broad-based political program. Workers could also have developed this broader understanding and acted accordingly if a well-developed program of political education existed. No such program was consistently made available to workers. Nor was the intellectual cadre ideologically homogeneous. All members placed a great emphasis upon the role of capitalist exploitation in explaining racial subordination but they differed in the degree to which they felt that white racism played a role independent of capitalist exploitation.

One group of cadre took a relatively pure Marxist—Leninist position and therefore placed prime organizational emphasis upon the worker and pushed an integrated fight against capitalism, racism, imperialism, and sexism. They believed that it was necessary to engage in principled cooperation with white radicals. The second group of cadre was closer to the orientation of the workers. They felt that capitalism was the main enemy but that whites were tinged with racism independent of the economic order. Thus they stressed the need for a primarily black fight against capitalism and racism. Their program envisaged a black-led socialist revolution that would culminate in separate black and white socialist states, which cooperated but maintained political independence.[11] The two groups of cadre had different ideas regarding the need for political education. The more national-oriented group saw little immediate need for political education as the attack upon racism should come first and it was relatively clear-cut and straightforward. It required no complex intellectual foundation. The more class-oriented group of cadre disagreed. They felt it was necessary to raise the workers' level of abstraction in order to help them to see the connection between racism, capitalism, sexism, and imperialism. The strain resulting from the possession of conflicting models of society became sufficiently strong that it was not possible to keep the diverse tendencies within a single organization. The League did not have sufficient strength or resources to enable either faction to survive without the other.

It would be a mistake to allow this section to end on a negative note. The League is dead but it did have a number of positive accomplishments. These must be recognized at this point.

Concrete accomplishments of the League

The black Marxist–Leninists' major focus was always the long-run objective of bringing about a socialist America, although there was disagreement as to whether there should be one or two (racially separate) socialist Americas. However, their strategy involved approaching black workers on the level of the concrete problems that faced them on the job. It was believed that workers could be organized initially in terms of concrete work conditions and then helped to develop revolutionary class consciousness through a program of political education. This approach involved the possibility of producing concrete short-run accomplishments even though these were not the primary organizational objective. The League left its mark on the auto industry by achieving significant concrete improvement in the situation of the black workers, even though some of its accomplishments were the result of attempts by management and the union to "buy off" workers in order to destroy the League. It is unlikely that these particular concessions would have been made if it were not for the fact that the League was perceived by both management and the union as a threat that had to be destroyed.

Both Douglas Fraser and Mike Hamlin agree that the activities of the League were responsible for observable changes.[12] There has been a significant increase in the number of black foremen and black union stewards. Some of the union locals that were points of contention are now under black control. It is not possible to precisely determine the impact of these changes. It is often thought that concessions made in response to militant action will produce a heightened sense of power and an escalation of demands.[13] However, in this case, the concessions may have partially accomplished their intended goal of weakening black worker support for the League. It is probable that management would attempt to make promotion and upgrading of blacks appear to be a consequence of the normal rewarding of seniority and skill. It is also probable that the union would attempt to make accession of blacks to political power appear to be a function of normal democratic union practices. This is exactly what Douglas Fraser did when he said that the best way to defeat the militants was to demonstrate that the system works, and cited a high degree of black representation in various union posts.[14]

This general attempt may have been facilitated by the policy eventually adopted by the League of providing electoral support, often covert, for blacks who were not League members. It would be quite difficult for the League to demonstrate that increased black representation in union decision-making positions resulted from the pressure it created. Thus many black workers may have become convinced that changes could be brought about through traditional assimilationist-oriented black pressure tactics. It is possible that they concluded that Marxism–Leninism was an unnecessary ideological trapping, constituting potentially more of a hindrance than a help.

Regardless of how one interprets the changes, it is true that blacks occupy more positions of authority in both the union and in the company after the League presented its challenge than they did before. It is also true that the plants are less unsafe and less dirty — although they are hardly clean and safe. The League was largely responsible for the idea of a Black United Fund or an International Black Appeal. They may claim at least partial credit for the various "Black United Fund" organizations now functioning around the country.[15] However it is possible that the greatest single accomplishment of the League was its contribution to the growing heritage of struggle experienced by black workers.

Legacy of struggle

It is possible that the most important single thing the League did was to provide more black workers with the experience of struggle. The act of coming together in united struggle leaves a legacy of commitment that cannot ever be wiped away.[16] The actual short-range outcome of the struggle may be irrelevant. Black workers came together and developed a sense of solidarity and unity of interests. They perceived the existence of a common enemy. They fought, and many of them suffered as a result of that fight. They won some victories through collective effort and solidarity. These experiences leave memories that will be activated the next time there is an effort to organize black workers in the plants. Just as the Garvey movement paved the way for the later development of the Nation of Islam, the League may have paved the way for the future organization of a black Marxist—Leninist worker movement.[17]

The potential value of the legacy of struggle for future organizing is illustrated by John Steinbeck in his novel, *In Dubious Battle*.[18] This novel told the story of an unwinnable apple strike organized by two Communists: Mac, an old experienced Communist, and Jim, a young Communist learning the ropes from Mac. The London referred to is one of the leaders of the local apple pickers. At one point Jim asks Mac whether the strike will be won and receives the following reply:

We ought to go to sleep, but you know, Jim, I wouldn't have told you this before to-night: No, I don't think we have a chance to win it. This valley's *organized*. They'll start shooting and they'll get away with it. We haven't a chance. I figure that these guys will start deserting as soon as much trouble starts. But you don't have to worry about that, Jim. The thing will carry on and on. It'll spread, and some day — it'll work. Some day we'll win.[19]

At a later point Mac explains to London:

Listen, he said, I guess we're going to lose this strike. But we raised enough hell so that maybe there won't be a strike in cotton. Now the papers say we're just causing trouble. But we're getting the stiffs used to working together; getting bigger and bigger bunches working together all the time, see? It doesn't make any difference if we lose. Here's nearly a thousand men who've learned how to strike. When we've got a whole slough of men working together — maybe Torgas valley, most of it, won't be owned by three men. Maybe a guy can get an apple for himself without going to jail for it, see? Maybe they won't dump apples in the river to keep up the price. When guys like you and me need an apple to keep our Goddamn bowels open, see? You've got to look at the whole thing, London, not just this little strike.[20]

Maybe this is the true meaning of the League of Revolutionary Black Workers and the real message embodied in the DRUM slogan that they borrowed from Mao Tse-Tung:

> DARE TO FIGHT! DARE TO WIN!
> FIGHT, FAIL,
> FIGHT AGAIN, FAIL AGAIN,
> FIGHT ON TO VICTORY.[21]

PART III

The present and the future

In Part I a portrait was presented of the background from which the League of Revolutionary Black Workers emerged, exploring those aspects in the history of the auto industry and UAW that contributed to the development of black worker insurgency. Conditions in Detroit facilitating the development of black pride, black militance, and black activism were examined. This Part attempted to ascertain the reasons why activism among black auto workers took a Marxist–Leninist bent, seeking the explanation in conditions prevalent in Detroit, the auto industry, and the UAW. In Part II the history of the League itself was examined with particular attention to the political development of its cadre, its growth, activities, and eventual death. Particularly close scrutiny was applied in examining the contribution that the League's ideology and class composition made to its demise.

Part III will be concerned with post-League developments. In Chapter 11 an attempt will be made to examine the continuing level of militancy among black auto workers in Detroit and to assess the relationship between that militancy and the earlier existence of the League. The organizational forms that post-League black worker activism has taken will also be explored. The book concludes with an attempt in Chapter 12 to assess the meaning of the League experience. The nature of conditions that could produce additional black Marxist–Leninist worker movements will be explored and the probability of their concrete development in the foreseeable future examined. I will also explore the theoretical developments implicit in this monograph and will attempt to assess the probable nature of the theoretical foundation for any such movements in terms of the type of racial stratification model that is likely to underlie their ideology.

189

11. Insurrectionary potential remains

The League of Revolutionary Black Workers has disappeared from Detroit and the revolutionary union movements are no longer active in Detroit's auto plants. This does not mean that all is quiet and that all black auto workers are contented with their jobs and their conditions of employment. A reservoir of discontent remains. Many black workers are convinced that they suffer from racism and that they work in unsafe plants under unhealthy conditions. Many are angry. There is a real possibility that this anger may be harnessed by future organizations similar to the League. The Black Workers' Congress has not made major inroads into the plants but workers have continued to engage in wildcat strikes and there is some radical organizational work taking place among dissidents.

Black militance in the auto plants

The summer of 1973 brought concrete manifestations of the continuing high level of militancy among black auto workers despite the absence of the League of Revolutionary Black Workers. On three separate occasions unauthorized worker actions halted production in one of the Detroit-area Chrysler plants. The actions were biracial in character, involving both black and white workers. However, the bulk of the participants were black and the majority of the issues primarily related to black workers. The three worker actions also demonstrated that Detroit's auto workers are, at the very least, not "turned off" by a Marxist rhetoric. In many cases they are quite responsive to it.

Workers pull the plug

Two workers, Isaac Shorter and Larry Carter, climbed a ten-foot wire fence, lowered themselves into a six-foot-square wire cage, and turned off the electricity — stopping the assembly line at the Jefferson Avenue

190

assembly plant for thirteen hours on July 24, 1973.[1] Five thousand workers were made idle and the production of 950 cars lost. Shorter and Carter presented a list of four demands: (1) Thomas Woolsey, utility superintendent, should be fired; (2) no reprisals; (3) this should be guaranteed in writing; and (4) the guarantee should be signed in their presence and in front of their fellow workers. These demands apparently struck a receptive chord in a number of workers as a crowd gathered around the cage shouting encouragement and supplying food and other forms of aid. The crowd supplied a cable and then chains and locks to aid in securing the cage. They also provided physical protection in preventing two skilled workers from using a torch to cut through the cable. Estimates of the size of the crowd vary. The low estimates appeared in the daily newpapers, which reported a crowd ranging from 100 to 300 people depending upon the hour. The high estimate of a crowd of 1,000 workers was provided by Neil Chacker, chief steward for Local 7.[2] All accounts agree that a jubilant crowd carried Shorter and Carter off on their shoulders when they came out of the cage at 7:11 P.M. after winning all demands. Both management and UAW representatives had previously attempted without success to talk the two workers out of the cage. When all other efforts failed, Chrysler capitulated.

Woolsey had been a subject of previous controversy. He had been transferred within Chrysler because of worker discontent, had been the subject of five grievances, and had been accused of racism and abusive behavior stimulating an earlier work stoppage. Workers accused Woolsey of abusing workers and using racist epithets, for example, calling a man a "black son-of-a-bitch." He was particularly charged with *abusing workers without cause — that is, over actions that were unrelated to production:*

Woolsey did not just harass people for the sake of production, he did it for fun. He tore out the chairs that people had built out of scrap in their work areas. He wrote people up [filed a written reprimand] for reading the paper when there were skips in the line. In the largely black department, he was considered an ardent racist.[3]

Woolsey had about 300 workers, 90 percent of whom were black, under his jurisdiction. Workers had collected 214 signatures on a petition demanding that Woolsey be fired. After four months of ineffectual protest, Shorter and Carter resorted to direct action. Shortly after the shutdown began the United Justice Caucus (UJC), a rank-and-file caucus within UAW Local 7, spread the word about what was happening and helped to rally supporters. Worker support contributed to the victory but it was primarily its timing that was responsible for Chrysler's concession. This was the last week of production on 1973 model cars and the run had to be completed so that the changeover to 1974 models could begin.

Chrysler justified firing Woolsey by saying that he had been guilty of "violation of company personnel policies."[4] Woolsey claimed that he had never been informed of exactly which personnel policies he had violated. He stated that he was considering hiring Ken Cockrel to represent him in an attempt to get his job back. It is unclear whether this was sarcasm or whether Woolsey was unaware of Cockrel's attitudes regarding black workers and their right to engage in direct action against undesirable working conditions. At any rate, Cockrel did not represent Woolsey in this matter. One consequence of the firing was an increase in insecurity among Chrysler line supervisors and foremen.[5] Serious discussion was initiated over the possible need to form a foremen's association.

Isaac Shorter and Larry Carter addressed a victory celebration sponsored by UJC on July 29.[6] Shorter did most of the talking and announced that he was a socialist who was "working to change the total structure of the capitalist system by scientific socialism."[7] Carter, who lived at the same address as Shorter, did not say whether he shared Shorter's political orientations. Shorter indicated that he was not a member of any socialist organization. He had been affiliated with the Black Panther Party in California but had no relation to them after coming to Detroit. He expressed the need for a vanguard party to lead the workers and indicated that the union was a part of the problem rather than a vehicle for its solution. He received an ovation in response to his statement that "Workers of the world must unite."[8] A *Free Press* editorial commented on the presentation and attacked Chrysler for submitting to anarchy. It accused them of encouraging a repetition of the same behavior by readily yielding to blackmail.

Shorter's view of the vanguard party appears to differ from that earlier espoused by the League. He was asked whether he felt that black workers were strategically located in industry and he responded:

In Detroit the percentage of black workers, just in the Jefferson plant, and in the plants in the city, is the majority. And the black workers in this city could control it. But at the same time there is no such thing as black control. It's workers control. Because it's not a racial thing. It's the system which is a capitalist system. It oppresses all people. Blacks, whites, Chicanos, just name it, yellow, brown. And that's the way we should look at it as being. As far as the workers working separate, I think the workers should work together, black workers should work with white workers, white workers should work with black workers. That's the only way we're going to accomplish our goals.[9]

Whatever the differences in views on the role of black workers as a vanguard, Shorter certainly shared with the League a belief in the need for workers to engage in direct action at the point of production, with the ultimate aim of creating a socialist society. It is also clear that many black workers were ready to lend their support to such actions. The major differences between Shorter's views and those of the League appear to concern the nature of the dialectic at a particular point in time. Shorter believed that it could be primarily a class dialectic while the League asserted that, for the present time, the dialectic had to be simultaneously waged in both race and class terms. The League saw the black worker as the basic unit of struggle while Shorter saw all workers united in a common unit of struggle.

Six-day wildcat at Detroit Forge

Workers at Detroit Forge walked out on August 8, barely two weeks after the Jefferson Avenue shutdown.[10] This walkout developed into a six-day wildcat strike involving a complex set of issues. There were many continuing complaints regarding unsafe and dirty working conditions but most discontent seemed to center on a double standard of discipline. Twelve workers were fired shortly after a supervisor returned from a thirty-day suspension (some of it with pay) for having been caught with company property in his car. It was charged that workers were fired for theft and suspended for being five minutes late while supervisors got wrist slappings for similar offenses. The fact that an estimated 60 percent of the work force had been required to work a seven-day week over a six-month period must have been a major contributing factor. It should be noted that Chrysler was the only one of the big three that *did not*, at that time, *have a clause in its contract that allowed workers to refuse overtime on a Sunday after having worked thirteen consecutive days.*[11]

Douglas Fraser, UAW vice-president in charge of Chrysler Division, initially charged that the strike was caused by outsiders.[12] His charge was largely based upon the fact that two nonworkers had passed out leaflets just prior to the first shift that did not report for work. He implied that workers from the Jefferson Avenue assembly plant had something to do with causing this strike but the charge was universally denied. The charge of outside agitation was not repeated when a high level of internal worker support was demonstrated. Fraser ordered the strikers back to work and Judge James Ryan issued a restraining order prohibiting picketing. The members of Local 47 met on August 9 and an interracial group of about 250 workers, consisting mostly of older workers, rejected the UAW plea that they return to work. The workers again expressed great concern over safety conditions. Twelve workers were informed later that day that they were fired for participating in the wildcat.[13]

In an apparent change of tactics, Douglas Fraser announced the next day that he would personally inspect working conditions at Detroit Forge and that other UAW officials would inspect twenty-one other plants.[14] He conducted the inspection on August 11 and concluded that the workers had a legitimate and pressing grievance in that working conditions were unsafe and dirty. He announced his findings just hours after Chrysler said that they welcomed his visit because that would demonstrate the falsity of the charges. They cited the fact that the plant had received three safety awards during 1972. On August 12 U.S. District Court Judge Cornelia Kennedy banned picketing or mass action by strikers. During the hearings preceding the issuance of the injunction, James Crawford, Chrysler Corporation's manager of employee safety, testified that working conditions in the plant were quite safe. However, under cross-examination he confirmed that Chrysler had been fined as a result of an inspection of the Detroit Forge plant made within the previous four months by the Occupational Health and Safety Administration.[15]

Douglas Fraser addressed a meeting of Local 47 on August 12. He reminded the assembled workers that there was a federal injunction against the strike. He told them that their grievances were just but that the UAW could not do anything as long as they were out on strike. He promised to authorize the local to conduct a strike vote on Friday, August 17, if they returned to work and Chrysler failed to clean up the plant. A show of hands was taken and sentiment was about evenly divided between going back and staying out.[16] Workers began returning to their jobs that evening. About one-third of the midnight shift reported to work and almost 95 percent of the following day shift returned to their jobs.

The six-day wildcat ended with a partial victory. Not only were working conditions improved at the Detroit Forge Chrysler plant but health and safety conditions were added as a major issue to be negotiated in the contract negotiations currently underway. Chrysler attempted to use both "the carrot and the stick" in an attempt to get the workers back at their jobs. Chrysler dismissed sixteen workers during the strike in addition to successfully seeking an injunction and a restraining order, and instituted a court suit specifically naming fifty-five workers. Chrysler also released a report on August 13 claiming that 50 percent of its Detroit area work force was now black, that sixteen minority members had been franchised as independent owners of MOPAR-associated enterprises, and that a heavy program of minority hiring had been followed since the Detroit Insurrection.[17] It is not possible to determine the relative contribution of the various factors to the workers' decision to end their walkout but it is at least plausible that the major factor was the belief that something would now be done to improve health and safety conditions.

Mack Avenue sit-in

Chrysler Corporation did not get a long respite from its labor troubles. An old-fashioned sit-in closed down Chrysler Corporation's Mack Avenue stamping plant on August 14.[18] Its origins must be traced back to three weeks earlier, when, William Gilbreth led a seventeen-man work stoppage in an attempt to force the company to install ventilation fans on the gate line next to the welding department, where the air was considered barely breathable. Gilbreth claims that the wildcat came after all grievance procedures were exhausted. On Friday, August 10, Gilbreth was fired, allegedly for falsifying his employment application, but Gilbreth claims that he was fired for leading the wildcat.

It is true that Gilbreth's application was incomplete. He did not include a year of college attendance and apparently did not admit that he had once been arrested and charged with assaulting a police officer. It is also true that many people do not list college educational experiences when applying for jobs in auto plants because they believe that they will not be hired if they are "overeducated" for the job. The omission of an arrest record could easily have the same motivation, that is, the desire to be hired. Gilbreth apparently met on Sunday, August 12, with two fellow Mack Avenue employees and seven nonemployees to discuss the possibility of shutting down the plant as a means of getting his job back. All ten were members of the Workers Action Movement (WAM) associated with the Progressive Labor Party.

Gilbreth somehow gained admission to the Mack Avenue plant on

Tuesday morning. Two guards tried to remove him and an altercation resulted. The two guards claimed to have been beaten by a lead pipe and Gilbreth claims to have been assaulted by the guards. Whatever happened, this touched off a sit-in in which an undetermined number of workers took control of the plant. Rumors circulated that Issac Shorter was among those sitting-in but the same issue of the *Detroit Free Press* that reported the rumor also printed a picture showing Shorter and Carter outside the fence with the sit-in participants inside. Two of the demands were that Gilbreth be reinstated and amnesty be granted for the strikers.

Douglas Fraser participated in the discussions in an attempt to get the plant operating again. He could hardly be viewed as a strong advocate of the workers' position as he told the press that he agreed with Chrysler's decision to close the plant rather than giving in to the workers. He added:

I don't think that you can capitulate in a situation like this. The agitators, regardless of who they are, represent only a very tiny fraction of the total Chrysler workers in the Detroit area and I advocate a policy of no surrender. If you surrender to this kind of blackmail there's no end to it. I'm for doing whatever we have to do as long as we don't surrender.[19]

Fraser continued to sound more like a Chrysler executive than a UAW vice-president in stating that "We don't place a premium on lawlessness." Fraser traced the trouble at the Mack stamping plant to Chrysler caving in to the demands of the two men who took over the Jefferson assembly plant. He said that the trouble at Detroit Forge was started by Chrysler workers and "continued by nonworkers." "The radicals exploited the situation at Detroit Forge but did not start the problem there," Fraser said. He said it was "absolutely" a mistake for Chrysler to give in during the Jefferson lock-in. He said he told Chrysler it had made the wrong decision there but he acknowledged it was not an easy decision. Then he added, "It was inexcusable if it was based on a mad desire to close out the 1973 model run."[20]

It is interesting to note that even Chrysler's industrial relations director, William F. Bavinger, Jr., did not take such a hard line. He felt that the decision at the Jefferson Avenue plant had been the correct one. But he did feel that no concessions could be made in the Mack sit-in.

Police expelled the strikers from the plant about 10:30 A.M. on August 15 despite the fact that they had no warrants for trespass or other violations against the majority of the strikers. The sequence of events that initiated the expulsion began about 9:30 when a number of the strikers came out of the plant to the gate in order to talk to reporters. They wished to explain that Gilbreth had had to defend himself when assaulted by the two guards who were injured the first day. Plant guards tried to prevent their return to the plant and a fight broke out. Several policemen entered the grounds at this point and tried to break up the fight. The strikers returned to the plant and then came outside again to demand that the guards be arrested for assaulting them. In the meantime fifty riot-equipped police had entered the grounds. They proceeded to round up the strikers, escort them off the company grounds, and release all except Gilbreth and Carlton Smith, who were charged with assault for the original altercation.

A temporary restraining order enjoining the workers from striking was issued by Federal Judge Fred W. Kaess at 11:30 A.M., one hour after the plant had been cleared.[21] Many of the expelled strikers attended a meeting at the Local 212 Hall where a stormy forty-minute meeting was held. The workers voted to continue to picket until their demands were met despite the restraining order enjoining them from such actions. The difficulty in telling management from union people continued as 1,000 UAW members wearing arm bands stating Sergeant-at-Arms assembled at the plant gates in order to insure that work was resumed. The "loyal unionists" prevented any picketing and physically roughed-up several workers who attempted to maintain a picket line. Among those who were beaten was Gilbreth. The *Detroit Free Press* reported: "Two workers said they saw a group of men wearing armbands beat up Gilbreth and an unidentified companion. The men reportedly chased Gilbreth from the Canfield gate to a parking lot, tackled him and punched him repeatedly until some supporters arrived."[22]

The UAW performance was praised by the *Detroit Free Press* in an editorial.[23] Everyone seemed to feel that it was about time that union and management demonstrated that they would no longer tolerate independent worker action, especially if it were carried out by "radicals." WAM claimed credit for the sit-in but the majority of the workers who participated were not WAM members. There is some doubt in Jordan Sims' mind as to whether WAM really had much to do with it.[24] He felt that WAM joined a spontaneous worker's movement protesting safety and health conditions and attempted to capitalize on it to their own advantage. The media were so preoccupied with radical revolutionary groups that all WAM had to do was say "this is our strike" and it was believed.

It is not possible to assess the role that WAM played. They certainly participated and were accepted by the workers. They never made any attempt to hide who they were and they consistently claimed that they had planned the strike in advance. WAM had members in the auto plants as did the Spartacist League, The Independent Socialists, and the Detroit Labor Committee. The sequence of three work stoppages clearly indicated that many of Detroit's auto workers were angry and ready to move against both company and union. They also demonstrated that this militance was displayed by both black and white workers although it was more heavily concentrated among black workers. Workers did not reject a person simply because he was labeled as "socialist," "Marxist," or "revolutionary." Actions were more important than political beliefs. It is fair to say that a reservoir of militance and receptivity to socialist ideology remained among Detroit's black auto workers despite the removal of the League from the scene. The League may have had some indirect influence upon developments. John Watson believes there was an overlap between membership in the revolutionary union movements and participation in the wildcat strikes.[25]

This sequence of work stoppages also demonstrated that concrete working conditions — especially health and safety conditions — remained as issues around which workers could be organized and galvanized into action. Conditions were actually bad. The UAW apparently allied itself with management to crush the insurgents but even they were finally forced to admit that conditions in the auto plants were seriously deficient. They announced that sixteen of the twenty-two plants visited in their inspection tour following the Detroit Forge strike had such bad health and safety conditions that strike votes would be justified. There was a general feeling that conditions at Chrysler were worse than in either Ford or General Motors because the plants were typically older. It is also true that Chrysler plants were more likely to be located in Detroit and to have a higher proportion of black workers. That combination of circumstances may account for the fact that much of the activity of the League's associated revolutionary union movements was concentrated in Chrysler and why Chrysler was harder hit by spontaneous work stoppages.

United National Caucus

A different style of opposition is embodied in the United National Caucus (UNC).[26] UNC is an organization that integrates a number of caucuses of dissident workers from various UAW local unions: e.g., Mack Safety Watchdog (Local 212, Mack Avenue stamping), United Justice Caucus (Local 7, Jefferson Avenue assembly), Strike Back (Local 3, Hamtramck assembly), Shifting Gears (Local 235, Chevrolet gear and axle), Democratic Caucus (Local 155, tool and die workers at 130 small plants). It includes both black and white workers but, because of its history, is primarily white.

The origins of UNC can be traced back to the revolt of skilled workers within the UAW.[27] Feelings of relative deprivation experienced by UAW craftsmen and skilled workers have produced protest and agitation over an extended period of time. Such feelings peaked during the late 1960s when auto companies contracted out increased numbers of jobs in the plants, creating situations in which UAW members and nonmembers worked side by side doing the same work for vastly different wage rates. This created resentment. A worker protest movement began and was generally referred to as the "dollar an hour, now" movement. UAW craftsmen wanted an immediate raise and, as a separate unit, the right to bargain with management for its own contract. They won some recognition but did not get what they felt was an adequate response to their grievances.

The skilled tradesmen began to form more permanent pressure groups and worker caucuses. This movement eventually coalesced into a central unifying organization, which began a newspaper, the *United Caucus*. As more diverse groups were attracted, the name was changed to the *United National Caucus*. At its outset the group was virtually all white. The ethnic composition of the skilled workers was primarily English, Scottish, and German.[28] This set them apart from the mass of the white production workers − mostly Eastern and Southern European and Appalachian white − as well as from the black production workers. This ethnic difference has proved to be a serious problem in attracting new recruits. Many black workers cannot relate to an organization that is primarily white.

In the years since the death of the League increasing numbers of dissident blacks have been attracted to the UNC. It has come to include in its membership the extremes of social background found within the UAW. Many of its members are craft workers of northern and western European ancestry. Many others are blacks working in the lowest status occupations within the automobile industry. It does not have very many members with Southern and Eastern European ancestry working at middle status jobs. Thus it includes members from the highest and lowest occupational and ethnic categories while not having very many members from the middle strata of either. This is not surprising. The majority of the UAW membership is drawn from the middle strata of jobs and the majority of members have southern and eastern ancestry. Consequently the UAW leadership and policies better represent the interests of the broad middle occupational and ethnic strata than they do the two extremes. Thus it is the white craftsmen and the black unskilled workers who are most likely to feel that the UAW does not represent their interests and, consequently, be attracted to UNC. This coalition is symbolized by the fact that the UNC chairman is Pete Kelly, a white skilled tradesman, and the co-chairman is Jordan Sims.

Jordan Sims

Jordan Sims is an interesting man who deserves separate examination within this section. His name surfaced in Chapter 2 during the discussion of postwar employment in the auto industry, in Chapter 4 as part of the discussion of the ELRUM wildcats, and in Chapter 5 in the course of the discussion of the ELRUM-backed electoral slates. In some ways he exemplifies the entire black auto worker movement and in many others he is unique. Jordan Sims was born around 1930 in Hamtramck. He was one of six people living in a three-room cold-water residence. He attended a primarily white school system (where he was an athlete, a decent student), graduated from high school in 1948, and worked in auto plants from then until 1971 when he was fired.

His experiences led Sims to conclude that he had no option but to develop a black perspective and to organize with other workers along racial lines. He sought an active role in local union affairs but was generally unsuccessful until the mid-1960s when large numbers of younger blacks began moving into the plants, and he was elected to lower-level union posts such as shop steward. When ELRUM began forming in the plant he felt a certain amount of empathy but he also had certain reservations. He strongly believed that health and safety conditions were bad at the Eldon Avenue plant and that black workers felt the brunt of the worst conditions. Sims believed that it was necessary for black workers to organize and to take direct action. On the other hand he could not accept all of ELRUM's rhetoric. He felt that the most pressing need of black workers was to do something to improve immediate working conditions. Whatever the merits of socialism, the possibility of a socialist America was temporally too far removed to do much good for the black worker. Thus ELRUM and Sims could collaborate on those aspects of common struggle involving concrete working conditions and remain separate on that part of the ELRUM platform relating to the Marxist–Leninist program for revolution.

Consequently Jordan Sims received ELRUM support in the election campaigns described in Chapter 5 and there was collaboration in the wildcat strikes cited in Chapter 4. The earlier account (Chapter 5) of Sims' electoral activities ended with the 1971 presidential campaign. Sims led the balloting in the first round with 806 votes to 739 for Frank McKinnon, a white.[29] Richardson, the incumbent, finished third and was eliminated from the runoff. It should be noted that Sims and McKinnon had both been fired during the May 1 wildcat. McKinnon had his discharge changed to a suspension and Sims was "on the street" as of the election date. McKinnon defeated Sims by a vote of 1,178 to 1,142 in the runoff held on May 28. Sims protested the vote because of the presence of armed guards, which intimidated voters, and because approximately 250 votes were invalidated. The invalidations concerned persons who were allegedly ineligible to vote because they had fallen behind in their dues during a period when the check-off was inoperative because the current contract had expired. The "ineligible" voters allegedly had not been notified of their delinquency as required by UAW rules.

The election committee rejected the protest and certified McKinnon as elected. The Sims protest was then carried to the UAW executive board where he won a partial victory as a new election was ordered.[30] He did not win all of his points. The executive board ruled in favor of a new election on the grounds there was a real confusion as to who should have been eligible to vote but it also ruled that the armed guards did not interfere with the members' right to vote. Jordan Sims lost the new election by twelve votes.[31] Still not rehired by Chrysler, Jordan Sims ran for president of Local 961 in 1973.[32] He finished first in the May 15 voting and was elected president in the May 23 runoff election.

Thus Jordan Sims is a link between various types of black workers. He is older than most members of the revolutionary union movements.

He experienced the extreme discrimination confronting most black pioneers in the auto plants but he did not become as conservative as many of the other older black workers. He is militant but not an avowed revolutionary. However, he does not find it necessary to repudiate or refuse to cooperate with black revolutionaries. Thus Jordan Sims is able to cooperate with, and provide the link between, many diverse elements among black workers. He is able to establish an effective working relationship with young and old, radical and moderate, and apparently with black and white, as long as all take a militant posture with regard to the struggle for worker rights.

United National Caucus policy

The UNC conducts programs in political education. It sponsored a conference on racism on February 6, 1972, which covered such topics as racism in the labor movement. It also published an article in which it was argued that red-baiting was an attempt to split workers and weaken the movement.[33] The article traced the history of the UAW and the use of "communist" charges in an attempt to destroy the UAW during its formative years. It also pointed out that all persons who have ever pursued a drive for black rights have been accused of being communist.

In another article they answer the question of who they are as follows:

If you ask your International Union representative about the UNC the response depends on where you stand in the UAW. *If you are a black production worker you will be told we are an elite, white, skilled trades group. If you are a skilled tradesman you will be told we are a bunch of "dummies . . . "*

The Caucus is an organization of members working within the structure of the UAW to make it more democratic and responsive to the needs of the membership. We believe that we as citizens and Union members should not relinquish our rights as individual human beings because we have crossed the Corporation's plant gates to make a living.

We believe that the profits of the corporations are put ahead of the welfare of people. *Far too many parasites are living off the back-breaking, dehumanizing working conditions suffered by workers on the production lines, in the foundaries and in the plants.*

We are not a political group, nor are we the substitute for a political party. We believe, however, that we need a political party that would run on a program for working people, for neither the Democratic nor the Republican parties have such a platform.

We hold many conferences and meetings in which every member is notified, issues are debated openly and decisions are reached democratically. We have Caucus chapters in many Locals throught the UAW.

We know that the structure of the UAW must be changed if we are to make it once again a fighting union. This can only be done if we have a rank-and-file move-ment throughout the UAW. No single Local or Region can survive the International Union, which can isolate and usurp such movements. It can only be done by a Na-tional movement. [emphasis in the original] [34]

The UNC grew and expanded. While remaining primarily white it ap-parently has attracted some of the black workers who were formerly affiliated with the various revolutionary union movements and/or with the League. It also apparently has attracted some of the black auto work-ers who are also loosely tied to the Black Workers' Congress. The Congress deserves a few comments before drawing this chapter to a close.

Black Workers' Congress

The Black Workers' Congress was formed on December 12, 1970, when people who had been members of black workers' groups in various cit-ies such as the League joined together with other black activists, stu-dents, and revolutionary intellectuals to form a black revolutionary communist organization.[35] It was originally planned that the League should constitute one of the major components of the Congress. How-ever, internal dissension (see Chapter 8) kept the League from forming any formal ties. Cockrel, Hamlin, and Watson joined as individuals after the split in June 1971. The Congress was active in organizing campaigns across the nation. They hoped that by the end of 1971 they would be in a position to build a mass antiimperialist movement in the ghetto but they got bogged down in an internal ideological struggle. The struggle continued throughout 1972 and early 1973, limiting their ability to make headway. The Congress was initially dominated by Forman's "cadre/mass" notion in which it was to be simultaneously a cadre and a mass party. This meant that there would be uneven development with-in the organization. An attempt was made to build a mass organization within which were cadres of politically educated Marxists–Leninists. This was expected to be reminiscent of the League structure. In both cases the executive committee was largely, but not entirely, comprised of a politically advanced cadre while the central staff included both cadre and less politically sophisticated activists.

This concept was challenged. It was argued that excessive concern with masses of people who were not committed, aware Marxists–Leninists allowed the level of organizational activity to degenerate into mass antiwar activities. There was a demand for a restriction of membership so that the Congress would be a cadre organization in which all members had a conscious understanding of Marxism—Leninism. More and more time was taken up in endless internal discussions and less and less actual organizational work got done.[36] Eventually Ken Cockrel became sufficiently fed-up and attacked James Forman as being egotistical and incompetent. Hearings were held by a Black Workers' Congress committee in February 1972 and Cockrel's charges were determined to be unproven. Cockrel and several other leadership cadre withdrew from the Congress at this point. John Watson took a leave of absence to return to Wayne State University in an attempt to complete his undergraduate work. In April 1973 the Congress executive body, headed by Mike Hamlin, reevaluated James Forman and expelled him from the Congress. The official indictment accused Forman of opportunism, responsibility for destroying the League, and for coming close to destroying the Congress. Mike Hamlin remained as chairman of the Black Workers' Congress until it experienced another split in 1975.

The Congress continued to evolve. In mid-1973 it came to believe that the communist movement had to be a multinational movement, that some black Communists must be in multinational parties, but that there must also be separate black communist parties on the order of the Congress. The evolution continued so that by mid-1974 the Congress was itself a multinational communist party. It no longer believed that it was theoretically sound for a communist movement to organize along strictly national lines.

As the Black Workers' Congress evolved it lost many of the characteristics that had enabled the League to attract black workers into its revolutionary union movements. When the Congress became a cadre it eliminated the possibility of attracting black workers who were not yet ready to commit themselves to a program of political education. When it became a multinational party it lost its appeal for the nationally oriented black workers. This is not the place to evaluate the correctness of these theoretical or organizational developments. However, it may be correctly asserted that as the Congress changed it attracted fewer black workers into its fold.

Conclusion

In this chapter I sought to demonstrate that a reservoir of militancy remains among black auto workers in Detroit and that these workers are either receptive to a socialist program or at the very least are not "turned off" by those who espouse it. There are many socialist groups forming caucuses among auto workers but none of them have been able to build a base of the size that the League had developed. The UNC exists as a multiracial nonideological organization of dissidents. It appears to be reasonably strong and includes some socialists, some former League affiliates, and some present or former Black Workers' Congress members. However, for the most part, the UNC is made up of white workers who are left of center but who are not Marxist–Leninist revolutionaries.

12. The meaning of it all

Barely four years elapsed between the founding of the Dodge Revolutionary Union Movement and the fading away of the successor League of Revolutionary Black Workers. The length of this span is no indicator of significance. The League may have constituted either a brief phenomenon without import or a highly significant harbinger of things to come. It was a product of circumstances existing in the auto industry, in Detroit, and in the American black community that enabled its ideology and organizational activities to strike a responsive chord. An adequate assessment of the meaning of the League has to consider the extent to which the auto industry is unique or representative of American industry, the extent to which Detroit is unique or representative of industrial cities, and the adequacy of the League's ideology as a possible foundation for a black movement.

The auto industry as a prototype of all industry

In Chapter 2 material was presented to support the thesis that the auto industry contributed to the rise of the League in several ways. Much of American industry shares with auto manufacturing the history of exclusion of blacks, or limitation of them to service occupations, until war-induced labor shortages made it necessary to open the employment doors.[1] The auto industry was not unique in the use of blacks as strikebreakers and in the tendency to treat blacks as a reserve labor force to be utilized in filling needs that could not be economically satisfied with white workers. Similarly much of the American labor movement shares with the UAW the historical pattern of excluding blacks until forced to admit them under the duress of necessity in strike action.[2] Nor has much of organized labor a better record than the UAW in the realm of commitment to black civil and work rights. This combination facilitates the organizational efforts of any black workers' movement that bases its campaign upon the charge of historical and continuing racism on the part of both industry and organized labor.

206

Other features of the auto industry that facilitated the rise of the League were its tendency to exhibit a high degree of concentration in one geographic area, to display health and safety deficiencies, and to rely increasingly upon black workers in production jobs. The auto industry is probably more highly concentrated geographically than any other major American industry. Nevertheless it is true that other forms of heavy industry, e.g., steel, have a high degree of concentration of productive facilities in certain urban centers. It also may be the case that a high degree of concentration is less essential to building a mass movement than it has been previously. The decade of the sixties produced a tremendous increase in both black and radical media outlets with national and/or regional circulation. It may be easier in the current context to communicate grievances and develop a common line of action among blacks in different geographic settings than it was at the time of the development of the League.

The health and safety deficiencies in the auto plants partially resulted from their age. These deficiencies are probably shared by manufacturing concerns that are still using production facilities of similar vintages. Other health and safety problems result from the nature of the job. These vary in seriousness from industry to industry with some worse than auto and others not so bad. Still other of the problematic health and safety conditions were a function of management neglect and were probably caused by the fact that time and money spent on safety conditions would have to be diverted from production and could be expected to reduce overall profit levels. These conditions exist in industries to the extent that organized labor tolerates them and will be cleaned up to the extent that organized labor is vigilant. There is undoubtedly great variation from union to union and local to local but it is difficult to believe that the UAW record is significantly worse than that of other unions.

The auto industry had increasingly come to rely on blacks as a source of labor. This was especially true on the least attractive shifts and in the least desirable departments and jobs. There is no direct measure of this type of utilization of blacks that is equally applicable to all industries. However, it can be indexed by the concentration of blacks within particular occupational classifications. Table 12.1 presents the data necessary for this analysis.

Blacks constitute less than 1 in 10 male workers in manufacturing but they comprise 1 in 8 of the male operatives, 1 in 6 male transport operatives, and 1 in 5 male laborers and service workers. The picture is

Table 12.1. *Percentage representation of black workers within occupations in selected industries, by sex, 1970*

	All occupations		Mining		Total manufacturing		Primary ferrous metals		Motor vehicle manufacturing	
	M	F	M	F	M	F	M	F	M	F
Professional	3.5	8.3	0.7	3.4	1.8	3.3	2.8	1.5	1.8	4.8
Managerial	2.2	4.4	0.3	1.5	0.9	2.0	1.3	3.9	0.8	9.8
Sales	2.5	4.0	a	a	1.8	3.0	1.3	8.7	1.6	a
Clerical	9.1	6.8	3.3	3.0	7.2	3.8	6.6	3.4	8.0	4.1
Craft	6.2	9.3	1.8	3.8	5.6	9.1	10.3	19.4	7.8	13.3
Operative	12.3	13.2	4.7	10.8	13.1	11.7	18.6	16.2	19.4	14.2
Transport operative	14.3	9.7	6.2	2.7	16.1	13.9	24.3	26.0	18.9	12.3
Labor	20.3	17.3	10.1	9.7	21.6	16.2	26.9	29.5	22.5	19.8
Farm labor	8.4	18.1	—	—	—	—	—	—	—	—
Service	16.8	24.3	8.9	12.2	19.7	26.3	17.8	24.5	25.9	26.0
Total	8.5	11.5	3.5	4.1	9.0	9.1	14.3	13.8	13.8	10.6

[a] Numbers too few to enable computation of meaningful percentages.

Source: Constructed from U.S. Department of Commerce, Bureau of the Census PC(2)-7C *Occupation by Industry*, Tables 1 and 2.

even more striking in the primary ferrous metals (including steel) industry and in motor vehicle manufacturing where blacks comprise over 1 in 8 male workers. In primary ferrous metals blacks comprise 1 in 5 male operatives, 1 in 4 transport operatives and laborers, and 1 in 5 male service workers. In the motor vehicle industry, blacks make up 1 in 5 male operatives and transport operatives, 2 in 9 male laborers, and 1 in 4 male service workers.

Blacks make up a smaller proportion of male craftsmen (1 in 20 in manufacturing, 1 in 10 in primary ferrous metals, and 2 in 9 in motor vehicles). As these figures indicate, blacks comprise a significant proportion of all male workers who are directly engaged in the productive processes in manufacturing and in these selected industries. In some factories the proportions are much higher, as indicated by the preceding discussion of the Detroit automobile plants.

Blacks constitute a larger proportion of the female labor force than of the male labor force. Approximately 1 in 9 working women is black. Black women are less well represented among manufacturing and mining sectors than they are in the total labor force. This is associated with their high degree of concentration in household service (52.5 percent of women so employed). They tend to be disproportionately concentrated in blue-collar occupations but, with the exception of steel, do not have as high a proportional representation in most categories as do black men. Nevertheless the numbers of black women in most industrial blue-collar occupations are large enough to represent a potent force. The militance displayed by black women contributed to the strength of the League and could certainly contribute to future movements.

Mining is a basic industry cited by the Black Workers' Congress as a potential base of organizational strength. It may be the case that black miners would respond to their programs but the proportion of blacks among miners is small. It does not exceed 1 in 10 in any occupational classification and black miners are not as likely as black industrial workers to be able to exert leverage within their industry.

The auto industry is not entirely typical of American industry. If anything, it should be viewed as the "ideal-type" industry epitomizing those characteristics that facilitate the development of black revolutionary worker movements. However, it does not differ from the rest of American industry to such a great extent that it would be safe to conclude that what happened in auto is unlikely to happen elsewhere. It is probably the case that most other industries, taken in isolation, are less likely than auto to provide the developmental context for a black movement of the order of the League. However, the existence of mass communications incorporating both radical and black media may minimize the significance of the developmental context. Movements can and do spread from factory to factory. Thus the nature of American industry is such that a new League may easily emerge and, under the proper conditions, develop into a national force.

Detroit as a prototype of American industrial cities

Thus the auto industry is not unique in providing those conditions that contributed to the rise of the League. The question remains as to whether there is anything unique about Detroit. Detroit contributed to League development through its industrial nature, its high concentration of blacks, its radical heritage, and its heavy reliance upon a single industry. Most industrial cities have high concentrations of blacks but few of them have as heavy a reliance upon a single industry as Detroit.[3] Reliance upon a single industry facilitated political development by providing a large portion of Detroit's black community with a common set of grievances and a common organizational enemy. This degree of commonality is diminished in cities with more diversified industry. Black workers will always have certain things in common around which organizational activity may concentrate but there is less commonality of experiences when workers are employed in different industries. Successful organizational activity may need to rely more upon the national question and a generalized class situation and less on specific work-related conditions.

It is also doubtful if any other city has quite the radical tradition of Detroit but contemporary situations may not demand as much in the way of indigenous radical developments when expanded mass media outlets facilitate the spread of radical ideas from community to community. It would appear that there are differences between Detroit and other industrial cities that might alter the form taken by organizational work, but they should not prevent the development of a revolutionary black worker movement. There may be advantages to industrial diversity in that a resulting movement would be less parochial and more related to class, *per se*. A black Marxist–Leninist worker's movement may easily develop in cities other than Detroit and industries other than auto. Its chances of success would be dependent upon the content of its ideological program and the proper set of external circumstances.

Evaluation of League ideology

Ultimately the soundness of the League's ideology rests upon the validity of the models of racial stratification it incorporates. Each model includes an analysis of society that suggests the nature of societal changes deemed necessary to create social justice. Consequently each model also suggests certain strategic and tactical lines of endeavor compatible with the achievement of desired changes. Thus it would appear that the selection of an appropriate model of racial stratification is crucial to the possibility of any oppressed group developing a viable program for collective advancement. Therefore it behooves us at this point to examine the degree of validity of the capitalist exploitation model, the colonial model, and of the emerging capitalist exploitation—colonial model that formed the analytic underpinnings of the League of Revolutionary Workers' ideology and program of action.

The capitalist exploitation model

The capitalist exploitation model has much to commend it, as most of the black population are workers and much of their experiences are determined by that fact. Table 12.2 presents the proportional distribution of blacks by type of occupation. Less than 1 black male in 10 is in managerial or professional occupations and 1 in 20 is in farm labor. The overwhelming majority of black males are in proletarian occupations. In addition to the 3 in 4 who are blue-collar workers, an additional 1 in 10 is in the new proletarian occupations (white-collar workers).[4] Thus 7 in 8 of all employed black males are proletarians, even excluding the agricultural proletariat. Over one-fourth (28.4 percent) of all black males meet the classical definition of the proletariat in that they are blue-collar workers in manufacturing industries.[5] Almost one-third (31 percent) of all black males work in manufacturing, all occupational levels included.

The occupational distribution of black women differs from that of black men. They are more likely to be in professional, clerical, and service occupations. Almost one-fifth (17.9 percent) of all black women in the labor force are employed in household service occupations. Over 3

Table 12.2. Percentage distribution of black workers within selected industries by occupation and sex, 1970

	All occupations		All occupations (farm excluded)		Mining		Total manufacturing		Primary ferrous metals		Motor vehicle manufacturing	
	M	F	M	F	M	F	M	F	M	F	M	F
Professional	5.8	11.3	6.1	11.5	2.4	7.0	2.5	1.4	1.3	0.8	1.2	1.4
Managerial	2.9	1.4	3.1	1.4	0.6	1.1	0.7	0.2	0.2	0.6	0.2	0.1
Sales	2.0	2.5	2.1	2.6	a	a	0.7	0.3	0.1	0.3	0.1	a
Clerical	8.1	20.7	8.5	21.0	3.7	52.5	5.2	11.4	3.1	24.4	3.6	13.2
Craft	15.4	1.4	16.1	1.5	14.1	3.2	16.1	4.6	24.9	15.6	14.2	4.8
Operative	19.6	16.0	20.5	16.2	49.2	28.4	47.6	75.3	41.1	36.2	63.9	71.6
Transport operative	9.9	0.4	10.4	0.4	13.7	0.5	7.6	0.3	5.4	1.7	4.8	0.6
Labor	15.7	1.5	16.5	1.5	12.3	1.5	13.7	3.2	19.9	9.6	6.5	2.9
Farm labor	4.5	1.3	—	—	—	—	—	—	—	—	—	—
Service	16.0	43.4	16.7	43.9	4.1	5.9	5.9	3.3	3.9	10.8	5.5	5.3
Total	99.9	99.9	100.0	100.0	100.1	100.1	100.0	100.0	99.9	100.0	100.0	99.9

^aNumbers too few to enable computation of meaningful percentages.

Source: Constructed from U.S. Department of Commerce, Bureau of the Census PC(2)-7C, *Occupation by Industry*, Tables 1 and 2.

in 5 employed black women are in a blue-collar occupation with another 1 in 5 a member of the white-collar proletariat (e.g., in a clerical occupation). Occupational concentration is even higher in manufacturing. Only 3 in 200 women employed in manufacturing have occupations other than clerical or blue-collar. The greater degree of concentration of black than of white women (see Table 3.1) undoubtedly reinforces charges of racism in the hiring and allocation of black women.

Racism is an essential component of the colonial model but it may also be explained within the capitalist exploitation model. Close examination of the history of slavery in America buttresses this interpretation.[6] Jordon demonstrated that Europeans had ethnocentric attitudes and racist preconceptions of Africans prior to the beginnings of the slave trade.[7] Nevertheless it was not attitudes that caused the selection of Africans for slavery. It was primarily the weakness of Africa and its remoteness from the capitalist core at the time when a cheap, easily exploited source of labor was needed. The weakness of Africa combined with emerging agricultural capitalism to determine the ultimate status of black Americans.

While Jordon, Boskin, Degler, and the Handlins disagree among themselves on the details of the historical evolution, they agree that the Africans who arrived in the colonies in 1619 were indentured servants, not chattel slaves. They also agree that over a period of time the status of the imported Africans degenerated to that of chattel slaves while the status of European indentured servants improved to that of free labor. Among the conditions accounting for this evolution was the relative strength of European societies, which enabled them to protect their immigrants, and the relative weakness of African societies, which made it impossible for them to do the same. Developments in colonial agricultural technology and economy produced a demand for an increased supply of cheap labor.[8] Immigration from Europe was largely voluntary while immigration from Africa totally involuntary. Communications back to country of origin reporting harsh or intolerable working conditions could reduce the flow of workers from Europe but would not affect that from Africa. Thus colonists had to be concerned with maintaining tolerable conditions for potential European immigrants but not for potential African immigrants.

The presence of the frontier with its free land also had its impact. White indentured servants could run away to the frontier and virtually disappear. In the absence of evidence to the contrary there would be no reason to question the assumption that they were free. However, the color of his skin set the African apart and make it natural to assume that a black man was a bondsman in the absence of proof to the contrary. The African was simply less able to escape his bonded state. The fact that Africans had previous experience with tropical agriculture, which would enable them to make a valuable contribution to southern plantation agricultural techniques, was simply an added plus.[9] The ability to control the labor supply and prevent labor dissipation through escapes at a time of labor need was a primary contributing factor to the decision to enslave blacks.

This fact becomes increasingly evident if one examines the reasons why American Indians were not enslaved.[10] It is true that Indians were less resistant to tropical diseases than Africans but it is doubtful that this was a major factor in the decision not to rely on Indians as the prime source of agricultural labor. Whites were willing to tolerate a great loss of African life in the middle passage and undoubtedly would have tolerated a similar Indian loss of life if by so doing they were assured of a stable work force. Far more crucial was the fact that the American colonies were the native home of American Indians. They knew the area and could readily escape to the protection of their people. Furthermore it is highly likely that the attempt to enslave Indians would have created a security problem for the slaveowners. It is likely that a wave of Indian wars and retaliatory raids would have been touched off by the practice of Indian slavery on a wide scale. Thus power and control factors were more crucial than any other in the selection of Africans as slaves.

We may conclude that existing racism was utilized and exacerbated as a rationalization for the enslavement of Africans even though the determining considerations involved economic and power relations. Racism, once evolved as an ideology, also served to divide and weaken the proletariat. Nonslaveowning whites in the South did not directly benefit from slavery and probably suffered economically from its competition. Nor was the poor white any better off after abolition transformed the slave into a peon. White industrial workers experienced low wages and poor working conditions as long as racism kept black and white workers apart and weakened the union movement. Thus there is considerable merit in the capitalist exploitation model but it, by itself, is inadequate to explain the realities of race in America. We must now turn to a consideration of the potential utility of the colonial model.

The colonial model

The colonial model closely resembles reality in several respects. Its central assumption is that blacks comprise a people (or nation) that has been exploited as a people (or nation). Much empirical evidence supports this assumption. The bulk of the black population in America between 1670 and 1860 was slaves. Between 8 and 14 percent of black Americans were free at each census count between 1790 and 1860.[11] However, free is a legal term and does not imply equality. There were innumerable restrictions placed upon the activities of free blacks, who continued to occupy a subordinate and exploited position.[12]

Nor did abolition bring an end to black exploitation. There was a continuing need for black labor in the agricultural South. Many blacks provided coerced labor either through debt peonage, sharecropping, or tenant farming.[13] Even those blacks who escaped North did not escape exploitation. Black workers were not accepted into industry on the basis of full equality.[14] Blacks were generally excluded from production jobs until after the outbreak of World War II. They were often excluded from labor unions. They had no real ally in either capital or labor except in times of labor strife. Capital was happy to use blacks as strikebreakers and labor was sometimes willing to admit blacks into their unions in order to prevent their use as strikebreakers. However, neither role led to lasting black gains. The end of periods of strife often meant the elimination of gains.

World War II did not change the general picture. The position of blacks advanced relative to that of whites but they did not achieve full equality. They still are concentrated in the dirtiest, most dangerous, least desirable, and poorest paid occupations. Blacks were eventually admitted into labor unions but they have never achieved equality within the unions themselves. They are still underrepresented in positions of authority in the union structure. Blacks are no less discriminated against in other areas of American life. There is evidence that they are less likely than whites to receive economic rewards for educational or occupational achievements.[15] It appears that blacks are discriminated against regardless of education, occupation, or place of residence. Even those blacks who are incorporated into the dominant capitalist system are incorporated in a status that falls short of full equality. This suggests that the internal colonial model has features that are useful in describing the American system of racial stratification.

The black community is not homogeneous. Most, but not all, blacks are workers. The increasing proportion of the black community possessing white-collar jobs is part of the proletariat. It must sell its labor for wages and it works under conditions that increasingly resemble those of blue-collar workers. However, there are black capitalists. They control enterprises that are small in comparison to the giant corporate conglomerates in America but they exist and cannot be ignored. In many ways this small class of petty black capitalists joins together with black professionals to function as agents of indirect rule in a manner analagous to that of the bourgeoisie among colonized peoples.[16] The ghetto is economically and politically controlled from the outside. Its prime export to the "mother country" is unskilled labor but it also supplies a pool of reserve labor that can remain underutilized until needed by industry.[17] The welfare and unemployment systems support this reserve army to the extent of preventing it from starving but at a minimal level so as to insure its receptivity to low-wage jobs when they become available.

Thus there is much of value incorporated in the colonial model but it, too, is not completely adequate by itself. It successfully explains the nature of racial exploitation in America and could account for the racial dialectic. However, it does not adequately explain the contribution that racial exploitation — the exploitation of black Americans — makes to class exploitation. That is, it does not adequately explain the increased exploitation of all workers, regardless of race, which is made possible by the practice of racial exploitation. The capitalist exploitation model explains both class exploitation and the class dialectic without adequately explaining racial exploitation. Therefore it is necessary to examine possible theoretical developments that would contribute to the development of a merged capitalist exploitation–colonial model.

A merged capitalist exploitation–colonial model

There are valuable features incorporated into the internal colonial or submerged nation model but there are also valuable features incorporated into the capitalist exploitation or class model. Each describes a portion of reality and provides valuable insights regarding the American system of racial stratification. Neither is sufficiently general to be capable of subsuming the other. Therefore it is necessary to merge the two models in order to provide a comprehensive basis for the analysis of racial stratification and the black revolt in America. Black Americans are a people who have been proletarianized and who, for the most part, are currently members of the proletariat. They experience exploitation primarily as members of the proletariat. However, they also experience exploitation as blacks. The black community is differentiated by class. Each of these features is more compatible with the internal colonial than the class model.

Space would not permit the presentation of a fully developed capitalist exploitation–colonial model of racial stratification, even if one were fully worked out. It is clear that there is need for such a theoretical development if we are to understand the nature of racial stratification in America, but much work remains before the colonial–class model can be fully elaborated. It is not possible to do more at this time than to indicate its broad outlines and to describe one of its central concepts. Any viable model must begin with an analysis of the historical role of exploitation in emerging labor systems. Such exploitation predated the development of modern capitalism but probably reached the heights of refinement in the capitalist era.

This merged model must begin with the insights of Robert Park and his students (see Chapter 1). It must recognize that race relations were initially created out of European expansion in the search for markets, raw materials, land, or labor. Europeans utilized power differentials to introduce systems of superordination–subordination that were rationalized through racist ideologies and institutionalized in systems of accommodation. Lind developed this analysis by noting that race relations differed by type of frontier situation.[18] The prime need of Europeans in plantation frontiers was for controllable labor. They were likely to either attempt to fill these needs by harnessing indigenous peoples or importing controllable labor from elsewhere. The prime need of Europeans in settler-farming frontiers was for land so they were likely to attempt to exterminate or expel the indigenous populations. Lind saw domination through capital investment as a third, and the most modern, type of frontier, in which market conditions and indirect rule were likely to be used to perpetuate European control. Park also noted that the frontier created by immigration was essentially the same as that created by colonial expansionism.

These insights provide the basis for a useful combined capitalist exploitation–colonial model. Blacks were initially imported into the United States and transformed into chattel slaves to meet the developing labor needs of an emerging plantation economy. Abolition may have brought an end to chattel slavery but it did not eliminate the plantations or the need for coerced labor. A number of devices (debt peonage, sharecropping, tenant farming, and sheer physical coercion) were used to insure that blacks continued to fill the need for agricultural labor. At the same time, industry was beginning to gear up in American society and was developing a need for industrial labor. Rather than compete with southern agriculture for the same labor pool, northern industry looked to European immigration to fill its labor needs. Immigrant workers in industry and black workers in agriculture were both exploited, both worked under undesirable conditions at minimal compensation, and both found their exploitation rationalized by ideologies stressing the alleged racial and/or cultural superiority of the exploiters.

Technological advances and the transformation of southern agriculture into capitalist agriculture did little to alter the basic facts of life for black workers. They were driven off the land but were not welcomed into industry except in a second-class role until wartime expansion made it impossible to keep them out. The present black population is largely an urban proletariat. Much of the white population remains as an urban proletariat. However, they do not occupy the same position. Black workers are still kept in the least desirable jobs. This tends to create a perception in white workers that they have a vested interest in racism and the status quo.

Thus present-day America is a capitalist society in which all workers are exploited but black workers more intensely than white workers. Racism divides white and black workers and contributes to the weakness of the proletariat and the perpetuation of the system that exploits it. Blacks who are not members of the proletariat also must confront racism and are deprived by it. Thus a concept is needed that would facilitate the examination of the simultaneous impact of class and national oppression within the American system of racial stratification. The concept of "ethclass" has great potential providing it is suitably modified.

The concept of ethclass becomes the concept of race–class

Gordon developed the concept of ethclass within an assimilationist perspective.[19] The concept may be transformed to fit a conflict perspective. Ethclass refers to the social space delineated by the intersection of the vertical dimension of ethnicity with the horizontal dimension of class.

	National or racial groupings	
Classes	White	Black
Capitalist class	White capitalists	Black capitalists
Proletariat	White workers	Black workers

Figure 12.1. The race–class concept. This is a simplified diagram.
It does not include either the lumpen or petty-bourgeoisie.

Every ethnic group in American society includes members of more than one class. Every class in American society includes members of more than one ethnic group. People share certain things (e.g., common history, culture, sense of peoplehood, etc.) with other members of their ethnic group. There are other things (certain aspects of culture, interests, etc.) that are shared among members of the same class. Social participation appears to be largely restricted to the ethnic group segment of one's social class (ethclass). The most significant unit of social behavior is then the ethclass.

All black Americans are simultaneously black and members of a particular social class. All whites are simultaneously white and members of a particular class. There are proportionately more blacks in the proletariat and proportionately more whites in the capitalist class, but each racial group is internally differentiated by class and each class is internally differentiated by race. There are a few black capitalists even though they are concentrated in peripheral concerns such as insurance, cosmetics and publishing. There are many proletarians among whites. We may assert at this time that all workers in a capitalist society have interests in common – interests that unite them and bring them into opposition with the capitalist class regardless of the racial identity of either workers or capitalists. The historical evolution of American society is such that all blacks experience oppression as blacks. Thus all blacks in American society have interests in common that unite them and bring them into opposition with whites regardless of the class of either blacks or whites. These two dimensions of race and class intersect to make the most meaningful unit of social analysis and social action: the race–class. Figure 12.1 represents this social formation.

A race–class is a social collectivity comprised of persons who are simultaneously members of the same class and the same race. It is this social grouping that possesses the maximum combination of shared interests. However, the same type of analysis may not be equally applicable to all cells in Figure 12.1. Black workers share common interests and common enemies. They always comprise a meaningful combination for political action. They share certain interests and enemies with white workers and share other interests and enemies with black capitalists. At times they may perceive it in their best interests to form united front coalitions with black capitalists on behalf of shared national (racial) objectives. At other times they may perceive it in their best interests to join together in united front coalitions with white workers on behalf of proletarian objectives. In either case, these perceptions may or may not be correct for existing situations and such alliances may or may not prove profitable. This will be determined by many factors external to the united front coalitions themselves.

It is equally true that black capitalists might develop perceptions that would lead them to form united front coalitions either with black workers in pursuit of national (racial) objectives or with white capitalists in pursuit of shared class objectives. There are real national (racial) interests in contemporary American society that sometimes provide a real basis for unified action between black capitalists and black workers. However, there is no such realistic basis for black capitalists joining together with white capitalists. Black capitalists occupy positions peripheral to the capitalist structure. They do not engage in basic production and they do not possess sufficient wealth or stock ownership to enable them to exert any significant influence within the national economic elite. Thus those perceptions are illusory that lead black capitalists to affiliate themselves with white capitalists.

White capitalists have a real basis for unification with either black capitalists or white workers. In both cases their interests are more manipulative than reflective of truly shared interests. White capitalists would gain from united front actions with black capitalists because this would inhibit the development of black united fronts that could threaten some vested interests of the white capitalist class. Similarly they would gain from white racial unity designed to protect white skin privilege because activities so directed inhibit the development of proletarian united front movements that could threaten some basic capitalist vested interests.

White workers have a realistic basis for unification with black workers on behalf of shared proletarian objectives, as was discussed above. They may easily develop the illusory perception that they have a basis for common action with white capitalists to protect white skin privilege. The entire history of American society has demonstrated that racial divisions of the working class are more harmful to blacks than whites but ultimately are detrimental for all workers. Those areas in which racial unity have been most successfully prevented are also the areas of lowest wages and poorest working conditions for all workers regardless of race.

Thus it would appear that race—class is the natural unit for both social analysis and political action. There is a realistic basis for united action combining black and white workers that would benefit both race—classes just as there is a realistic basis for united action combining black workers and black capitalists. Any common action combining either white capitalists and black capitalists or white capitalists and white workers would ultimately prove to benefit only the white capitalists. Which alliances will actually be formed at any given time and place will be a function of external conditions affecting consciousness formation, perceptions of probable success for particular lines of struggle, and the willingness of all parties to form such alliances.

It is clear that the best approach to the study of the black revolt rests upon an integrated capitalist exploitation—colonial model of racial stratification incorporating a concept such as race—class. However, this merely provides the starting point for a structural analysis. Black workers may form the "proper" nucleus for a black revolt, which objectively should pursue a strategic line centering around race—class. However, this theoretical insight cannot, by itself, trigger an effective black worker movement. Before this is possible there must be a major black activist-theorist who can translate the insights incorporated in the above analysis into a more programmatic formulation. This presentation would have to make sense to black activists and also incorporate a set of carefully delineated programmatic implications. While no such fully developed formulation of a program for action is completely spelled out, Baraka has taken major strides in this direction.[20]

Baraka on the capitalist exploitation—colonial model

Baraka begins his theoretical statement at its logical starting place — the intrusion of imperialism into Africa. He argues that the exploitation of Africa and African labor contributed to the growth of capital accumulation. The end to the slave trade coincided with the replacement of competitive capitalism by monopoly capitalism. Racism, which requires the ability to dominate through physical force, developed as a part of the capitalist mode of production. Assimilation came to replace force as the means of enforcing domination. Black liberation requires an attack upon racism and imperialism as an integrated functioning unit. It goes without saying that the destruction of imperialism produces the simultaneous destruction of capitalism — for the latter cannot exist without the former.

The black liberation struggle is seen as resting upon the organized political expression of black culture. Baraka sees the struggle against racial oppression in America as a struggle for national liberation. This involves the striving for socialism:

It is critical that we always keep in mind that we are struggling to liberate ourselves as people and also to bring about socialism. Racism in America is real, not theoretical. Just as our racial distinction is real. We make an error when we posit our struggle as simply a class struggle, or render ourselves invisible within phraseology describing the essential struggle in America as one between the working masses and the ruling class, with no further revelation of the essential racism of American society.[21]

Baraka feels that the real accomplishment of racism in the United States was to split black and white workers and moderate the general contradiction of capitalist accumulation. He feels that the nationalistic character of the black struggle against oppression has to be modified to involve a simultaneous class struggle. He acknowledges that the ruling class is primarily white but he asserts that its racial behavior is less important than its class identity. Baraka draws upon Cox, Cabral, and Nkrumah in developing his version of the concept of nation–class. The struggle for national liberation becomes a struggle against capital as it involves striving to free the national productive forces.

Baraka believes that the class struggle is both international and intranational. Integration has been carried out in order to facilitate the exploitation of all blacks. He portrays the black liberation struggle as moving from nationalism, through Pan-Afrikanism, to socialism. Nationalism was the initial battle against racism. Pan-Afrikanism is at a higher level because it involves an international battle against imperialism. The struggle for socialism is the ultimate objective — that which the entire struggle is all about.

Baraka's theory, still in the process of development, has great potential. It recognizes the appropriate starting point in linking racism and exploitation to capitalism and imperialism. It recognizes the fact that racism is a potent force that cannot be subsumed under the class struggle. It warns against the dual dangers of allowing nationalism to lead one to reject the valuable teachings of Marx and of letting a concentration upon class lead to the denial of the need to modify Marx to handle the realities of racism. This is a basic line of analysis that enables potential recruits to be approached on their own levels. It matters little whether they are initially attracted to a movement for its racial or its class analysis. The theory has a basic soundness and richness that enables it to be used as the basis for a program in political education directed at either type of recruit.

Baraka advocates a line of activity that parallels the original League program. He proposes that there be a vanguard party and a united front. The vanguard party could be limited to the politically advanced elements who fully comprehend the entire analysis and the entire program. The united front enables the politically advanced segments to cooperate with others on common endeavors, to expose others to a program of political education, and to seek new recruits. This avoids some of the internal problems faced by the Black Workers' Congress when it attempted to operate as a cadre/mass party. It somewhat parallels the dichotomy between the League of Revolutionary Black Workers and the revolutionary union movements — although the League was never fully able to keep the lines drawn as clearly as it desired.

Relationship between ideology and constituency

An ideology will not appeal to its intended constituency simply by virtue of its derivation from a valid model of society. The life situations of potential participants condition the manner in which they view the world. Their perceptions of reality condition their responses to ideological appeals. Although the bulk of the male black population may objectively be defined as proletarian it does not necessarily follow that they will so define themselves. The nature of the contemporary black experience in America is such that black workers are more likely to define themselves as blacks than as workers. The most that can be reasonably expected at present is that they will define themselves as black workers rather than simply as blacks. This results from a combination of several factors.

The economic consequences to blacks of the existence of white skin privilege are all too evident.[22] Black median income remains less than two-thirds that of whites. Blacks are concentrated in lower-status and less desirable occupations. Differences in amount of education do not adequately account for lower-status jobs, lower levels of income or higher unemployment rates. Blacks and whites having the same level of education, the same job, and living in the same region of the country have an average difference in annual earnings in excess of $1,000. Blacks with four years of college earn less than white high school graduates. Blacks are closing the educational gap vis-à-vis whites but neither income nor occupational gaps are closing at corresponding rates. In all parts of the nation, white workers have been observed resisting black attempts at occupational upgrading and/or to break into previously all-white occupations. All of this is conducive to black workers developing a conception of whites as enemies. They see no reason to make an exception of white workers. Their knowledge of the history of organized labor and observation of contemporary job-consciousness exhibited by whites makes it difficult for them to perceive white workers as being very different from the larger white population.

It is unlikely that black workers will, at present, be attracted to a multinational worker movement designed to bring about a socialist revolution. However, they may be attracted to a black worker movement. It is probable that its initial appeal would have to be stated in tactical terms. National consciousness would be the major direction of the appeal but the focus upon black workers would have to be based upon a power analysis. It would be necessary to convince black workers that they occupy a strategic position in industry that gives them a degree of leverage out of proportion to their numbers. It would appear that Baraka's distinction between vanguard party and united front activities could facilitate these developments.

Whatever form it takes, organization would be facilitated by the existence of a separate black community. Segregation confines large numbers of blacks within a limited geographic area. This facilitates communications. The ease of communications among persons sharing a common set of life chances and experiencing a common set of problems encourages the development of a political class.[23] Grievances experienced individually become social when they are communicated to similarly aggrieved persons. The definition of a common enemy may lead to a unified movement against that enemy. Given the high proportion of workers in the black community, it would not be surprising if such a movement took on a black proletarian flavor.

There is little question that the League was correct in its belief that the lumpen-proletariat lacks the power base to conduct a successful revolution. It can riot, cause disturbances, and disrupt a community for a period of time, but it has no real leverage. If its disruptions prove too costly to the ruling class, the lumpen can be isolated and starved into submission or simply crushed by overwhelming force. However, black workers derive power from their strategic location at the point of production (see Tables 12.1 and 12.2). To destroy them also destroys production. This is a price that the ruling class could not afford.

The primary ferrous metal industry and the motor vehicle industry occupy key positions in the American economy. A general strike of black workers would cripple these industries and, indirectly, cripple the entire American economy. This provides black workers with great potential power. A solid organization of politically conscious black workers would have the leverage to create tremendous change. It is this power potential that may help to create a positive black response to an ideology that locates the base of the black liberation struggle in the black proletariat.

Organizational steps

If any ideology derived from an integrated capitalist exploitation—colonial model is successfully to attract a large black following, the following sequence of steps will in all likelihood be necessary: (1) blacks must be recruited to a united front movement on the basis of national consciousness; (2) they must develop a perception of the power distribution of society that encourages them to recognize that power lies at the point of production; (3) a program of political education must be carried on that enables black workers to see that capitalism and imperialism are the enemies behind racism, that they are responsible for racism; thus (4) black workers will be prepared for the unification of their movement with a movement of white workers into a united class struggle against capitalism.

If this is to be successful, there must be a simultaneous movement among white workers that must educate them to see (1) that capitalism and imperialism are enemies that exploit them; (2) that black workers are also exploited by the same system; (3) that racism divides black workers from white workers to the disadvantage of both; and (4) this educational process must prepare them for the unification of black and white worker movements into a combined worker movement against capitalism.

The experience of the League of Revolutionary Black Workers suggests that this developmental process currently breaks down at a number of points. One is the almost total absence of such a movement among white workers. A second point of weakness is the overriding strength of national consciousness among black workers. This hurt the League in many ways. Political education became almost impossible. A movement without a program of political education is opportunistic and issue oriented. The movement dies if the opposition moves to eliminate the issues. The only way a white worker movement could have been started was through the efforts of white radicals. Coordinated efforts were necessary to prevent blacks and whites from pulling in opposite directions. Yet all such efforts at coordination or cooperation were impeded by the high level of national consciousness.

It may well be the case that the ideological line most likely to succeed is one that emphasizes the unique role of the black worker and leaves the question of ultimate unification with whites for the indefinite future. But this indefinite future may never come. The alternative is to follow the route of the Black Workers' Congress and begin with the development of a multiracial party and work back to organizing black workers. This approach might not succeed in appealing to black workers because of their high level of national consciousness. The dilemma cannot be resolved at this point in time. It is possible that it will only be resolved through concrete actions. This important question will now be set aside and attention shifted to an examination of the possible effects of the economy upon the course of development of black worker revolutionary activities.

The impact of the economy

The foregoing analysis suggests that the League of Revolutionary Black Workers is more likely to have been a significant harbinger of things to come than it is to have been a passing epiphenomenon. The increase in the number and proportion of blacks working in the nation's basic industries is creating a massive black industrial proletariat. Their experiences incline them to see themselves as victims of racism although they are responsive to approaches that link racism to capitalist exploitation. They have proven themselves willing to engage in direct actions ranging from wildcat strikes to urban insurrections. A unified capitalist exploitation—colonial model underlies a theoretical approach taken by Baraka that is likely to strike a responsive chord among black workers. This approach integrates cultural nationalism, revolutionary nationalism, and class consciousness. It appears inevitable that the United States will be hearing more from black Marxist—Leninists — especially those inclined toward the thoughts of Mao Tse-Tung.

However, this prediction does not have a specific time dimension to it. The birth, rise, fall, growth, decline, and death of social movements are all influenced by external circumstances. One of the most significant of these is the economy.[24] Movements are less likely to be active during times of recession and more likely to be active during times of prosperity. The maximal times for gaining adherents may have exactly the reverse effect. The typical pattern in the American economy is for a period of recession to hit the black community much harder than it does the white community. The differential pattern of suffering may bring black consciousness of racism even more to the forefront of consciousness. Many blacks who thought that it was possible to succeed within the system may become angry when they lose their jobs.

Periods of depression also tend to bring an increase in critical evaluation of the economy and an increased receptivity to socialism. A recession may facilitate the program of recruitment and political education of a black Marxist—Leninist movement but it will not facilitate action. Blacks who are out of work are also removed from their source of potential power. One cannot stop the forces of production if one is isolated from them. It is during periods of prosperity and full employment that potential black power is at its zenith. More blacks are working then than at any other time and, therefore, are in a position to halt production and the generation of profit. But this is the period in which one is likely to attract the fewest recruits. The set of economic circumstances that would be expected to yield both the maximum number of adherents to a black Marxist—Leninist program and maximum black worker access to power is a period of increased prosperity following a major, prolonged, economic slump. We should expect to observe a wave of black worker revolutionary activities at a time when the American economy comes out of a prolonged recession or depression, is expanding, and is moving into a period of prosperity and full employment.

THE LEAGUE IS GONE, DRUM HAS BEEN STILLED,
BUT THE BEAT GOES ON.[25]

Notes

Chapter 1. Sociology and the dialectics of class and race

1 Immanuel Wallerstein, *The Modern World-System: Capitalist Agriculture and the Origins of the European World-Economy in the Sixteenth Century* (New York: Academic Press, 1974), p. 67.
2 *Ibid.*, pp. 87–91.
3 See Oscar Handlin and Mary Handlin, "Origins of the Southern Labor System," *William and Mary Quarterly* 7 (April 1950), 199–222; Donald L. Noel, "A Theory of the Origin of Ethnic Stratification," *Social Problems* 16 (Fall 1968), 157–72.
4 See George P. Rawick, *From Sundown to Sunup: The Making of the Black Community* (Westport: Greenwood, 1972), esp. Chap. 6; Herbert Aptheker, *American Negro Slave Revolts* (New York: Columbia University Press, 1945); Herbert Aptheker, *To Be Free: Studies in Negro History* (New York: International Publishers. 1948).
5 W. E. B. DuBois, *Black Reconstruction in America, 1860–1880* (New York: Atheneum, 1973), esp. Chap. 4.
6 See Pete Daniel, *The Shadow of Slavery: Peonage in the South, 1901–1969* (New York: Oxford University Press, 1972).
7 Mark D. Naison, "The Southern Tenant Farmers Union and the CIO," *Radical America* 2 (September–October 1968), 246–68; Mark D. Naison, "Black Agrarian Radicalism in the Great Depression: The Threads of a Lost Tradition," *Journal of Ethnic Studies* 1 (Fall 1973), 47–65; Martin Dann, "Black Populism. A Study of the Colored Farmer's Alliance Through 1891," *Journal of Ethnic Studies* 2 (Fall 1974), 58–71.
8 Stanley Aronowitz, *False Promises: The Shaping of American Working Class Consciousness* (New York: McGraw-Hill, 1973), Chap. 3.
9 *Ibid.* Gunner Myrdal, *An American Dilemma* (New York: Harper & Row, 1962), esp. Chaps. 8, 13, and 19.
10 See Herbert R. Northrup, *Organized Labor and the Negro* (New York: Harper & Row, 1944); Ray Marshall, *The Negro and Organized Labor* (New York: Wiley, 1965); Julius Jacobson (ed.), *The Negro and the American Labor Movement* (Garden City, N.Y.: Doubleday-Anchor, 1968); and John H. Bracey, Jr., August Meier, and Elliott Rudwick (eds.), *Black Workers and Organized Labor* (Belmont: Wadsworth, 1971); Sterling D. Spero and Abram L. Harris, *The Black Worker* (New York: Atheneum, 1972).
11 See Gerhard Lenski, *Power and Privilege: A Theory of Social Stratification* (New York: McGraw-Hill, 1966), pp. 24–42.
12 Steven A. Marglin, "What Do Bosses Do?" *Review of Radical Political Economics* 7 (Summer 1974), 60–112; Harry Braverman, *Labor and Monopoly Capital: The Degradation of Work in the Twentieth Century* (New York: Monthly Review Press, 1974).
13 See Oliver C. Cox, *Caste, Class and Race: A Study in Social Dynamics* (New York: Monthly Review Press, 1970 – original copyright 1948).
14 Robert Ezra Park, "Our Racial Frontier on the Pacific," pp. 138–51 in Everett C. Hughes, Charles S. Johnson, Jitsuichi Masuoka, Robert Redfield, and Louis Wirth (eds.), *Race and Culture, Vol. I, The Collected Papers of Robert Ezra Park* (Glencoe: Free Press, 1950), p. 150.

15 Robert Ezra Park, "The Nature of Race Relations," pp. 3—45 in Edgar T. Thompson (ed.), *Race Relations and the Race Problem* (Raleigh: Duke University Press), pp. 25, 43—5.

16 Robert Ezra Park, "A Race Relations Survey," pp. 158—66 in Hughes *et al.* (eds.), *Race and Culture*, pp. 159—60.

17 Park, "The Nature of Race Relations," p. 4.

18 *Ibid.*, p. 36; Park, "Our Racial Frontier," p. 150.

19 Park, "The Nature of Race Relations," pp. 23—4.

20 Robert Ezra Park, "Racial Assimilation in Secondary Groups," pp. 204—20 in Hughes *et al.* (eds.), *Race and Culture*, pp. 219—20; Park, "Our Racial Frontier," p. 144.

21 Park, "Racial Assimilation," p. 219—20; Park, "The Nature of Race Relations," p. 31; Robert Ezra Park, "Race Prejudice and Japanese—American Relations," pp. 223—9 in Hughes *et al.* (eds.), *Race and Culture.*

22 Park, "Race Prejudice and Japanese—American Relations," pp. 228—9; Robert Ezra Park, "The Race Relations Cycle in Hawaii," pp. 189—95 in Hughes *et al.* (eds.), *Race and Culture*, p. 190.

23 Park, "Racial Assimilation," p. 220.

24 *Ibid.*, p. 205.

25 Park, "The Nature of Race Relations," p. 45.

26 Oscar Handlin, *The Newcomers: Negroes and Puerto Ricans in a Changing Metropolis* (Cambridge: Harvard University Press, 1959).

27 Nathan Glazer and Daniel P. Moynihan, *Beyond the Melting Pot: The Negroes, Puerto Ricans, Jews, Italians, and Irish of New York City*, First and Second Editions (Cambridge: M.I.T. Press, 1963 and 1970).

28 Irving Kristol, "The Negro Today Is Like the Immigrant of Yesterday," pp. 197—210 in Peter I. Rose (ed.), *Nation of Nations: The Ethnic Experience and the Racial Crisis* (New York: Random House, 1966); Nathan Glazer, "Blacks and Ethnic Groups: The Difference and the Political Difference It Makes," *Social Problems* 18 (Spring 1971), 444—61; Glazer and Moynihan, *Beyond the Melting Pot.*

29 Glazer, "Blacks and Ethnic Groups," p. 458.

30 Otto Kerner *et al.*, *Report of the National Advisory Commission on Civil Disorders* (New York: Bantam Books, 1968), pp. 278—82.

31 Winthrop D. Jordan, *White Over Black: American Attitudes Toward the Negro 1550—1812* (Baltimore: Penguin Books, 1968).

32 James A. Geschwender, *Racial Stratification in America* (Dubuque: Brown, 1977).

33 See Gordon W. Allport, *The Nature of Prejudice* (Garden City, N.Y.: Doubleday-Anchor, 1958); Bruno Bettelheim and Morris Janowicz, *Social Change and Prejudice: A Systematic Theoretical Review and Propositional Inventory of the American Social Psychological Study of Prejudice* (New York: Wiley, 1973); George Eaton Simpson and J. Milton Yinger, *Racial and Cultural Minorities: An Analysis of Prejudice and Discrimination*, Fourth Edition (New York: Harper & Row, 1972).

34 See Cox, *Caste, Class and Race*; Paul A. Baran and Paul M. Sweezy, *Monopoly Capital: An Essay on the American Economic and Social Order* (New York: Monthly Review Press, 1966), pp. 249—80; Harry Braverman, *Labor and Monopoly Capital: The Degradation of Work in the Twentieth Century* (New York: Monthly Review Press, 1974); C. L. R. James, "The Revolutionary Solution to the Negro Problem in the United States (1947)," *Facing Reality* 4 (May 1947), 12—18; John C. Leggett, *Class, Race and Labor: Working Class Consciousness in Detroit* (New York: Oxford University Press, 1968); Martin Oppenheimer, "The Sub-Proletariat: Dark Skins and Dirty Work," *The Insurgent Socialist* 4 (Winter 1974), 6—20; William K. Tabb, "Race Relations Models and Social Change," *Social Problems* 18 (Spring 1971), 431—44; Henry Winston, *Strategy for a Black Agenda: A Critique of New Theories*

of *Black Liberation in the United States and Africa* (New York: International Publishers, 1973).

35 Harry Haywood, *Negro Liberation* (New York: International Publishers, 1948); William Z. Foster, *The Negro People in American History* (New York: International Publishers, 1954), pp. 463—6.

36 Foster, *The Negro People*, p. 463.

37 Robert L. Allen, *Black Awakening in Capitalist America: An Analytic History* (Garden City, N.Y.: Doubleday—Anchor, 1970); Robert Blauner, *Racial Oppression in America* (New York: Harper & Row, 1972); Stokely Carmichael and Charles V. Hamilton, *Black Power The Politics of Liberation in America* (New York: Vintage, 1965); Kenneth B. Clark, *Dark Ghetto* (New York: Harper & Row, 1965); William K. Tabb, *The Political Economy of the Black Ghetto* (New York: Norton, 1970).

Chapter 2. Black workers, the auto industry, and the UAW

1 Herbert R. Northrup, *Organized Labor and the Negro* (New York: Harper & Row, 1944), p. 186.

2 Lloyd H. Bailer, "The Negro Automobile Worker," *Journal of Political Economy* 51 (October 1943), 415.

3 B. J. Widick, *Detroit: City of Race and Class Violence* (Chicago: Quadrangle, 1972), p. 26.

4 *Ibid.*, p. 27.

5 *Ibid.*

6 Bailer, "Negro Automobile Worker," p. 415.

7 John G. Van Deusen, *The Black Man in White America* (Washington: Associated Publishers, 1944), cited in Widick, *Detroit*, p. 27.

8 Widick, *Detroit*, p. 27.

9 Bailer, "Negro Automobile Worker," pp. 415—6.

10 *Ibid.*, p. 416.

11 *Ibid.*

12 Robert W. Dunn, *Labor and Automobiles* (New York, 1929) cited in Northrup, *Organized Labor and the Negro*, p. 187.

13 Bailer, "Negro Automobile Worker," p. 417.

14 *Ibid.*

15 *Ibid.*, p. 419.

16 Glen E. Carlson, "The Negro in the Industries of Detroit" (Ann Arbor: University of Michigan unpublished doctoral dissertation, 1929) cited in Bailer, "Negro Automobile Worker," p. 417.

17 Bailer, "Negro Automobile Worker," p. 419.

18 Northrup, *Organized Labor and the Negro*, pp. 189—90.

19 Herbert R. Northrup, "The Negro in the Automobile Industry," pp. 43—126 in Herbert R. Northrup (ed.), *Negro Employment in Basic Industries I* (Philadelphia: Wharton School of Finance, University of Pennsylvania, 1970), p. 56.

20 Northrup, *Organized Labor and the Negro*, p. 190.

21 *Ibid.*

22 *Ibid.*

23 Northrup, "The Negro in the Automobile Industry," p. 58.

24 Irving Howe and B. J. Widick, *The UAW and Walter Reuther* (New York: Random House, 1949), pp. 216—17.

25 Northrup, *Organized Labor and the Negro*, p. 193.

26 *Ibid.*

27 Lloyd H. Bailer, "Negro Labor in the Automobile Industry" (Ann Arbor: University of Michigan unpublished doctoral dissertation, 1943), cited in Howe and Widick, *UAW and Walter Reuther*, p. 216.

28 Howe and Widick, *UAW and Walter Reuther*, p. 217.

29 Northrup, *Organized Labor and the Negro*, p. 194.

30 Horace A. White, "Who Owns the Negro Churches?" *Christian Century* 55 (February 9, 1938), 176—77.

31 Northrup, "The Negro in the Automobile Industry," p. 57.

32 Widick, *Detroit*, pp. 58—9.

33 *Ibid.*, p. 59.

34 *Ibid.*, p. 66.

35 Bailer, "Negro Automobile Worker," p. 421; and Northrup, *Organized Labor and the Negro*, p. 189.

36 Widick, *Detroit*, p. 28.

37 Bailer, "Negro Automobile Worker," p. 421.

38 Lloyd H. Bailer, "The Automobile Unions and Negro Labor," *Political Science Quarterly* 59 (December 1944), 550—1.

39 Howe and Widick, *UAW and Walter Reuther*, p. 210.

40 Bailer, "Auto Unions and Negro Labor," p. 551.

41 For an illustration, see John Bracey, Jr., August Meier, and Elliott Rudwick (eds.), *Black Workers and Organized Labor* (Belmont: Wadsworth, 1971).

42 Howe and Widick, *UAW and Walter Reuther*, p. 211.

43 *Ibid.*, pp. 211—12.

44 Bailer, "Auto Unions and Negro Labor," pp. 551—2.

45 *Ibid.*, pp. 553—4.

46 *Ibid.*; and Widick, *Detroit*, pp. 74—6.

47 Howe and Widick, *UAW and Walter Reuther*, pp. 96—7; Bailer, "Auto Unions and Negro Labor," p. 552.

48 Bailer, "Auto Unions and Negro Labor," p. 554.

49 *Ibid.*

50 Lloyd H. Bailer, unpublished manuscript furnished to Northrup, apparently an early version of "Auto Unions and Negro Labor," cited in Northrup, *Organized Labor and the Negro*, p. 195.

51 This account is primarily derived from Howe and Widick, *UAW and Walter Reuther*, pp. 100—6.

52 Northrup, *Organized Labor and the Negro*, p. 196.

53 Howe and Widick, *UAW and Walter Reuther*, p. 103 with the portion within quotation marks taken from the *Detroit News*, April 2, 1941.

54 Walter White, *A Man Called White* (New York: Viking, 1948), p. 213; Northrup, *Organized Labor and the Negro*, p. 196.

55 Howe and Widick, *UAW and Walter Reuther*, p. 104.

56 White, *A Man Called White*, pp. 213—23.

57 *Ibid.*, p. 216.

58 Bailer manuscript cited in Northrup, *Organized Labor and the Negro*, p. 196.

59 Northrup, *Organized Labor and the Negro*, p. 196.

60 *Ibid.*, p. 198.

61 Bailer, "Negro Automobile Worker," p. 424.

62 Northrup, "The Negro in the Automobile Industry," p. 60.

63 Bailer, "Auto Unions and Negro Labor," p. 562.

64 *Ibid.*, pp. 562—6; Northrup, "The Negro in the Automobile Industry," p. 60.

65 Bailer, "Auto Unions and Negro Labor," p. 566.

66 *Ibid.*

67 Northrup, *Organized Labor and the Negro*, p. 199.

68 Bailer, "Negro Automobile Worker," p. 424.

69 *Ibid.*, p. 568.

70 Much of the following discussion of the wildcat strikes is based upon Bailer, "Auto Unions and Negro Labor," pp. 568–72, and Northrup, *Organized Labor and the Negro*, pp. 199–210.

71 For a discussion of internal political developments and conflicts within the UAW, see B. J. Widick, *Labor Today* (Boston: Houghton Mifflin, 1964); Widick, *Detroit*; and Howe and Widick, *UAW and Walter Reuther*. These are valuable sources in that their portrayal of events is reasonably accurate. The author does not agree with their interpretation of these events, however.

72 Northrup, *Organized Labor and the Negro*, pp. 201–3.

73 *Ibid.*, p. 203.

74 Northrup, "The Negro in the Automobile Industry," p. 61.

75 This discussion of policy changes is based upon Northrup, *Organized Labor and the Negro*, pp. 204–5.

76 Widick, *Detroit*, p. 125.

77 *Ibid.*, pp. 125–6.

78 *Ibid.*, pp. 126–7.

79 Howe and Widick, *UAW and Walter Reuther*, p. 228.

80 *Ibid.*, pp. 228–30.

81 *Ibid.*, p. 230.

82 Interview with Jordan Sims, January 1974.

83 *Ibid.*

84 Northrup, "The Negro in the Automobile Industry," p. 77.

85 *Ibid.*, pp. 66–8.

86 *Ibid.*, pp. 68–72.

87 Widick, *Detroit*, pp. 127–35.

88 Brian Peterson, "Working Class Communism: A Review of the Literature," *Radical America* 5 (January–February 1971), 44.

89 Northrup, "The Negro in the Automobile Industry," pp. 72–75.

90 Widick, *Detroit*, p. 148.

91 This estimate is computed by the following formula: number of experienced black auto workers in Detroit X (number of employed black auto workers in Michigan ÷ number of experienced black auto workers in Michigan) = estimated number of employed black auto workers in Detroit. This is computed separately by sex.

92 Northrup, "The Negro in the Automobile Industry," p. 77.

93 *Ibid.*, pp. 89–90.

94 Sidney Lens, *The Labor Wars: From the Molly Maguires to the Sit-Downs* (Garden City, N.Y.: Doubleday, 1973), p. 299.

95 Sidney Lens, *The Crisis of American Labor* (New York: Sagamore, 1959), p. 192.

96 Lens, *The Labor Wars*, pp. 187, 237–9, 274.

97 Keith Sward, *The Legend of Henry Ford* (New York: Holt, Rinehart and Winston, 1948), pp. 231–42.

98 Lens, *The Crisis*, pp. 195–8, 187–9.

99 *Ibid.*, p. 187.

100 *Ibid.*

101 Saul Alinsky quoted in William Z. Foster, *History of the Communist Party of the United States* (New York: Greenwood, 1968), p. 353 (original copyright, 1952).

102 *Ibid.*, pp. 351–3.

103 Sidney Lens, *Left, Right and Center: Conflicting Forces in American Labor* (Hinsdale: Henry Regency, 1949), p. 323.

104 Theodore Draper, *American Communism and Soviet Russia* (New York: Viking, 1960), pp. 315–56.

105 Howe and Widick, *UAW and Walter Reuther*, p. 106.

106 *Ibid.*

107 William Z. Foster, *The Negro People in American History* (updated version), (New York: New World Paperbacks, 1954), p. 504.

108 Lens, *Left, Right and Center*, pp. 309, 326; Sward, *The Legend of Henry Ford*, p. 381.

109 Foster, *History of the Communist Party*, p. 353; Howe and Widick, *UAW and Walter Reuther*, pp. 70–8; Martin Glaberman, "A Note on Walter Reuther," *Radical America* 7 (November–December 1973), 113–17.

110 Howe and Widick, *UAW and Walter Reuther*, pp. 70–8.

111 *Ibid.*, p. 115.

112 *Ibid.*, pp. 118–47.

113 For an extended discussion of this drive for representation, see Howe and Widick, *UAW and Walter Reuther*, pp. 223–31.

114 Ray Marshall, *The Negro and Organized Labor* (New York: Wiley, 1965), pp. 83–4; and Northrup, "The Negro in the Automobile Industry," pp. 99–103.

115 This discussion is based partially on material in David A. Shannon, *The Decline of American Communism: A History of the Communist Party Since 1945* (New York: Harcourt Brace Jovanovich, 1959), pp. 47, 103–4, and Widick, *Detroit*, pp. 127–35; but it is primarily based on interviews conducted by Herbert Hill with blacks who had been active in the UAW in the thirties and forties.

116 For a discussion of the history of TULC, see Marshall, *The Negro and Organized Labor*, pp. 68–70; and Widick, *Detroit*, pp. 149–51, 159–60.

117 See Reinhard Bendix and Seymour Martin Lipset, "Karl Marx Theory of Social Classes," pp. 26–35 in Reinhard Bendix and Seymour Martin Lipset (eds.), *Class, Status, and Power* (New York: Free Press, 1953) for a discussion of the manner in which class consciousness may emerge out of the interaction of a number of persons sharing a common set of grievances. See also Karl Marx, "The Eighteenth Brumaire of Louis Bonaparte," in Karl Marx and Frederick Engels, *Selected Works* (New York: International Publishers, 1968), pp. 171–2, for a discussion of the inability of the French peasantry to develop class consciousness due to the lack of a network of communications.

Chapter 3. Detroit: evolution of a black industrial city

1 Robert D. Swartz, John M. Ball, Fred E. Dohrs, and Merrill K. Ridd (eds.), *Metropolitan America: Geographic Perspectives and Teaching Strategies* (Oak Park: National Council for Geographic Education, 1972), p. 11.

2 *Ibid.*, p. 12.

3 Computed from United States Department of Commerce, Bureau of the Census: PC(1)-D24, Detailed Characteristics, Michigan, Table 184.

4 Frank B. Woodford and Arthur M. Woodford, *All Our Yesterdays: A Brief History of Detroit* (Detroit: Wayne State University Press, 1969), p. 179.

5 David M. Katzman, *Before the Ghetto: Black Detroit in the Nineteenth Century* (Urbana: University of Illinois Press, 1973), pp. 6–7.

6 *Ibid.*, pp. 8–12.

7 *Ibid.*, pp. 5–6.

8 *Ibid.*, pp. 5, 33–9, 175–6.

9 *Ibid.*, pp. 23, 50, 85; Woodford and Woodford, *All Our Yesterdays*, p. 148.

10 See Katzman, *Before the Ghetto*, pp. 44—7; Woodford and Woodford, *All Our Yesterdays*, p. 184.

11 Katzman, *Before the Ghetto*, p. 48.

12 *Ibid.*, pp. 104—7, 110, 116, 119—23, 217—22.

13 For a discussion of the role of ethnic minorities as buffer groups see Tamotsu Shibutani and Kian M. Kwan, *Ethnic Stratification: A Comparative Approach* (New York: Macmillan, 1965), pp. 196—7, 382.

14 Sidney Glazer, *Detroit: A Study in Urban Development* (New York: Bookman, 1965), p. 107; George Edmund Haynes, "Negro Newcomers in Detroit," pp. 1—42 in William Loren Katz (ed.), *Haynes and Brown: The Negro in Detroit and Washington* (New York: Arno and the *New York Times*, 1969).

15 Donald R. Deskins, Jr., *Residential Mobility of Negroes in Detroit, 1837—1965* (Ann Arbor: University of Michigan, Department of Geography, 1972), pp. 259—60.

16 See *ibid.*, p. 138; Woodford and Woodford, *All Our Yesterdays*, pp. 341—3; B. J. Widick, *Detroit: City of Race and Class Violence* (Chicago: Quadrangle, 1972), pp. 3—5, 343—4.

17 See Widick, *Detroit*, pp. 5—22; Woodford and Woodford, *All Our Yesterdays*, pp. 343—4; John C. Dancey, *Sand Against the Wind: The Memoirs of John C. Dancey* (Detroit: Wayne State University Press, 1966), pp. 21—34.

18 See Widick, *Detroit*, pp. 95—7; Woodford and Woodford, *All Our Yesterdays*, pp. 344—5.

19 See Widick, *Detroit*, pp. 88—112; Dancey, *Sand Against the Wind*, pp. 21—34; Woodford and Woodford, *All Our Yesterdays*, pp. 346—8; Alfred McClung Lee and Norman D. Humphrey, *Race Riot: Detroit, 1943* (New York: Octagon, 1968); Robert Shogan and Tom Craig, *The Detroit Race Riot: A Study in Violence* (New York: Chilton, 1964).

20 Albert J. Mayer and Thomas F. Hoult, "Race and Residence in Detroit," pp. 3—13 in Leonard Gordon (ed.), *A City in Racial Crisis: The Case of Detroit Pre- and Post- the 1967 Riot* (Dubuque: Brown, 1971).

21 Dancey, *Sand Against the Wind*, pp. 215—16.

22 Widick, *Detroit*, pp. 123—4.

23 Shogan and Craig, *Detroit Race Riot*, pp. 122—8.

24 Joel D. Aberbach and Jack L. Walker, *Race in the City: Political Trust and Public Policy in the New Urban System* (Boston: Little, Brown, 1973), p. 9.

25 Benjamin D. Singer, Richard W. Osborn, and James A. Geschwender, *Black Rioters: A Study of Social Factors and Communication in the Detroit Riot* (Lexington: Heath Lexington, 1970), pp. 26—9.

26 See Shogan and Craig, *Detroit Race Riot*, pp. 122—37; Woodford and Woodford, *All Our Yesterdays*, pp. 344—50; Widick, *Detroit*, pp. 157—8.

27 Shogan and Craig, *Detroit Race Riot*, p. 136.

28 See Widick, *Detroit*, pp. 161—2; Hubert G. Locke, *The Detroit Riot of 1967* (Detroit: Wayne State University Press, 1969), pp. 62—5.

29 See Widick, *Detroit*, p. 164; Locke, *The Detroit Riot*, pp. 65—6.

30 Locke, *The Detroit Riot*, pp. 67—9, 105; Widick, *Detroit*, pp. 161—5; Singer, Osborn, and Geschwender, *Black Rioters*, pp. 98—9.

31 See Locke, *The Detroit Riot*; Singer, Osborn, and Geschwender, *Black Rioters*; Van Gordon Sauter and Burleigh Hines, *Nightmare in Detroit* (Chicago: Henry Regency, 1968); Widick, *Detroit*, pp. 166—85.

32 *Detroit Free Press*, September 3, 1967.

33 This description of the insurrection participants is often questioned by readers. Several persons have asked, "Why is there a discrepancy between this account and that normally reported in the literature?" and, "If these figures are based upon arrest statistics, may they

not be misleading?" Both questions deserve a response. It is true that the primary source for these statistics are data collected by interviewing arrestees. These data are reported in Singer, Osborn, and Geschwender, *Black Rioters*. However, I should note that the data usually used to refute it — that published by the Kerner Commission — were based, in part, upon material submitted by Benjamin D. Singer to the Kerner Commission prior to its complete analysis and subsequently included in *Black Rioters* [Otto Kerner, *et al., Report of the National Advisory Commission on Civil Disorders* (New York: Bantam Books, 1968)]. The data reported by the Kerner Commission were not age controlled and were superficially examined. The data were presented in a form that suggested that the insurrection participant was better educated and economically better off than the nonparticipant. Later age-controlled analysis revealed exactly the reverse. The typical insurrection participant was less well educated than the nonparticipant of the same age, was likely to be an employed worker, but was also likely to have experienced a great deal more unemployment over the preceding year than that experienced by the nonparticipant and was less well paid. Thus it may be concluded that the participant was typically a member of the marginal working class or part of that reserve army of workers who are called upon when needed by an expanding industry and laid off by a contracting industry. In order to evaluate the validity of arrest data I compared the social characteristics of our sample of arrestees with an unpublished list of characteristics of all arrestees and of a sample of arrestees furnished to me by Robert Mendelsohn from a study he conducted and with published characteristics of self-reported participants (see Nathan S. Caplan and Jeffrey M. Paige, "A Study of Ghetto Rioters," *Scientific American* 219 (August 1968), 15–21). There was a great similarity in comparable social characteristics among all four data sets. Therefore I am convinced that the Singer, Osborn, and Geschwender report of participant characteristics is accurate.

34 See Widick, *Detroit*, pp. 186–208.

35 The Smith Act was passed in 1940 and made it illegal to teach, advise, or advocate the overthrow of the government of the United States. Twelve top members of the Communist Party were indicted on July 20, 1948, by a Federal Grand Jury in New York City on charges of violating the Smith Act. They were actually charged with conspiracy to form a party to teach and advocate the overthrow of the United States government. The case of one defendent was severed due to ill health. George W. Crockett was one of the five principal defense attorneys. The defense strategy was to use the trial as a vehicle to expose the class nature of justice in American society rather than to concentrate efforts on an attempt to win an acquittal. Thus jury selection techniques were attacked. It was charged, with more than a little validity, that the jury was stacked with middle-class whites; blacks, in particular, were systematically excluded. The Judge, Harold Medina, was attacked for his racial biases as well as his prejudicial handling of the case. The defense attorneys constantly clashed with the Judge, as is inevitable in political trials. Consequently, after the defendents were found guilty and sentenced, the Judge then charged Crockett, among others, with contempt, convicted him, and sentenced him. There is little question that the Smith Act trials were aimed at destroying the Communist Party. They took place in the "witch-hunt" atmosphere of McCarthyism and were so conducted by Judge Medina as to constitute a travesty on justice. Nevertheless they did succeed in severely damaging the Communist Party in America. For a nonobjective account of the trials from the frame of reference of a very hostile anti-Communist see Davis A. Shannon, *The Decline of American Communism: A History of the Communist Party of the United States Since 1945* (New York: Harcourt Brace Jovanovich, 1959), pp. 195–203.

36 Verbal communication from Herbert Hill based upon his interviews with black Communists who had been in the UAW.

37 Widick, *Detroit*, pp. 127–35.

38 See C. Eric Lincoln, *The Black Muslims in America* (Boston: Beacon Press, 1961), pp. 10–21; Locke, *The Detroit Riot*, pp. 110–22.

Chapter 4. The birth of the League

1 "Storm in Auto," reprinted in Robert Dudnick, *Black Workers in Revolt*, a *Guardian Pamphlet*. Originally appeared in the *Guardian*, March 8, 1969, p. 4.

2 "To the Point of Production: An Interview with John Watson of the League of Revolutionary Black Workers," *Fifth Estate*. Reprinted as a Bay Area Radical Education Project Publication, p. 1.

3 Uhuru was a militant organization of blacks centering on the Wayne State University campus in the early 1960s.

4 *Detroit News*, October 14, 1963.

5 *Detroit News*, February 24, 1966.

6 Interview with Luke Tripp and John Williams late July 1971.

7 Dan Georgakas and Marvin Surkin, "BWC Leader Looks at Past, Sees New Stage of Struggle. An Interview with Mike Hamlin," *Guardian*, February 28, 1963, pp. 8—9.

8 Mike Hamlin quoted in Jim Jacobs and David Wellman, "An interview with Ken Cockrel and Mike Hamlin of the League of Revolutionary Black Workers," *Leviathon*, June 1970. Reprinted as *Our Thing Is Drum*.

9 This discussion is largely based upon interviews with Marty Glaberman and George Rawick, July 1971.

10 Dudnick, *Black Workers in Revolt*; the *Michigan Chronicle*, August 24, 1968; the *Detroit News*, August 19, 1968; *Detroit Free Press*, August 16, 1968.

11 Luke Tripp, "D.R.U.M. — Vanguard of the Black Revolution: Dodge Revolutionary Union Movement States History, Purpose, and Aims," special issue of *The South End*, January 23, 1969, pp. 8—9.

12 *Michigan Chronicle*, August 24, 1968.

13 Chuck Wooten, "Why I Joined DRUM," *Guardian*, March 8, 1969. Reprinted in Dudnick, *Black Workers in Revolt*, p. 13.

14 Mike Hamlin quoted in Jacobs and Wellman, "An Interview with Ken Cockrel," p. 11.

15 This and all subsequent references to *drum* newsletters were taken from the originals in my collection.

16 *Michigan Chronicle*, August 24, 1968; *Detroit News*, August 19, 1968; *Detroit Free Press*, August 16, 1968.

17 *Ibid.*, Interview with Douglas Fraser, July 1971.

18 *Ibid.*

19 *drum*, 1, #2.

20 Tripp, "D.R.U.M.," p. 9.

21 *Ibid.*, pp. 9—10.

22 The shutdown was legal in that it violated no laws. However, it was a violation of the UAW contract with Dodge and of the UAW bylaws.

23 Dudnick, *Black Workers in Revolt*, p. 4, sets the date of the wildcat as July 8. Tripp, "D.R.U.M.," pp. 9—10, states that the meeting was the day before the wildcat.

24 *Detroit Free Press*, August 16, 1968.

25 Tripp, D.R.U.M.," pp. 10, 12.

26 *Detroit Free Press*, August 16, 1968.

27 Tripp, "D.R.U.M.," p. 5.

28 This was indicated in the original ELRUM and FRUM newsletters in my collection as well as by Mike Hamlin as quoted in Jacobs and Wellman, "An Interview with Ken Cockrel," p. 15.

29 *Speak Out*, 2, #3 (March 1969), 3.

30 Dudnick, *Black Workers in Revolt*, p. 5.

31 *Detroit Free Press*, March 12, 1969.

32 Mike Hamlin quoted in Jacobs and Wellman, "An Interview with Ken Cockrel," pp. 15—16.

33 *Detroit Free Press*, August 16, 1968.
34 Interview with Homer Jolly, UAW executive, May 1, 1974.
35 John Watson quoted in "To the Point of Production," p. 20.
36 Dudnick, *Black Workers in Revolt*, p. 5.
37 This account is largely based upon the undated, untitled, four-page newspaper issue put out by the League of Revolutionary Black Workers; *Detroit News*, November 8 and 9; *Detroit Free Press*, November 9 and 10.
38 *Spear*, 1, #4.
39 Gabriel N. Alexander, "Jordan Sims Grievance Decision," mimeograph of UAW decision, December 15, 1970.
40 *elrum*, 1' #1—7. (Elrum publications will herein be capitalized or not as they are in the originals.)
41 *Inner City Voice*, 2, #6 (June 1970), p. 8.
42 *Eldon Wildcat*, #8 (May 4, 1970); Homer Jolly stated that Scott was reinstated the next day: Jolly, in an interview May 1, 1974.
43 Most of the following discussion is taken from Alexander, "Jordan Sims."
44 *ELRUM*, 3, #3.
45 *Inner City Voice*, 2, #6 (June 1970).
46 Undated *ELRUM*.
47 Jolly, in an interview May 1, 1974.
48 Undated *ELRUM* from week of September 1; *Eldon Wildcat*, #20 (September 2, 1970).
49 *ELRUM*, 3, #4.
50 Alexander, "Jordan Sims"; interview with Jordan Sims, September 1973.
51 Reprinted in *Eldon Wildcat*, #19 (August 20, 1970).

Chapter 5. Union electoral politics

1 Thomas R. Brooks, "DRUMbeats in Detroit," *Dissent* 7 (January—February 1970), 23.
2 Luke Tripp, "D.R.U.M. — Vanguard of the Black Revolution: Dodge Revolutionary Union Movement States History, Purpose, and Aims," special issue of the *South End*, January 23, 1969, pp. 8—9.
3 *drum* 1, #13, 14, 15.
4 Dereck Morrison, "Dodge Revolutionary Union Movement," *Young Socialist* 12 (November, 1968), 11, 18.
5 *Ibid.*, p. 18.
6 *Battleline* 1 (July 1968), 1.
7 "The Dodge Rebellion," *Ramparts* 7 (November 30, 1968), 12.
8 Morrison, "Dodge Revolutionary Union Movement," p. 8.
9 *Ibid.*, pp. 11, 18; "The Dodge Rebellion."
10 *drum* 1, #15.
11 *drum* 1, #15.
12 *drum* 1, #8, 9.
13 *drum* 1, #8, 9, 10.
14 *Detroit News*, March 16, 1969.
15 *drum* 2, #11.
16 Undated *drum*.
17 *drum* 2, #15.
18 *Ibid.*
19 *Inner City Voice*, 2 (March 16—April 1, 1970), 8—9.
20 *Ibid.*, p. 8.

21 *drum* 3, #5.

22 *Detroit News*, May 4, 1971.

23 See Dan Georgakas and Marvin Surkin, *Detroit: I Do Mind Dying: A Study in Urban Revolution* (New York: St. Martins Press, 1975), pp. 90—1, 96—8, 161.

24 *Detroit Free Press*, May 18, 1969.

25 *Detroit Free Press*, May 29, 1971.

26 *Ibid.*

27 Unnumbered *ELRUM; ELRUM* 3, #3.

28 *ELRUM* 3, #3.

29 Interview with Douglas Fraser, UAW vice-president, July 1971.

30 *Eldon Wildcat* #5 (April 1, 1970); *ELRUM*, undated; several undated election flyers and leaflets; *Inner City Voice* 2 (March 16—April 1), 13.

31 Brooks, "DRUMbeats," p. 21.

Chapter 6. Ideology

1 League of Revolutionary Black Workers, *The General Policy Statement and the Labor Program of the League of Revolutionary Black Workers*, pamphlet, no date or publisher; *Inner City Voice* 2 (October 1970), 11—12; 2 (November—December 1970), 11—13; 3 (February 1971), 11—13.

2 *Inner City Voice* 2 (November—December 1970), 10.

3 *Ibid.*, pp. 10—11.

4 *Inner City Voice* 3 (February 1971), 10.

5 *Ibid.*, pp. 10—11.

6 League of Revolutionary Black Workers, *The General Policy Statement*, p. 15.

7 *Ibid.*, p. 29.

8 *Ibid.*, pp. 30—3.

9 Oliver C. Cox, *Caste, Class, and Race* (New York: Monthly Review Press, 1948).

10 For a description of the populist movement see C. Vann Woodward, *The Strange Career of Jim Crow* (New York: Crowell, 1961).

11 Watson presents a well-reasoned discussion of the populist movement including an analysis of the role of racism in its ultimate demise. This is quoted in "To the Point of Production: An Interview with John Watson of the League of Revolutionary Black Workers," *Fifth Estate*. Reprinted as a Bay Area Radical Education Project Publication, pp. 12—13.

12 Robert Blauner, *Racial Oppression in America* (New York: Harper & Row, 1972).

13 Personal communication from Immanuel Wallerstein.

14 See Franz Fanon, *The Wretched of the Earth* (New York: Grove Press, 1968); see also Robert L. Allen, *Black Awakening in Capitalist America: An Analytic History* (Garden City, N.Y.: Doubleday-Anchor, 1970), p. 14; William K. Tabb, *The Political Economy of the Black Ghetto* (New York: Norton, 1970), pp. 22—3; Blauner, *Racial Oppression*.

15 John Williams stated essentially this point in an interview, November 11, 1971.

Chapter 7. League organizational activities

1 "To the Point of Production: An Interview with John Watson of the League of Revolutionary Black Workers," *Fifth Estate*. Reprinted as a Bay Area Radical Education Project Publication, p. 6.

2 Dan Georgakas, "League of Revolutionary Black Workers: Interview with John Watson," *Liberated Guardian* 2, #1 (May 1, 1971), 12.

3 *Fifth Estate*, "To the Point of Production," pp. 6—7.

4 Interview with John Watson, July 7, 1971; Ken Cockrel quoted in Jim Jacobs and David Wellman, "An Interview with Ken Cockrel and Mike Hamlin of the League of Revolutionary Black Workers," *Leviathon*, June 1970. Reprinted as *Our Thing is Drum*.

5 *Detroit News*, June 11, 1969; January 5, 1970; June 16, 1970.

6 *Time*, June 7, 1971.

7 Interview with Luke Tripp and John Williams, July 1971.

8 See Gene Marine, *The Black Panthers* (New York: New American Library, 1969).

9 John Watson, "Perspectives: A Summary Session," the final presentation of the first year of the Control, Conflict, and Change Book Club, June 8, 1971.

10 Cited in Thomas R. Brooks, "DRUMbeats in Detroit," *Dissent* 7 (January—February 1970), 23.

11 Ken Cockrel quoted in Jacobs and Wellman, "An Interview with Ken Cockrel," p. 19.

12 Mike Hamlin quoted in *ibid.*, p. 22.

13 *Detroit Free Press*, August 18, 1968.

14 Black Star Publishing (eds.), *The Political Thought of James Forman* (Detroit: Black Star, 1970), pp. i—ii, 1—69; Jim Jacobs, "The Midwest and the League," in Jacobs and Wellman, "An Interview with Ken Cockrel," p. 10; and Robert S. Lecky and H. Elliott Wright (eds.), *Black Manifesto* (New York: Sheed and Ward, 1969); Dan Georgakas and Marvin Surkin, *Detroit: I Do Mind Dying: A Study in Urban Revolution* (New York: St. Martins Press, 1975), pp. 94—9.

15 Black Star Publishing, *The Political Thought of James Forman*, pp. 59—62.

16 Interview with John Williams and Luke Tripp, late July 1971. The book was Black Star Publishing, *The Political Thought of James Forman*; the pamphlet was *Revolutionary Nationalism and the Class Struggle*.

17 Pamphlets on the IBA in my collection and interviews with John Williams and Luke Tripp, July 1971.

18 Mike Hamlin quoted in Jacobs and Wellman, "An Interview with Ken Cockrel," pp. 15—16.

19 Most of this section is based upon material appearing in the *Detroit News* between November 3, 1968 and March 2, 1969. This is supplemented by material appearing in *The South End* during the same time period.

20 Interviews with Luke Tripp and John Williams, June 1971; interview with John Watson, June 1971; Georgakas and Surkin, *Detroit*, pp. 91—3.

21 Watson, "Perspectives."

Chapter 8. The League splits and dies

1 The discussion of the split is based upon interviews with John Watson, November 11, 1971, and with John Williams and Luke Tripp later the same day; Ken Cockrel, Mike Hamlin, and John Watson, "The Split in the League of Revolutionary Black Workers: Three Lines and Three Headquarters," privately circulated manuscript; and an untitled packet of materials on the split privately circulated by John Williams, Rufus Burke, and Clint Marbury.

2 This discussion is based on a series of discussions with the participants and upon the account appearing in Dan Georgakas and Marvin Surkin, *Detroit: I Do Mind Dying: A Study in Urban Revolution* (New York: St. Martins Press, 1975), pp. 159—81.

3 Cockrel, Hamlin, and Watson, "The Split in the League."

4 *Ibid.*, pp. 7—8.

5 *Ibid.*, p. 8.

6 *Ibid.*, p. 16.

7 *Ibid.*, pp. 17—20.

8 *Ibid.* pp. 24—5.

9 Williams, Burke, and Marbury, privately circulated materials.
10 *Ibid.*, pp. 1—2.
11 *Ibid.*, pp. 4—5.
12 *Ibid.*, p. 5.
13 *Ibid.*, p. 6.
14 Interview with Watson; interview with Williams and Tripp.

Chapter 9. Why was the League initially so successful?

1 See James A. Geschwender, "Social Structure and the Negro Revolt: An Examination of Some Hypotheses," *Social Forces* 43 (December 1964), 250—6; James A. Geschwender, "Negro Education: The False Faith," *Phylon* 29 (Winter 1968), 371—8; James A. Geschwender, "The Changing Role of Violence in the Black Revolt," *Sociological Symposium* 9 (Spring 1973), pp. 403—11.

2 See Richard M. Dalfiume, "The Forgotten Years of the Negro Revolution," *The Journal of American History* 55 (June 1968), 90—106; Herbert Garfinkle, *When Negroes March* (New York: Free Press, 1959); Murray Kempton, "The Choice Mr. President," pp. 450—5 in Robert B. Luce (ed.), *The Faces of Five Decades: Selections from the New Republic* (New York: Simon and Shuster, n.d.).

3 Donald R. Mathews and James W. Prothro, *Negroes and the New Southern Politics* (New York: Harcourt Brace Jovanovich, 1966).

4 Donald Von Eschen, Jerome Kirk, and Maurice Pinard, "The Disintegration of the Negro Non-Violent Movement," pp. 113—34 in John H. Bracey, August Meier, and Elliott Rudwick (eds.), *Conflict and Competition: Studies in the Recent Black Protest Movement* (Belmont: Wadsworth, 1969).

5 Sidney M. Wilhelm, *Who Needs the Negro* (Garden City, N.Y.: Doubleday-Anchor, 1971), pp. 103—59.

6 See Len Holt, "Eyewitness: The Police Terror at Birmingham," pp. 344—9 in Joanne Grant (ed.), *Black Protest: History, Documents, and Analyses* (New York: St. Martins Press, 1968); August Meier and Elliott Rudwick, "Black Violence in the Twentieth Century: A Study in Rhetoric and Retaliation," pp. 399—412 in Hugh Davis Graham and Ted Robert Gurr (eds.), *The History of Violence in America* (New York: Bantam Books, 1969); Harold A. Nelson, "The Defenders: A Case Study of an Informal Police Organization," *Social Problems* 15 (Fall 1967), 127—47; Charles R. Sims, "Armed Defense," pp. 357—65 in Grant, *Black Protest*; Robert F. Williams, "Negroes With Guns," pp. 149—61 in Floyd B. Barbour (ed.), *The Black Power Revolt* (Boston: F. Porter Sargent, 1968).

7 James A. Geschwender, "Civil Rights Protest and Riots: A Disappearing Distinction," *Social Science Quarterly* 49 (December 1968), 474—84.

8 Robert L. Allen, *Black Awakening in Capitalist America: An Analytic History* (Garden City, N.Y.: Doubleday-Anchor, 1970).

9 Malcolm X, *The Autobiography of Malcolm X* (New York: Grove Press, 1966).

10 Stokely Carmichael and Charles V. Hamilton, *Black Power: The Politics of Liberation in America* (New York: Vintage, 1967).

11 John R. Howard, *The Cutting Edge: Social Movements and Social Change in America* (New York: Lippincott, 1974).

12 Seymour Martin Lipset and Sheldon S. Wolin, *The Berkeley Student Revolt: Facts and Interpretations* (Garden City, N.Y.: Doubleday-Anchor, 1965).

13 See Carmichael and Hamilton, *Black Power*; Gene Marine, *The Black Panthers* (New York: Signet, 1969); Roderick Aya and Norman Miller (eds.), *The New American Revolution* (New York: Free Press, 1971); Harold Jacobs (ed.), *Weatherman* (Ramparts Press, 1970);

Jerome H. Skolnick, *The Politics of Protest* (New York: Ballantine Books, 1969).

14 Eleanor Paperno Wolf and Charles N. Lebeaux, *Change and Renewal in an Urban Community: Five Case Studies of Detroit* (New York: Praeger, 1969).

15 See Philip S. Foner, *Organized Labor and the Black Worker 1619—1973* (New York: Praeger, 1974), p. 411.

16 *Progress Report of the New Detroit Committee, April 1968*, pp. 55—7.

17 Interviews with Ken Cockrel, John Watson, and John Williams, October 1975.

18 Dan Georgakas and Marvin Surkin, *Detroit: I Do Mind Dying: A Study in Urban Revolution* (New York: St. Martins Press, 1975), p. 62.

19 *Ibid.*, p. 19.

20 *Ibid.*, p. 23.

21 *Detroit News*, October 14, 1973.

Chapter 10. Why did the League die?

1 I heard these rumors while living in Detroit in August and September 1967. They were considered serious enough that they were denied on local TV stations and a rumor control center was set up with a phone number where one could call and check out any rumors that were circulating. Daily newpapers were on strike beginning in October 1967 and rumors were a major source of news.

2 Ken Cockrel, Mike Hamlin, and John Watson, "The Split in the League of Revolutionary Black Workers: Three Lines of Development and Three Headquarters," privately circulated manuscript, p. 2; interview with John Watson, November 11, 1971; interview with John Williams and Luke Tripp, November 11, 1971.

3 Quoted in Dan Georgakas and Marvin Surkin, "BWC Leader Looks at Past. Sees New Stage of Struggle, an Interview with Mike Hamlin," *Guardian* (February 28, 1973), 8—9.

4 Cockrel, Hamlin, and Watson, "The Split in the League," pp. 20—22.

5 *Ibid.*, pp. 21—2.

6 Quoted in Georgakas and Surkin, "BWC Leader Looks at Past," p. 8.

7 *Ibid.*, pp. 7—8.

8 *Ibid.*, p. 9.

9 See Philip S. Foner, *Organized Labor and the Black Worker 1619—1973* (New York: Praeger, 1974), p. 421.

10 Interview with John Watson, November 11, 1971.

11 Interviews with John Williams and Luke Tripp, July 1971, November 11, 1971.

12 Quoted in Georgakas and Surkin, "BWC Leader Looks at Past," p. 8; and interview with Douglas Fraser, November 1971.

13 See Lewis M. Killian and Charles Grigg, *Racial Crisis in America: Leadership in Conflict* (Englewood Cliffs: Prentice-Hall, 1964), pp. 81—90, 131—3.

14 Interview with Douglas Fraser, November 1971.

15 Conversation with Joseph Merchant of IFCO, February 1973.

16 The impact of a public act or statement upon the development of commitment is described by Ralph H. Turner and Lewis M. Killian, *Collective Behavior* (Englewood Cliffs: Prentice-Hall, 1972), pp. 94, 364—5.

17 See C. Eric Lincoln, *The Black Muslims in America* (Boston: Beacon Press, 1961), pp. 50—66.

18 John Steinbeck, *In Dubious Battle* (New York: Bantam Books, 1961).

19 From *IN DUBIOUS BATTLE* by John Steinbeck, p. 111.
Copyright 1936, ©1964 by John Steinbeck
Reprinted by permission of the Viking Press, Inc.

20 *Ibid.*, p. 206.

21 *Inner City Voice*, 2 (March 16—April 1, 1970), 11.

Chapter 11. Insurrectionary potential remains

1 See the *Detroit News*, July 25 and 26, 1973; *Detroit Free Press*, July 25 and 26, 1973.

2 *United National Caucus* 5 (August, 1973).

3 *Ibid.*

4 *Detroit News*, July 25 and 26, 1973; *Detroit Free Press*, July 25 and 26, 1973.

5 *Detroit Free Press*, August 1 and 13, 1973.

6 *Detroit Free Press*, July 30, 1973.

7 *Ibid.*

8 *Ibid.*

9 Frank Joyce and John Taylor, "Jefferson Shut-Down: Interview," the *Journey* 1 (August 1973).

10 *Detroit Free Press*, August 8, 1973; *Detroit News*, August 8, 1973.

11 *Detroit News*, August 10, 1973.

12 *Detroit News*, August 10, 1973; *Detroit Free Press*, August 10, 1973.

13 *Detroit News*, August 10, 1973.

14 *Detroit Free Press*, August 11 and 12, 1973; *Detroit News*, August 11 and 12, 1973.

15 *Detroit Free Press*, August 12, 1973.

16 *Detroit Free Press*, August 14, 1973.

17 *Detroit News*, August 13, 1973.

18 See *Detroit Free Press*, August 15—19, 1973; *Detroit News*, August 15—19, 1973.

19 *Detroit News*, August 15, 1973.

20 *Detroit Free Press*, August 15, 1973.

21 *Ibid.*

22 *Detroit Free Press*, August 17, 1973.

23 *Detroit Free Press*, August 18, 1973.

24 Interview with Jordan Sims, January 1974.

25 Interview with John Watson, September 1973.

26 Most of this discussion is taken from the interview with Sims; *Detroit News*, August 19, 1973; *United National Caucus* 1 (November 1969); *United National Caucus* 2 (December 1970); 5 (February 1974).

27 "Walter Reuther: 'He's Got To Walk That Last Mile,'" *Fortune* (July 1967) pp. 87—9, 141—2, 144, 149.

28 *Ibid.*, p. 141.

29 *Detroit Free Press*, May 29, 1971.

30 *Detroit Free Press*, November 11, 1971.

31 Interview with Homer Jolly, May 1, 1974.

32 *United National Caucus* 5 (August, 1973).

33 *United National Caucus* 4 (March—April, 1973).

34 *United National Caucus* 5 (August, 1973).

35 This discussion is primarily based upon the following series of materials from the Black Workers' Congress as supplemented by selected discussions with informal observers and participants: *The Black Liberation Struggle, The Black Workers Congress, and Proletarian Revolution*, pamphlet; *The Struggle Against Revisionism and Opportunism: Against the Communist League and the Revolutionary Union*, pamphlet; *Struggle in the RU: In Opposition to the Consolidation of the Revisionist Line on the Black National Question*, pamphlet; Mike Hamlin, "What Road to Building a New Communist Party," address March 23, 1973; *The Communist* 1 (August 14—November 15, 1974).

36 The account of the development within the Congress leading up to the expulsion of James Forman is largely taken from Dan Georgakas and Marvin Surkin, *Detroit: I Do Mind Dying: A Study in Urban Revolution* (New York: St. Martin's Press, 1975), pp. 173—7.

Chapter 12. The meaning of it all

1 See Herbert R. Northrup (ed.), *Negro Employment in Basic Industries* (Philadelphia: Wharton School of Finance, University of Pennsylvania, 1970).

2 See Herbert R. Northrup, *Organized Labor and the Negro* (New York: Harper & Row, 1944); Ray Marshall, *The Negro and Organized Labor* (New York: Wiley, 1965); Julius Jacobsen (ed.), *The Negro and the American Labor Movement* (Garden City, N.Y.: Doubleday-Anchor, 1968); and John M. Bracey, Jr., August Meier, and Elliott Rudwick (eds.), *Black Workers and Organized Labor* (Belmont: Wadsworth, 1971); Philip S. Foner, *Organized Labor and the Black Worker 1619—1973* (New York: Praeger, 1974).

3 See Karl E. Tauber and Alma F. Tauber, *Negroes in Cities* (New York: Atheneum, 1965).

4 See Harry Braverman, *Labor and Monopoly Capital: The Degradation of Work in the Twentieth Century* (New York: Monthly Review, 1974), esp. Chap. 15.

5 Computed from data presented in United States Department of Commerce, Bureau of the Census, PC(2)-7C, *Occupation by Industry*, Tables 1 and 2.

6 This discussion is primarily based upon Oscar Handlin and Mary Handlin, "Origins of the Southern Labor System," *William and Mary Quarterly* 7 (April 1950), 199—222; Winthrop D. Jordan, "Modern Tensions and the Origin of American Slavery," *Journal of Southern History* 28 (February 1962), 18—30; Joseph Boskin, "Race Relations in Seventeenth Century America: The Problem of the Origins of Negro Slavery," *Sociology and Social Research* 49 (July 1964), 446—55; Carl Degler, "Slavery and the Genesis of American Race Prejudice," *Comparative Studies in Society and History* 2 (October 1959), 49—66; and a rejoinder to the latter by the Handlins along with Degler's response to the rejoinder, pp. 488—95.

7 See Winthrop D. Jordan, *White Over Black: American Attitudes Toward the Negro, 1550—1812* (Baltimore: Penguin, 1968).

8 For an integration of the relevant literature see Donald L. Noel, "A Theory of the Origin of Ethnic Stratification," *Social Problems* 16 (Fall 1968), 157—72.

9 See Eric Foner, *America's Black Past: A Reader in Afro-American History* (New York: Harper & Row, 1970), p. 29; Marvin Harris, *Patterns of Race in the Americas* (New York: Walker, 1964), p. 14; Herbert S. Klein, "Patterns of Settlement of the Afro-American Population in the New World," pp. 99—115 in Nathan I. Huggins, Martin Kilson, and Daniel M. Fox (eds.), *Key Issues in the Afro-American Experience*, Vol. 1 (New York: Harcourt Brace Jovanovich, 1971), p. 103.

10 Eric Foner, *America's Black Past*, pp. 19, 20, 28—31; Harris, *Patterns of Race*, pp. 11—14; Jordan, *White Over Black*, pp. 89—90; Noel, "Theory of the Origin of Ethnic Stratification," p. 170; Kenneth M. Stampp, *The Peculiar Institution: Slavery in the Ante-Bellum South* (New York: Vintage, 1956), p. 23; Edgar T. Thompson, "The Plantation: The Physical Basis for Traditional Race Relations," pp. 180—218 in Edgar T. Thompson (ed.), *Race Relations and the Race Problem: A Definition and Analysis* (New York: Greenwood, 1968), pp. 184—7; William J. Wilson, *Power, Racism and Privilege: Race Relations in Theoretical and Sociohistorical Perspectives* (New York: Macmillan, 1973), pp. 74—5; Eric Williams, *Capitalism and Slavery* (New York: Capricorn, 1966), pp. 7—9.

11 Harris, *Patterns of Race*, p. 120.

12 Jordan, *White over Black*, pp. 122—8, 406—22; Eugene D. Genovese, "The Slave States of North America," pp. 258—77 in David W. Cohen and Jack P. Greene (eds.), *Neither Slave Nor Free: The Freedman of African Descent in the Slave Societies of the New World* (Baltimore: Johns Hopkins University Press, 1972).

13 Pete Daniel, *The Shadow of Slavery: Peonage in the South 1901—1969* (New York: Oxford University Press, 1972); E. Franklin Frazier, *The Negro in the United States* (New York: Macmillan, 1949), pp. 147—68; August Meier and Elliott Rudwick, *From Plantation to Ghetto* (New York: Hill and Wang, 1970), pp. 137—76.

14 Philip S. Foner, *Organized Labor.*

15 James A Geschwender, "Negro Education: The False Faith," *Phylon* 29 (Winter 1968), 371—8.

16 See William K. Tabb, *The Political Economy of the Black Ghetto* (New York: Norton, 1970), especially pp. 35—60; Robert L. Allen, *Black Awakening in Capitalist America* (Garden City, N.Y.: Doubleday, 1970), especially pp. 128—245; and Frantz Fanon, *Wretched of the Earth* (New York: Random House, 1968).

17 Tabb, *Political Economy*, pp. 24—30; and Charles Killingsworth, "Jobs and Income for Negroes," pp. 194—273 in Irwin Katz and Patricia Gurin (eds.), *Race and the Social Sciences* (New York: Basic Books, 1969).

18 Andrew W. Lind, "Occupation and Race on Certain Frontiers," pp. 49—70 in Andrew W. Lind (ed.), *Race Relations in World Perspective: Papers Read at the Conference on Race Relations in World Perspective: Honolulu, 1954* (Honolulu: University of Hawaii Press, 1955).

19 Milton M. Gordon, *Assimilation in American Life: The Role of Race, Religion, and National Origins* (New York: Oxford University Press, 1964), pp. 51—4.

20 Imamu Amiri Baraka, "Toward Ideological Clarity," *Black World* (November 1970), pp. 24—33, 84—95.

21 *Ibid.*, pp. 33—4.

22 For a sample of sources of documentation for this statement see Charles Killingsworth, "Jobs and Income for Negroes," pp. 194—273 in Irwin Katz and Patricia Gurin (eds.), *Race and the Social Sciences* (New York: Basic Books, 1969); James A. Geschwender, "Social Structure and the Negro Revolt: An Examination of Some Hypotheses," *Social Forces* 43 (December 1964), 250—6; James A. Geschwender, "Negro Education: The False Faith," *Phylon* 29 (Winter 1968); 371—8; Benjamin D. Singer, Richard W. Osborn, and James A. Geschwender, *Black Rioters: A Study of Social Factors and Communication in the Detroit Riot* (Lexington: Heath, 1970), pp. 25—29; and John D. Kain (ed.), *Race and Poverty: The Economics of Discrimination* (Englewood Cliffs: Prentice-Hall, 1969).

23 The concentration of blacks in ghettos allows for ready communication of grievances. The development of racial and class consciousness is facilitated by this communication process. Common interests and common enemies may come to be defined. In contrast, note Marx's discussion of the inability of the French peasantry to communicate and their consequent lack of political activism. Karl Marx, "The Eighteenth Brumaire of Louis Bonaparte," esp. pp. 171—2 in Karl Marx and Frederick Engels, *Selected Works* (New York: International Publishers, 1968).

24 For a discussion of the relationship between strike activity and economic conditions, which parallels the present analysis, see Albert Rees, "Industrial Conflict and Business Fluctuations," pp. 213—20 in Arthur Kornhauser, Robert Dubin, and Arthur M. Ross, *Industrial Conflict* (New York: McGraw-Hill, 1954).

25 This closing relates back to my original choice of titles for this work (*But The Beat Goes On*) and was meant to reemphasize one of the major messages growing out of my analysis — organizational forms may die out or change but the basic thrust of rebellion among black workers will continue so long as race/class exploitation persists in anything approximating its present form.

Index